Witt's End

The neighborhood where I lived, as well as other areas, had residents of various ethnic origins. Ours was about eighty per cent Caucasian, but social contacts were nil or for business purposes only. The saying "And never the twain shall meet" was symbolic of racial relationships in Woodlawn. I was 16, living across the railroad tracks downhill called "the bottom" by blacks and "niggertown" by whites who lived on Oakridge Hill. It was so close and yet so far away.

To: Micaiah
Sarter,
Happy Reading

Edwin T. Witt, MD

6-13-'98

Witt's End

by
Edwin T. Witt

First Printing — 1997
Second printing — April 1998

ISBN No. 0-9663700-0-7

Published by:
                        E & C Publishers
                        8714 S.V.L. Box
                        Victorville, CA 92392

Printed in the U.S.A.

This book is written by one who survived the financial paralysis of the great depression of 1929 with bank closings and no jobs, reared in a home where bootlegging, alcoholism and family discord was initiated by an abusive father.

It is dedicated to all boys, girls, adolescents and parents of the world, rich and poor.

Study and make ready by doing well in school and some day your chance will come.

Get that high school diploma and college degree, just hang them on the wall if you want to delay using them. They can always be activated and utilized whenever you are ready.

Add some fur to them, but don't try to hustle them as an adult, for something you should have earned while growing up.

I paid for my pre-Med educated at Miles College throwing a sixteen cent (16¢) daily newspaper.

Unfortunately, World War II was in progress and I was fortunate enough to have the education to be admitted to Meharry Medical College, Nashville, Tennessee, and earn my MD degree.

It provided me security for life.

Develop early spirituality, through your love and dedication to Jesus and your family.

Make sure all is right with your soul.

An old spiritual says: "You've got to stand your test in the judgment, you've got to stand it for yourself, there's nobody here can stand it for you, you've got to stand it for yourself, in life and after death."

Parents take care of the spiritual, educational and physical needs of your children.

The facts of life, sexuality, drugs, gangs and unwanted pregnancies, should be a family project, beginning at age eight years.

That learned from the streets is dangerous for everyone's mental health and physical well-being.

I became sterile at age seventeen due to a sexual misgiving. My parents were negligent, after seeing symptoms, by doing nothing.

Thanks to the responsible community role model adults who praised me for being polite to them and predicting that I'd make something of myself some day.

Last, but not least, my sincerest gratitude to my divine wife, Cordelia, who critiqued and typed the whole thing. I could never have written and completed this book without her.

CONTENTS

INTRODUCTION

by Walter J. Mueller

In April 1993, my wife and I took one of our periodic rail trips across the continent.

Aboard the Desert Wind on the Los Angeles-Chicago leg of the journey, we met an outgoing, cultured African American couple, Dr. Edwin T. Witt and his wife Cordelia. I do not recall which one of us first mentioned that he was far advanced in writing his memoirs, but our mutual interest was immediately aroused. I concluded from what Dr. Witt told me that he had a significant story to relate, that of an African American born in Birmingham, Alabama, and growing up and living there in the third, fourth and fifth decades of this century, undergoing the exigencies of life in that era. These experiences I soon visualized as Part I of *An American Life*. Part II, covering Dr. Witt's determination to break out of the limitations the times placed on a black person before the advent of civil rights legislation—and his subsequent remarkable professional career—must be saved for a separate volume. However, the highlights of that career are summarized in the epilogue to Part I, so that the reader has an overview of the entire story.

Dr. Witt's narrative struck me as so compelling that I, a retired Foreign Service Officer, University Professor and Dean, volunteered to assist in putting this manuscript in final form, for I quickly recognized it as a valuable chapter in American history. The manuscript, I believe, must be preserved in published form for future generations to learn from what Dr. Witt has to say. His is an African American Horatio Alger story and an inspiration for all who read it.

This autobiography comes at an opportune time, for there is a recently published book by Paul Hemphill, *Leaving Birmingham* (Viking, 1993), which relates a white's experience of that city in more recent decades (after Dr. Witt's departure). The juxtaposition of the two accounts, even though they cover different time periods, is a revealing experience.

Edwin Witt and Cordelia Freeman Witt were married in June, 1956. Mrs. Witt was born in Nebraska, attended the University of Southern California and had a banking career. It was she who typed and retyped the manuscript patiently, without complaint, concerned only that her husband's life story appear in print.

As for me, I am grateful for whatever part I have been able to play in moving Dr. Witt's memoirs forward toward publication. Our chance meeting aboard an AMTRAK train has convinced both of us of the serendipity accompanying train travel where passenger speaks with passenger and we all become more human.

Williamsburg, Virginia

Chapter 1
My Beginning Up Life's Slippery, Sliding Slope

I was born in Birmingham, Alabama, January 9, 1920, in what was often called a shotgun house, situated on a twenty-five by fifty foot lot in South Woodlawn, six miles east of downtown. Father bought the house from Mr. James Nunnally for $750 in 1919.

My father, Thomas Jesse Witt, the fifth of eight children, was born in Livingston, Alabama, a small town 105 miles south of Birmingham. Mother, Virginia Alberta Ogletree Witt, the older of two, was born in Union Springs, Alabama, eighty-eight miles south of Birmingham. My sister, Annie Ruth, was born October 27, 1922, and brother, Thomas Jr., was born January 6, 1935.

The house sat on pillars about three feet high, providing protection underneath for plenty of firewood, hard coal, my pet goat, two dogs and one cat. It consisted of a front porch, front room, one bedroom, dining room, kitchen and a screened-in back porch. Our hens were quite clandestine about where they laid their eggs. They always came from underneath the front porch cackling so Daddy knew something was going on. One day he sent his nephew, Sandy Witt, Jr., to see what the cackling was about. He discovered so many eggs, he crawled out hurriedly, exclaiming excitedly, "Uncle Tom, Uncle Tom, there's many, many eggs back there." Father was elated when Sandy brought them out. From that day on, I gathered them regularly.

The small front yard, with green grass which I cut with a hand sickle, neat flower beds, colorful potted plants and a big rose bush, extended to the unpaved street.

Our front room was small, with beautiful hardwood floors covered with a colorful rug which we called an odd square. The floor around the edge of the rug glistened from linseed oil applied with a floppy dust mop. That was my job. The plasterboard walls were covered with colorful wallpaper which sister and I were emphatically warned not to touch. There were several chairs in that room with a swastika carving on the back of each one. They were unique and a real novelty, as was our self playing piano with tunes on rolls of paper with holes punched in them. There was a restraint to keep the keys locked to prevent straining them. I would release the lever, pump the foot pedals and watch the keys plunking out a tinkling tune. I was fascinated by their movements. Mother would reprimand me if she caught me.

A long table in the center of the room and a graphanola which had to be wound to play records, mainly by Bessie Smith, a superb black blues singer; a davenport which could be converted to a bed, where I was relegated to sleep at age nine, completed the furnishings in that room.

Our only bedroom was small. There were two double beds, sister and I slept in one and mother and father across the room in the other. The bed-

posts almost met in the walkway between the front
and dining rooms. There were two emergency pot-
ties made of plain white porcelain at the foot of
sister's and my bed. We called the larger one with
a lid a slop-jar and the smaller one, for sister, a
chamber. They were very handy, especially on cold
winter nights when the outdoor toilet seemed far
away. Sister never wanted to go until long after
dark and I always had to stand guard by the door
of the outhouse until she completed her action. I
protested loudly but mother made me go with her.
Sister's excuse was "I can't go until the pain strikes
me". Guess she was right.

A large, colorful odd square covered the floor
and only a small portion of the shiny, waxed, hardwood showed between mother's trunk at the foot
of our bed which was right by one of two windows
on either side of the room. The odd square was
cleaned with mother's small Eureka vacuum. Once
in a while the rug was slid from underneath the
furniture, taken to the yard, spread over the clothes
line and beaten to remove some of the dirt. I took
the handle of the broom and slugged it vigorously.
Dust flew everywhere. Finally, it became less and
less. I wasn't aware of the danger of inhaling dust
and didn't wear anything over my face.

A chest for shirts and underwear stood at the
foot of Mother and Daddy's bed. Atop the chest an
old fashioned clock, which struck loudly every
hour, set in all its glory. An old rocking chair with
a thin cushion sat by their bed. A chiffonier, which
held our wearing apparel, and mother's dressing
table were squeezed into that small room. As
crowded as it was, I felt snug and secure. It didn't
cramp my style.

The dining room was the largest and where we
sat most of the time. The floor was covered with

linoleum. It maintained a sparkling gloss from my slinging hot soap suds backwards, forwards and side ways as often as mother thought necessary. A large heater, which burned hard coal, was our source of heat during the very cold winters. There was plenty of frost, but not much snow. A rip-roaring fire that turned the outside of the heater cherry red with the kitchen and bedroom doors closed, kept us nice and toasty warm. Before going to bed, we opened the bedroom door for the heat to warm it. Sometimes we banked the fire, covering it with ashes. The next morning Daddy stirred the ashes and added coal to the dormant embers.

We ate in the dining room occasionally on the large round oak table which covered most of the room. Mother outfitted it with a white linen tablecloth and matching napkins for Sunday dinner only. Beef roast, meat loaf, chicken and dumplings, mashed potatoes, string beans, collard greens and a green salad from week to week was our standard menu. This was topped off with peach or apple cobbler, ice cream which I cranked out in the two quart tin freezer, and a plain cake or cookies for those very special feasts. Rubber-like Jello mixed with fruit cocktail was our most frequent dessert. I was burned out by it when I became an adult.

We had a little room adjacent to the dining room where only a bathtub stood. It was to have been a bathroom, complete with a toilet, tub and wash bowl, but the tub wore out and the room became a storeroom for 500-1,000 bottles of homemade beer before the original plans were completed. A number three tin tub was for bathing. We bathed behind the heater in the dining room or the kitchen stove.

Many a card game, Florida Flip, Five Up and Coon-Can were played for drinks and small stakes by Father and his cronies. Once my maternal Uncle "Dare", Shedrick Gray from Detroit, visited us. He was playing against Father in a foursome. I was sitting between Uncle Dare and Daddy. I was nine years old and knew card values. It was Father's time to play, he reached for his king of trumps.] saw Uncle Dare's ace and warned Father with a knee bump. Uncle Dare saw me, his green eyes flashed like lightning; his very fair cheeks reddened as he angrily said, "Thomas, that boy touched you."

"Oh naw," Father replied. He prevailed and everything smoothed over. I never had another similar experience and didn't want one.

In a small corner behind the stove were three shelves where Mother placed her pots and pans. The trusty, old, big black skillet set in place on the shelf as did the six-inch-high, round container of Sally Myles salt, handy for Mother's educated fingers to get the exact amount to season our food.

A rounded glass china closet containing Mother's fine china dishes and crystal glassware stood on one side of the dining room. Across the room was a mirrored bureau with drawers full of clothes, tablecloths and napkins. A shelf below the mirror held a beautiful crystal punch bowl, scalloped around the top where fancy little hooks held six or eight matching cups. Mother sometimes made punch during the hot summer days and at Christmas filled it with delicious, spicy, alcoholic eggnog. Sister and I sneaked a little sip occasionally.

Daddy always sat in his leather, oversized barber's chair that he bought from Mr. Huffman. He slept off many a drunk in it. Mama's favorite seat was a rocking chair with comfortable arms which always set in front of the heater. A straight chair behind the heater was my favorite. I was driven from that seat in the winter many times when it got red hot. Sister inherited a large chair next to the china closet with a back that could be folded forward and converted to a table top. We never used it in that capacity. Four chairs around the large dining room table were utilized by sister and me to do our homework and studies or sometimes play games.

A dresser with a large mirror stood in another corner and Mother's Singer sewing machine was between Daddy's chair and the dresser in front of the only window in that room. I couldn't resist pedaling it just as I did the self-playing piano, placing my toes underneath the fast moving pedal, painfully mashing them. That didn't stop an occasional venture again with the same results.

Ninety-five per cent of our meals were eaten in the kitchen which was small. The floor was covered with linoleum. My parents sat at the small kitchen table above which was a shelf for Mother's condiments and other necessities for preparing our meals. Below it was a drippy faucet where a large pan was always in place to catch the water. Sister and I sat at the kitchen cabinet which had a small shelf where we placed our plates. Our coal stove was large with an oven below and two warmers above. A dishpan sat on the end of the stove which sometimes served as my table. The cabinet contained all of our every-day dishes. On the upper level was a large flour bin which held twenty-four pounds of Roller Champion flour, Mother's favorite. We had biscuits three-hundred-sixty days or more of the year, even though a large loaf of bread cost five to ten cents depending on the bakery. Saving money was most important. A sack of flour cost fifty cents and made many biscuits. A loaf of white bread was a very special treat and a rarity in our home. Cornbread for dinner was a three-hundred-sixty day affair. We sometimes had corn pone, cornmeal mixed with water, instead of all the good ingredients in cornbread. It was very tough and hard to chew. A glass of crumbled corn bread saturated with buttermilk flecked with big chunks of butter and eaten with a spoon was a delicious treat.

We had no refrigerator in those days, however, the ice man came by daily and delivered a twenty-five pound piece of ice. It cost a dime. He would bring it into the house on a pair of hooks, place it in the ice box, collect his money, visit awhile and go on his way. Our vegetables, meat, milk and leftovers were now preserved until another day when he returned.

Just outside the kitchen door on the screened back porch was a table where we occasionally ate dinner in the hot, sultry summer weather. We often sat out there in the evening in an attempt to cool off. There was an apple crate in the corner by the back door where an enamel washbasin set, which we filled with water to wash our hands and face.

I always brushed my teeth by the back door and used Pepsodent or Colgate toothpaste when we had some, otherwise soda and salt filled the bill.

Our outhouse was connected to the city sewer system and could be flushed. The door lacked two or three inches of closing completely and flies swarmed in huge numbers inside and out, frequently making me almost jump through the roof when they ascended from below. Old newspapers piled on the floor served as toilet paper and as a

fan to shoo those pesky critters away or for interesting reading in the confines of my solitary, private library. When the newspapers ran out stiff
pages torn from discarded magazines were reluctantly utilized and, as a last resort, corn cobs filled
the bill.

We had city water with meters. The charge was
$2.75 for three months. We turned the water off
during below freezing nights. Three feet of the water
pipe underneath the kitchen floor was exposed and
despite being wrapped with burlap would freeze
and burst as would the faucet in the kitchen.
Mother stored water in buckets and a large pan in
case of a freeze. When thawed, by applying burning newspaper to the unwrapped pipe, it would
burst and water flew everywhere until I rushed to
the meter and turned it off. The plumber who lived
two doors away had to be summoned.

A stalwart, dependable two-foot high hydrant
located in a corner of the yard to which a hose
could be connected to water the flowers and grass
and the dusty street was wrapped during the winter and didn't freeze as did the pipes in the kitchen
and underneath the house.

We had a low heavy wire fence which enclosed
our front yard. Midway in the fence was a five foot
gate with heavy lead pipe supports on either side
and across the top and bottom. A wood fence, about
five feet high connected to it and extended all the
way to the alley. There were two side gates: one by
the back door and one further back where Daddy
parked his truck. He had a sidewalk installed from
the front porch to the gate to enhance the beauty
of our modest home and had the front porch enclosed with a three-foot, buff-colored brick wall
with a huge pillar at each corner. There were two
rocking chairs and a swing where we enjoyed sit-

ting on hot, humid, late afternoons and evenings watching cars go by and visiting with neighbors out for an evening stroll.

The garage, outhouse and barn sat a short distance behind the house. After Father replaced his horse "Ole Sugar" with a truck, the barn became a chicken house. We had many chickens and Daddy built four two-foot high straw-filled nests inside the barn for the hens to lay their eggs and hatch their little biddies. Some hens liked to build their own nests on the ground underneath the front porch. The house sat high on pillars and was a perfect hiding place for them as well as a storage area for the hard coal, kindling and wood for fires to cook and heat the house.

Five steps descended from the back porch to the yard where Mother's wash tub set on an apple crate beside the top step. We carried water from the kitchen faucet by the bucketful to the wash-tubs. A huge, black pot stood nearby filled with sudsy water and a dash of lye. She stirred and plunged the clothes with a broom handle to get them sparkling white. The handle was slowly consumed over time by the lye in the soapy solution.

I must say, those often referred to "good old days" left much to be desired.

A tall china berry tree grew alongside the dining room window and shaded it very well. There was one in the backyard, too. The berries, light brown color on maturity, were about half the size of a red cherry. I liked to step on them just to hear them pop. They were very bitter. Even the chickens wouldn't eat them.

As a little boy I was heir to a private playground, my own park, before I became aware there were no playgrounds for Negroes in Woodlawn. We had an unobstructed view of 62nd Street and 4th Avenue South over the vacant lot adjacent to our home. I never thought about who owned it nor did I care. I had a good time romping and playing on the pretty green grass under one of the huge elm trees and sitting on its protruding, above-ground roots to cool off. There were two other very tall umbrella-like shade trees, one smaller elm and a large oak. I often rode my tricycle or played all alone with a broom handle and a tennis ball.

My adopted park served as a passageway for people who lived atop Oakridge Hill beyond the railroad tracks. It was a short cut to 62nd Street on their way to visit Dr. Broughton or to 1st Avenue North to catch the streetcar to go downtown. There were two huge signboards on the lot, targets for some leisurely rock throwing. I bounced enough rocks off the back of them to make the ground look like a gravel pit. The lot eventually became a baseball diamond for my friends and me. We often played cowboys and robbers, too. I spent countless hours throwing rocks at those billboards trying to perfect my aim for throwing strikes when pitching for my team.

The neighborhood where I lived, as well as other areas, had residents of various ethnic origins. Ours was about eighty per cent Caucasian, but social contacts were nil or for business purposes only. The saying "And never the twain shall meet" was symbolic of racial relationships in Woodlawn. Mr. Paul Hemphill, author of *Leaving Birmingham,* which was published by the Viking Press in 1993, lived within view of my home. His family moved to 60th Street and Fifth Court South when he was six years of age. I was 16, living across the railroad tracks downhill called "the bottom" by blacks and "niggertown" by whites who lived on Oakridge Hill. I could see the little green, one story house where he lived atop the hill that he so vividly described in his book. It was so close and yet so far away.

Circuit Court Judge J. W. Wilkinson, a heavy set man, lived on Georgia Road, three blocks from my home. I often passed his beautiful big abode where he would sometimes be sitting in the swing on the screened porch. The house sat back quite a distance from the sidewalk surrounded by many colorful flower beds, green trees and a lush green lawn. I looked that way often but never said anything to him. Aunt Edna Temple, an elderly lady who lived a stone's throw from our home, worked for him and liked him very much.

Dr. Kyle J. Kinkead lived just around the corner from him. He was a kindly white physician who treated me for gunshot wounds twice and father several times for various ailments.

The Coroner of Jefferson County, Gip M. Evans, lived three blocks further from Judge Wilkinson. I delivered beer and cigarettes to him during the couple of weeks I worked for Nick's Delicatessen. He was a small, expressionless man. I never saw a stranger acting person in my life. He would come to the door after I rang the bell, open it, and point to where I was to put his package. He never said a word, even after I said good morning or afternoon. He always gave me a dime tip. I would smile and say, "Thank you," pausing a moment awaiting a reply of some sort, but that never happened. I just turned and slowly walked away.

The City of Woodlawn had a unique, conveniently located shopping area for the merchandising, medical and entertainment needs of the neighborhood situated between 53rd and 57th Streets and First Avenue South and First Avenue North, the main artery between east and west Birmingham. Traveling four miles west by automobile or on streetcar No. 2 going to west end, or No. 27 going to Ensley would put you right in the heart of downtown Birmingham.

Morgan Brothers Department Store, a very large general mercantile establishment, was located in the middle of the business district. Next door was the large Woodlawn Hardware Store.

I liked to go to the first class Woodlawn Theater, but it was five miles away and I had to go through the white section to get there. A small gang of white hoodlums always hung around Nick's Delicatessen where I had to pass. Hard Hardy, a big red-headed youth from Mississippi didn't like blacks. One day Curtis Canada, a neighbor friend, passed the delicatessen alone and was attacked viciously by them. He was struck across the mouth with a pair of brass knuckles. His mouth swelled so large he couldn't eat for a week.

Fear was deeply embedded in my mind. With trepidation, I passed Hard Hardy and his associates on my way to the theater once, but wasn't bothered. I was relieved!

I couldn't buy popcorn in the lobby, a real deprivation especially while watching the movie. Blacks had to climb twenty-four steps to the balcony which we named "Buzzards' Roost". Whites sat on the main floor. The view of the movie was O.K., especially for a hard-to-get dime.

There were two Rexall drugstores in the area. Blacks couldn't sit at the beautiful soda fountain but could have prescriptions filled.

Woodlawn Medical Arts Building was located at 54th Street and 1st Avenue North where Doctors Wallace, Lovelace, Trucks and Kirby practiced. They treated the few black patients brave enough to go to them.

The firehouse was located on the edge of a large, beautifully manicured lawn at 57th Street and 1st Avenue North. All firemen were white.

W. C. Vice's Undertaking building was located at 56th Street and 1st Avenue North. Rideouts and Dillons Mortuaries from across town, as well as Vice's ambulances, often went by our home flying to answer emergency calls.

L. W. Sanks, when his ambulance would run, and Echols & Strong and Smith & Gaston from across town answered colored emergency calls. Whites were never summoned. Dr. Broughton, a black physician in the neighborhood, saw the blacks who didn't go downtown where most black physicians were located.

Woodlawn Bakery, next to the theater, was large and had many delicacies, especially big cinnamon rolls, four for a nickel, with plenty of raisins and lots of thick white icing. Also located in the area was a small police substation, a huge ice house behind Morgan's Department Store, Woodlawn Bank, a large old Methodist Church, Bon Marché Cleaners and a library, which I never entered. East of the library was the post office. Stamps to mail a letter cost two cents and postal cards a penny. Our postman drove a horse and buggy to a field adjacent to our home where he left the horse tethered to a heavy iron weight about the size of a large grapefruit while he delivered the mail. Mail boxes were on the front porch of every home in the community. All-white Woodlawn High School was a block away.

One year Woodlawn High enrolled an anomaly, a very dark-complexioned adolescent male from South America. The girls were crazy about him. One afternoon after school Sam Simmons, a black friend of mine, and some of our cronies passed him on the street close to the school and said "What you say, ma nigger?" a common expression used among neighborhood black youths. We didn't appreciate that expression when used by whites, however. The South American adolescent didn't seem disturbed. I saw him several times walking among his friends. He was six feet tall, handsome and had black straight hair. I don't know how long he remained there.

Woodlawn Bank was a large business located in front of the theater. Dr. Ed Samson was the president. A strange irony came about when all banks closed after the stock market crash in 1929 at the beginning of the Great Depression. It was circulated throughout the black community that he notified his influential white customers to withdraw their deposits before the bank closed. My parents had a few hundred there as did Mrs. Annie Green, our next door neighbor. We felt sorry for her because she had deposited the $10,000 there that she recently received from the Louisville and Nashville Railroad Company where her late husband had worked in the engine repair section for many years. He died from a stroke early one morning while sitting on the curb awaiting the streetcar to go to work.

Blacks weren't notified of the pending closure. The story goes that Dr. Samson went to south Alabama and supposedly drowned. A black man was killed and thrown into the river. When the body was recovered it was badly decomposed. It was declared to be Dr. Samson. Rumors circulated that he had taken most of the money and left for South America. That was the end of that saga and made the depression just that much more difficult for blacks to endure.

South Woodlawn was bordered on the east by

a white section called East Lake and the west by 59th Street. Several hundred black families lived in the community. Four churches, three grocery stores, Sanks Mortuary and Worth's Cleaners were the local businesses. Patterson Elementary School was located in the middle of the community.

Dusty, black, dirt streets with many pot holes were all over the black community, from 59th Street North to 66 Street. The holes were filled with grayish gravel, eventually ending up all over the street. It gradually wore away and was replaced from time to time.

Whites lived north and south of those streets. Theirs were paved and had sidewalks.

Clouds of dust flew and settled everywhere from the many automobiles that traversed Georgia Road on their way to Atlanta, Georgia. The "skeeter water" wagon, a truck with rear end sprinklers, came by daily spraying water to settle the dust. Many times I sprinkled the street with a hose and also the rear end of the streetcar, as a devilish entertaining prank. First Avenue North and First Avenue South, thoroughfares to downtown Birmingham, were paved.

We were happy when in 1930 Georgia Road was paved. I got a bang from chewing the remnants of tar atop the 500 pound drum left roadside by the workers. Some kids said chewing that black stuff would whiten teeth. Our parents said it would rot them. Guess who won. I chewed quite a bit of that black, bitter stuff and experienced no decayed teeth. It was like chewing gum to me.

As a young lad I was fascinated with naming cars that passed our house on Highway 78, which was called Georgia Road, on the way to Atlanta, Georgia, 177 miles north.

Father had a new 1928, four door, Buick sedan, which I was extremely proud of. I frequently went into the garage to manipulate the steering wheel as if I were driving, and from time to time bounced up and down in the back seat. It resembled a fresh air taxi. The detachable curtains with isinglass windows, flapped wildly on windy days, but served the purpose during inclement weather.

When I was about nine, father's hooch customers would stop by to relax awhile on one of two benches or a straight chair under the huge elm tree covering the watermelon stand adjacent to our house.

Mr. Quilla Ware, who always called me "Brother", had heard me naming cars as they sped by and gave me a little quiz, as did Mr. Daisy Johnson and others.

They were amazed with my knowledge.

The biggest and sharpest car that I had seen was the Packard with shiny chrome decorating the front. It was only for "The Folks", a hand-me-down slave reference to wealthy whites by under-educated blacks. Chauffeurs always drove those spectacles. Cadillacs were high class; Lincolns, very respected. Chryslers and Chalmers conjured up a lower level of discussion. La Salles, the sharpest of sport cars with a spare tire on either side by the front fender, were eye catching. Chandlers, Dodges, Fords, Chevrolets, Hupmobiles, Plymouths, Studebakers, Hudsons, Stanley Steamers, De Sotos, Whippets and the Essex were moderate in numbers.

I felt proud when I heard father's friends say, "He sure knows those cars."

Flat tires were a sign of the times back then and not an easy chore to repair. The wheel had to be laboriously removed, the inner tube pulled out of the casing and a search begun for the leak. If one was lucky enough to be at home, the tube could be dunked in a tub of water and the leak readily discovered.

Upon locating the hole, the area was roughened with the lid from the can of patches, moistened amply with mucilage and a square patch applied and heated through a process called vulcanization for permanency.

The initial wish for my first pair of skates popped into my head when Georgia Road was paved. I wore out quite a few pairs. I had never heard of skating rinks. When I did, they were for whites only.

Before my parents moved to Woodlawn a settlement of fine stable citizens were pillared very solidly. There were quite a few shotgun houses in our neighborhood and some big, pretty homes, too. There were no two story ones. They all had a comfortable inviting front porch, a swing and rocking chairs where one could relax and cool out in the late afternoon and night after the extreme heat and high humidity of summer. Air-conditioning was unheard of in our neighborhood as the hard financial times made it prohibitive.

Many had beautiful well groomed lawns with neatly trimmed hedges or a wood wire fence around the front yard. Some had huge pear, black walnut, peach, plum, apple and white fig trees in their yards. The fruit trees shared space with well-tended vegetable gardens that supplemented their food budgets so tightly squeezed by the depression. Not an inch of ground was wasted.

Railroad shop workers, Mr. John Tank, Mr. Cleve Moore, Bob and James Cornelius and Mr. Johnny Worthy had the best paying jobs. They all had lovely homes. Their children were my peers. I should say ninety-nine per cent of our neighbors were two parent families who owned their homes and had good jobs.

All of our neighbors were good law abiding citizens. Mother and Father taught sister and me to be polite to all adults, whenever or wherever we met them. I never forgot that advice. I always felt rewarded when I heard one of them say "He's such a mannerly young boy, he's going to make something of himself some day." Their praises sank in and helped sustain me in later childhood when my family became dysfunctional due to the psychological abuse from my evil minded, alcoholic father. Mother was the direct opposite of him and was a positive factor in helping me maintain my sanity.

Every neighborhood adult had an automatic parental surrogate disciplinary license to chastise any child they knew for any kind of misbehavior without rebuke from the child's parents. The parents of the guilty thanked every adult for their deeds and had proper verbal confrontation when the child returned home.

Church socials, where we played pinning the tail on the donkey, plucking an apple from a tub of water with your mouth while on your knees and dancing to records played on the graphanola were good clean fun. One of my favorite games went like this: one player holding a stick in his or hand said "Bet you can't do this, just like this," casually clearing his or her throat and striking the floor simultaneously with the stick. Players, when called upon, would eagerly jump up and strike the floor with the stick all kinds of ways but fail to clear their throats. The catch was to hit the floor with the stick and clear ones throat. It took a long time for me to figure out the trick.

Naughtiness reared its ugly head on Sunday

afternoons when crowds of early and mid-teens gathered at Mr. Lawson's cafe on 62nd Street. We slow-dragged awhile to Rockola music. I was fond of "Weary Blues" by Erskine Hawkins' orchestra featuring Avery Parrish on piano. He was reared less than two blocks from the cafe before joining Erskine Hawkins' band in New York City.

Mrs. Farley, an old settler, had a big home on Oakridge Hill with a large basement which she turned into a dance hall. We went there on some Sunday afternoons. I liked to dance with plump Julia Mae Sims. We bounced, rocked and rolled awhile. Her main man was Cheet Berry, an old first grade classmate of mine. I was just a slight passing fancy to her.

I enjoyed those rendezvous. It cost a nickel per record. We youngsters scraped up a few for those occasions, even during the depression.

I shan't ever forget those mellow days; however, Mother would have read the riot act to me if she had known where I had been. Other mothers would have felt the same way.

It was against the law in Birmingham, at that time, to dance on Sunday.

Chapter 2

Alabama, As It Was

Alabama was one of twelve southern states known as the Confederacy that fought the Northern troops during the Civil War, which Southerners like to refer to as "The War between the States" to preserve slavery and racial segregation.

Montgomery, the capital, was called the "Cradle of the Confederacy" and is 105 miles south of Birmingham. A post slavery mentality persisted and Negroes were looked upon as sub-humans. This perception has been handed down from generation to generation, nurtured consciously and subconsciously into permanency. References to Negroes among whites as niggers, darkies, Sambos, smokies, shines, zigaboos, coons, spooks, skoges, boys or girls made them feel superior. Blacks countered behind their backs with crackers, Honkies, Paddies, peckerwoods, poor white trash and Mr. Charley. Always Mr. or Mrs. whatever their last names and yes sir or ma'am. They controlled the wealth, all governments and educational institutions, which refused admittance to blacks.

Birmingham is located in Jefferson County, the largest of sixty-seven counties, and is Alabama's largest city with a population of about 125,000.

Just like every other city or town in Alabama, there were signs posted in all public places, over water fountains, restroom doors, streetcar and bus station doors, clearly stating, "WHITE-COLORED".

Birmingham's slogan as far as human rights for Blacks during the 20s, 30s and 40s was concerned could have been, "A bastion for the preservation of racial segregation".

Birmingham, established in 1871, is a beautiful city with rather flat terrain until going south on 20th Street where "Red Mountain" ascends to an elevation less than a thousand feet. It is called Red Mountain because of the fiery red clay. Originally an emblem atop the mountain with the hand of a man holding a flashing green light indicated no traffic fatality in the city at that time. It changed to red when one had occurred. It collapsed and the city fathers introduced the idea of a permanent monument in the form of an iron statue to be named Vulcan, after the Greek mythological God of Fire.

Vulcan, a big tourist attraction, now stands atop Red Mountain, symbolic of Birmingham's huge steel industry, the source of its prosperity and industrial might. Spectators can see the entire metropolis from that vantage point.

To me, "Vulcan" is to Birmingham what the Statue of Liberty is to New York City.

Above that red clay hill is Shades Mountain, twenty-five hundred feet tall, the highest point in Birmingham. Atop it developers established Homewood, a super business community. Five entrances into that suburb were appropriately named "Five Points." Ritzy shops, theaters, supermarkets, restaurants, drug stores and the beautiful Pickwick Night Club were located there. Wealthy whites had spacious homes tucked among the huge, straight, very tall pine trees spread over the entire area in all directions.

Whites really had it made. The Pickwick Club, atop Shades Mountain in Five Points was a very large fabulous night club, beautifully decorated. A big band played very beautiful music. The leader was decked out in white tie and tails. He looked very sharp.

One night Grover Price, Jr., a seat mate of mine, and I were taken there by a friend of his father's, an employee, Mr. Walton, to bus tables. It was my first time, at age 15, to see men in tuxedos and black ties and women in long dresses.

I don't know if there were any child labor laws in Alabama, it didn't matter because we were brought in by an adult employee for the first time and were black. A police officer was there for security and asked no questions. Maybe if we had returned, someone from management would have confronted us about our ages.

Grover and I collected an assortment of booze from the many discarded bottles that contained a little corner of alcohol. We salvaged about a half-pint, mixing the various contents into one bottle, retired to a back room, imbibed awhile and had ourselves a private party. We became a little looped, almost high as a Georgia Pine as that old expression goes, and felt good. We didn't have to worry about getting home safely, as Mr. Walton drove us. Our parents never found out what we had done. It remained our deep secret experiment.

We never worked there again. It was an interesting, eye-opening experience, seeing how well and pleasureful whites in Birmingham lived. There were no such happenings in our neighborhood.

A few miles south of Homewood was Mountain Brook, which was real money. Beautiful homes and a fabulous country club were tucked behind thick, tall pine trees obstructing the general public's view of the area.

My most outstanding memory of the Pickwick Club was a newspaper account of the slaying by a robber one Saturday night, of police officer, F. J. Harris, who was working there as a security officer. To my knowledge, that was the only episode of a violent nature that took place in that exclusive area during my childhood.

Rosedale, on the edge of Homewood, was where most of the two to three thousand blacks lived. Some resided in run-down shacks, others in modern, very nice, well maintained homes. Many worked as domestics, gardeners, chauffeurs and handymen in the homes of wealthy whites. Husband and wife teams lived in servants quarters at the rear of the mansions, just as they did during slavery.

Rosedale High School was an excellent school. I knew of its good football teams and academic reputation. Mr. B. M. Montgomery was principal there for many years. He married my seventh-senior-grade teacher after female teachers were, at long last, allowed to marry.

The only Negro business in the area was a large grocery store operated by the Lee family. Damon was the owner. The news of its popularity and prosperity became a mouth piece from the lips of blacks, with pride, for the biggest and best known, black-owned grocery business in Birmingham.

Birmingham had a commission form of government, five commissioners and a mayor. Cooper Green was mayor for twenty years. The Department of Public Safety controlled the police department which was openly anti-black. Eugene H. (Bull) Conner, a small man less than five-feet-eight inches tall, who always wore a hat and had one eye, was the tyrannical racist boss. He came to Birmingham from Selma, Alabama, 105 miles to the south and was a staunch advocate of racial segregation. His first job, in Birmingham, was as a radio broadcaster for the Birmingham Barons baseball club, a white professional team, one of the eight member Southern Association. I loved baseball and listened to him from age eight, many dozens of times and enjoyed his plain, country, flat-talking delivery. He wasn't too well educated. He really liked the Barons and so did I. As I listened to him and heard him holler "There she goes, a single, double, triple," or, "Into the nigger bleachers for a home run!" really irked me. Don't know if he was intentionally insulting blacks or just exhibiting inherited behavior. It never changed. That didn't stop me from listening to him.

Prohibition was the law of Alabama in 1932 when Mr. Conner initiated a campaign for a referendum to repeal it and allow 3.2% beer to be sold. His popularity caused a successful repeal of the law and increased his status throughout the city. Prohibition, which began in 1917, was repealed in 1933 in the United States for the sale of alcoholic beverages.

In 1932 he ran for the City Commission, won and became Commissioner of Public Safety. His reign of terror began against blacks with the police force and lasted for more than twenty years.

His downfall came when two vice-squad detectives found wet towels in the bathroom of a hotel where he and a young woman were cohabitating and arrested him. His popularity waned and he lost the next election.

The lid on racism was sealed tightly by the segregation mentality of whites in order to prevent humane social relationships between the races in Birmingham.

The police department had a mandate for open homicidal season on black males even before the advent of Mr. Conner. When I was about eight or nine years of age I remember Father's sister, Katie Knox, who lived in a suburb of Birmingham called Avondale, telling us of a most horrific killing of a black man on Taylor's Hill very close to her home. She and her family lived at the foot of that hill. A policeman killed him, draped his body across the hood of his car and carried it to the police headquarters downtown. We never heard if anything was done to the perpetrators. He was just another dead "nigger," in their way of thinking. The racism pot boiled, but didn't spill.

After Mr. Conner was elected Commissioner of Public Safety the lid became tighter. Race hatred continued to smolder and, as Governor George C. Wallace once said, "Segregation now, segregation forever," remained status quo.

The Birmingham Police headquarters, with an all white department, was located at 19th Street and 4th Avenue North. The one hundred piece police band, decked out in white uniforms, was super and beautiful. It wasn't second to the great million dollar Crimson Tide larger band of the University of Alabama, which I saw in Birmingham when they played Auburn or another southeastern conference foe. A detective who played clarinet in the band was a friend of Father's and visited us often.

Chief of Police, Fred H McDuff, held that office for a long time. He successfully ran for sheriff of Jefferson County, won and remained there a long time, too.

The Jefferson County Courthouse, twelve stories high, was at 19th Street and 8th Avenue North.

Ex-governor, George C. Wallace, was a circuit court judge. The Heflins, including Senator Howell Heflin, were well known all the way to the Alabama State Supreme Court when I was growing up in Birmingham.

"Don't go before that city judge; he'll throw the book at ya!" was the word around Birmingham, referring to Judge John Martin. Judges in the criminal court system didn't mean perhaps. Municipal Court Judge Martin's theme song for misdemeanors was "One-hundred dollars and six months on the street cleaning detail." There were vast numbers of streets to be cleaned. In addition to the fine, court costs of $3 had to be paid.

Judge Martin was on the bench for many years. I never faced him but Father did.

Judge J. M. Abernathy of the Jefferson County Circuit Court was on the bench forever and meted out rough sentences. Prisoners were sent to Ketona where "Cap'n Powell" was in charge of a rock quarry and worked the inmates exceedingly long and hard. Some were shackled with leg irons. Father faced Judge Abernathy on several occasions and paid fines of fifty-three dollars for possession of illegal corn whiskey.

Judge George C. Wallace of the Circuit Court and the Heflins, including Senator Howell Heflin, were a judiciary dynasty in Alabama.

Attorney Roderick Beddow was the criminal defense lawyer in Birmingham. I read about him often in The Birmingham News newspaper.

Greenwood's huge restaurant and the equally large Britling Cafeteria on 20th Street North, for whites only, looked beautiful from the outside. All clerks in stores and waitresses in restaurants were white. Blacks worked as custodians in many of the stores.

The Bankhead and Tutwiler Hotels, for white guests only, were multi-storied buildings and visually beautiful.

Birmingham was an all around convenient city for meeting the needs of its citizens. The University of Alabama's Medical School, in Tuscaloosa, Alabama, 105 miles south of Birmingham, was a two year school until 1948. Prior to that time students had to be accepted elsewhere for their last two years of study. The third and fourth years were added in 1948 when the school moved to Birmingham and took over the operation of Hillman-Jefferson County Hospital at 23rd Street and 8th Avenue, South. It has extended six blocks to 14th Street and is now known as The University of Alabama Medical Center.

There were five white high schools and one large Negro high school, Industrial High, with three thousand students. There were also two small Catholic high schools for Negroes, Immaculata and St. Marks. That situation existed through the 1960s. The city had two large colleges, Birmingham Southern, a Methodist school, and Howard College, a Baptist school (now Samford University), located on opposite sides of town; west and east, respectively. Neither admitted Negroes. Miles College, a four-year, liberal arts, Colored Methodist Episcopal denominational school, and Paine College, a two-year, struggling teachers training school, accepted Negroes before integration.

There were many fine white hospitals which admitted Negroes to the basement -St. Vincent's, South Highland, Lloyd Nolan, West End Baptist, T C I, operated by the Tennessee Coal and Iron Company for its employees, and Hillman Hospital, operated by Jefferson County where Negroes were automatically admitted to the basement as standard procedure. There was always the fear of being poisoned by mean white nurses administering "medicine" from that infamous black bottle.

Children's Home Hospital had ten beds for obstetrics and surgery. It was run by the Red Cross, was small and for Negroes only. Most blacks died at home from lingering illnesses following strokes and congestive heart failure. They were treated by their family doctors. There were twenty black doctors with offices located strategically among blacks all over Birmingham. There were three in North Birmingham, one at 14th Street and 8th Avenue downtown, one in Avondale, one in Woodlawn where I lived, seven in the Masonic Temple Building downtown at 17th Street and 4th Avenue, four in the Pythias Temple Building on 18th Street between 3rd and 4th Avenue North, two on the south side and one in Fairfield. Four were specialists, two surgeons, one in eye diseases, the other an obstetrician-gynecologist. There were hundreds of white doctors located in large office buildings all over the city.

Three high school chums and I went into medicine after college. One went to Cincinnati, Ohio, one to Dayton, Ohio, and two of us returned to Birmingham to practice. We eventually left. One of the old time black physicians went to Shaw University in Raleigh, North Carolina, one to Western Reserve in Cleveland, one to Michigan University, the others either to Howard University, Washington, D.C. or Meharry Medical College in Nashville, Tennessee.

Slossfield Health Center for blacks, located in North Birmingham, was sponsored by the Jefferson County Health Department. Infectious diseases and obstetrical clinics operated daily. Tuberculosis was diagnosed and treated there. Dr.

Kelly Joseph, Jewish, was in charge.

Dr. T. M Boulware, white, the leading obstetrical specialist in Birmingham and Chairman of Obstetrics at the University of Alabama Medical School, supervised white residents from the university in conducting prenatal care and deliveries. He trained Dr. Robert Stewart, a black physician, who later became certified by the American Board of Obstetrics and Gynecology.

Black county public health nurses worked in the clinics and made follow-up, community health calls on clinic patients.

Rickwood Field, home of the Birmingham Barons, the only place in Birmingham where blacks and whites were in close proximity for several hours, was located in Elyton between downtown Birmingham and West End, a large white upscale community. The park was named "Rickwood" for the owner, Mr. Richard Woodward. He also owned that most magnificent stadium and a coal mine, from whence he gained his wealth. No big league ball field superseded it in beauty. It could seat twenty-five thousand.

The Barons were very popular, always drawing big crowds. I listened to hundreds of broadcasts and remember the players very well. Ray Beres and "Yam" Yaryan were catchers. Henry Shoaf, Clay Touchstone, Ray Caldwell and Kirby Higby were right-handed pitchers. Clay Touchstone was the only cross-firing-delivery pitcher at that time. Big Jim Edwards and Jimmy Walkup were left-handers. Since my name was Edwin and I was plump in size, Hall Wells, a playmate, named me Big Jim Edwards.

Ray Caldwell, the elder statesman of the pitching corps, was Hall Wells' idol. We called him "Uncle Ray". Mule Shirley and Pete Susko, first basemen, Billy Bancroft, second base, "Shine" Cortazzo, short stop, Brute Pickering, third base and Art Weis, Wally Berger and Joe Prevost, outfielders, were the players back then. Prevost had a right arm like a cannon, throwing out many base runners who erred by attempting to stretch a single to a double or trying to go from first to third on a single. He also threw strikes to home plate to cut down a runner on second base trying to score on a single to right field. Yaryan, Pickering and Mule Shirley were the home run hitters. Clyde Milan was the manager.

I witnessed the strangest and rarest sight one will ever see. One hot and sunny afternoon at Rickwood Field I was sitting in the bleachers watching Birmingham play the New Orleans Pelicans when a pigeon flew over left field. As the pitcher released the ball to Eddie Rose, outfielder for the Pelicans, he swung, hitting the ball aloft. It soared high into the outfield and struck a pigeon in flight, killing it instantly. Art Weis, the left fielder, picked it up and put it into his left hip pocket as the crowd groaned in disbelief. He returned to his position in left field after throwing the missile to the infield. I was shocked and saddened by this incident but enjoyed the rest of the game.

Old man "Jim Crow," raised his ugly head there in the wide open spaces where plenty of hot sunshine, blue skies and clean air embraced the park. It was located a long way from the belching steel mills of Tennessee Coal and Ironworks that contaminated the air in Fairfield, a few miles away. The large covered horseshoe-shaped grandstand, for whites only, was bordered by bleachers for whites on the north side and blacks on the south. Blacks could sit in a small portion of the south side of the white grandstand in an extension known as "The colored grandstand." A gulch separated them. All bleacher seats cost fifteen cents, colored and white; the colored grandstand cost a quarter.

The Barons were members of the Southern Association. The other members were: The Memphis Chicks, Knoxville Smokies, Nashville Vols, Chattanooga Lookouts, Mobile Bears, New Orleans Pelicans, Little Rock Travelers and the Atlanta Crackers.

Birmingham had a good team and won the annual Dixie Series in 1931 from the Houston Buffaloes of the Texas League.

I rode the streetcar to the Barons games for fourteen cents round trip. Daddy never went. He occasionally went to see the Birmingham Black Barons (a Negro League team) play mid-weekly, coming home at noon from his fruit and vegetable route and heading for Rickwood Park. Negroes sat in the regular stands for their games.

Daddy took me to see the Barons when I was seven years old. They were members of the old Negro baseball League. I remember seeing Satchel Page pitch. He was tall, thin and had a big shiny toothed smile and threw very hard. He was an excellent pitcher, one of the best ever. He pitched at age forty-four for the St. Louis Browns of the American Baseball League and was the first black to pitch in the major leagues.

The swinging jump tune, Tuxedo Junction, was named for a small community, eight miles from downtown Birmingham on the old Tidewater streetcar line. A large picnic ground was located there. There were many tall green trees, beautiful green grass, benches and water fountains. Several swings, a sand box and a slide were for our enjoyment. Mother carried sister and me to Tuxedo Park for one of our Sunday School picnics. We enjoyed it very much, especially the market basket of goodies she brought -cake, potato salad, potted meat between crackers and ham sandwiches.

Erskine Hawkins, born in Birmingham, wrote Tuxedo Junction; the theme song for his weekly N.B.C. thirty-minute radio show. It's a legend in the annals of popular music. Glenn Miller's recording of it sold millions of copies.

A statue of Mr. Hawkins, who expired in 1993, stands in Tuxedo Park located at Tuxedo Junction in Birmingham.

Legion Field stadium was very large. Football as well as track and field events were held there. It was located about a mile west of Industrial High, seated thirty thousand at that time and was used mainly by the University of Alabama for home games against Southeastern Conference foes. The game against Auburn University was an annual event and a big, big affair.

The Alabama State Fair was a huge annual affair, held in Ensley three miles from downtown on 3rd Avenue North.

When I was a child a Negro youth was slain there by a policeman. Thereafter, Negroes weren't allowed to attend. Birmingham's Municipal Airport opened in July 1928. It was located six miles east of downtown in an area of northern Woodlawn, called Groveland. A large number of blacks lived in that vicinity.

Colonel Charles A Lindbergh, an ace flier in World War I and the first person to fly solo across the Atlantic Ocean in 1927, was at the dedication. Father drove Mr. Cleve Moore, a neighbor, and me to the opening festivities. There were many, many people milling around. The landscaping had not been completed and huge clouds of dust were so thick one couldn't see very far. We didn't witness the ceremonies, we were just three, tired, curious spectators in attendance on that hot, humid day. Father bought himself and me a five-cent bottle of coca cola. It went down "real good" and cooled us off temporarily. After drifting off, mingling amongst the crowd, Mr. Moore returned and told us of a man he saw with a Number 3 wash tub filled with water, a fifty-pound piece of ice floating in it, selling ice water for five cents a glass, attracting many customers. That bit of information brought about a little chuckle, but not enough excitement to encourage us to stay around any longer. We trudged to the car and headed home. The airport has come a very long way since then. In the early 1900s Birmingham was a very prosperous city. Its principal industry was steel. The city was labeled "The Pittsburgh of the South" because its steel production rivaled that of a city in Pennsylvania with the same name and the largest steel producer in the United States. Tennessee Coal and Iron Works, commonly called T.C.I. was the largest steel mill in Birmingham, with several thousand employees, black and white. Many were the times on my way to downtown via the streetcar, over the viaduct from 31st to 26th Street North, I observed a large stream of radiant red hot molten steel on the move at the Sloss-Sheffield Steel Works, a huge operation. Men with masks and aprons, carrying buckets made me think, "How could I adapt to that hot kind of work?"

There was a steel mill in Bessemer, twenty-two miles south of Birmingham, one in North Birmingham and another in Woodlawn, a mile and a half from my house.

They all had full employment until the great depression, beginning October 29, 1929, when the

New York Stock Market crashed. Eleven thousand financial institutions failed. T.C.I. was located in a suburb called Fairfield, twelve miles northwest of downtown Birmingham. Black workers lived in communities all over the city, had nice homes and were prosperous.

The powers that be, all white, were proud of the city and created the slogan, "The Heart of Dixie" which was exhibited on all automobile license plates.

The old Tidewater streetcar exited from a two block long, dark tunnel at 26th Street and 5th Avenue North on the way to downtown Birmingham where there was a huge sign the width of the exit displaying the slogan "BIRMINGHAM, THE MAGIC CITY."

Herbert Hoover was President in 1929 and his slogan was "A chicken in every pot". Things didn't work out that way for many people. He became known as "Hard Times Hoover".

Eventually, the government ordered the banks to begin small percentage payments to their depositors. Mother withdrew the mere pittances whenever she received a notice from the bank that funds were available.

One day when she returned home with the cash Father met her at the front door and snatched her pocketbook. A scuffle ensued as he tried to take the money from her. She put up a good struggle and several of the bills were torn, but he finally got most of it to buy whiskey for himself to drink and sell to his customers. That was a very depressing time. Mother was left holding an empty bag and a handful of torn bills. She avoided having that happen again. The meager sums received from their savings were carefully used to buy food, clothing and pay bills. The money disbursed from the bank accounts and that earned from Father's vegetable route and whiskey sales made it possible for us to survive without assistance from public welfare.

Twenty, fifty and hundred-dollar bills were a soft yellow-gold color during the twenties. I saw my parents with quite a few. Five, ten, twenty and fifty dollar gold coins were also in circulation. Mother had many of all denominations. She kept them under the rug in the bedroom and in the vanity drawers. When the depression hit, they slowly disappeared. At the end of World War I, in 1918, before Father met Mother, economic times were good. He and his older brother, Sandy, procured employment at the Red Ore Mines in Huffman, Alabama, 22 miles north of Woodlawn. The mines closed in 1923, four years after Father and Mother were married. At the urging of his brother-in-law who sold fruits and vegetables all over Birmingham, he decided to purchase a horse and wagon and begin the same type occupation.

In the 1920s, Prohibition was the law in the United States. Alcoholic beverages for personal use or sale meant nothing to me. Even though Father was an adult and understood the meaning of prohibition, he began to sell whiskey on his vegetable and fruit route and by the drink or bottle at home.

Our family lived well until the stock market crash plunged the nation into a deep depression. Fortunately, my parents were thrifty and had substantial savings in Traders National Bank, First National Bank, Woodlawn Savings Bank and Industrial Savings Bank where school children could put their savings. I banked ten cents to a quarter every week. We continued to live well, Mother dressed me like Little Lord Fauntleroy: pongee shirts, knickered suits, Buster Brown shoes and stingy brimmed hats. Sister was dressed in frilly dresses, bonnets, patent leather shoes and pocket books with a strap handle. Her ear lobes were pierced. Unfortunately she couldn't wear her little gold earrings because of allergy to the metal but kept the holes open with burned broom straws.

Public Welfare enrolled many families. We were never on welfare. Flour, butter, navy beans, black-eyed peas, lard and sugar were distributed to those who were unemployed. Twenty-four pound sacks of flour with a huge red cross printed on the back and an admonition not to be sold, were issued to needy families. Some recipients sold their sacks for fifty cents. Underwear and shirts were made from them. Some wearers, especially school children, were teased by their peers. Father bought a few sacks.

The hub of the business enterprises was 20th Street and First Avenue North in industrial-laden Birmingham. The commercial rim thinned at 18th Street to 17th Street and between 3rd and 8th Avenue North, the colored section.

The largest building downtown was the City Auditorium at 19th Street and 8th Avenue North. Blacks used it mainly to feature big bands such as Jimmy Lunceford, Benny Carter, Count Basie, Earl "Fatha" Hines, Duke Ellington and Cab Calloway. I was a teenager and had no desire to go. Mama would have declared me crazy if I had expressed such an ideation. Having no money and reports of the behavior at such gatherings left much to be desired. The main post office was next door.

Blacks held their gatherings at the Masonic Temple or the Elks Rest, buildings owned by the respective lodges.

Father was a 32nd Degree Mason. They met every Monday night at 7:30 p.m. I was fascinated hearing him tell of initiations when the inductees rode a goat. A big celebration followed the ceremony.

Mother was an Eastern Star, a sister to the Masons. I can see her in her white dress with a purple sash from her left shoulder, diagonally across her chest, tucked in at the waist. They met on a weekday afternoon. I sometimes carried her dues to the meeting when she was unable to attend. Climbing two steep flights of stairs to the meeting room was a tiresome task. It seemed to take forever for me to reach the top.

The two-story Knights of the Pythias Lodge Hall, where their meetings were held was the tallest building in our community, located one block from our home.

The year 1948 was hectic politically and racially for blacks. The "States Rights Party" was formed during that summer at the City Auditorium. It was referred to by the media as "The Dixiecratic Party." Governor Wright of Mississippi was their presidential nominee and Senator J. Strom Thurmond of South Carolina the vice-presidential nominee. There was no television but the radio stations were hot and heavy with "nigger this and nigger that". It was gut-wrenching to listen to that vociferous barrage. Fortunately they got nowhere, but awoke some quiescent minds, which wasn't good.

Governor Jim Folsom from Cullman, Alabama, fifty-two miles north of Birmingham where Negroes had to pull down the shades on the train as they went from Birmingham, northward, was a kind man and didn't attend the convention. They jumped on him with all the force of their venomous minds, totally denouncing him. He was defeated in his return bid for a second term.

He was accused in a paternity suit of fathering a little boy, who at age two looked very much like him. The Governor was seven feet tall with red hair and the little boy was large at age two with red hair, big feet and hands, which only helped to further confirm their assumption. That accusation undoubtedly helped to defeat him in his bid for reelection

What Little Tokyo is to the Japanese, Koreatown to Koreans and Chinatown to the Chinese in the city of Los Angeles, 17th and 18th Streets and 4th Avenue had equal significance to Blacks, being the prominent location of Negro businesses and professional activities. The Number 27 streetcar from East Lake to Ensley stopped at 17th Street and Fourth Avenue.

The Masonic Temple Building, owned by lodge brothers of the Colored Masonic Order, was located on the northwest corner. It was a seven story cement block building. There was a modern pharmacy on the main floor which filled prescriptions of patients seen by the seven physicians with offices in the building. It had a large soda fountain, one of two for blacks downtown, where I once worked and magazines, newspapers and various kinds of novelties could also be purchased.

Pilgrim Life Insurance, Atlanta Life and North Carolina Mutual, all large black-owned insurance companies, occupied some of the upper floors. Two dentists and two realty offices were also located on upper floors. It was a busy place every weekday. Foot traffic was very heavy.

Next to the pharmacy was a branch of the Jefferson County Library (for the colored). It was stocked with plenty of books, encyclopedias and periodicals. I used it on several occasions, but having to walk about five miles from Industrial

High made it rather inconvenient. I would have used it more often if it had been closer. I passed the Woodlawn Public Library on the streetcar going downtown and on my few visits to the theater, but never darkened its interior.

Lindsay's Tailoring Shop was next to the library.

The Birmingham Times was the first local and statewide newspaper owned and operated by blacks in the late twenties. It sold for a nickel and consisted of eight pages. It ceased publication after a short existence in the early thirties. Going toward 3rd Avenue on 17th Street, mid-block, was the home of *The Birmingham World* the second black newspaper printed in Birmingham. Emery O. Jackson, a dark complexioned, very glib graduate of prestigious Morehouse College, a four-year, liberal arts school in Atlanta, Georgia, was the editor. Solidly built, raspy voiced, very outspoken and an easy man to meet, he was the spokesman of the protest to the evils of racism in Birmingham and all of Alabama. He was threatened with violence by the Birmingham Police and Sheriffs Departments, the K.K.K. and malicious race-hating white organizations in general. He was never intimidated and kept up his critical editorial and reporting until he died in the early sixties. The paper cost a nickel and grew from four to a dozen pages.

The Pittsburgh Courier and *The Chicago Defender* were old standards and published weekly. They sold for ten cents and carried a wide variety of news of the black communities around the country.

From the pulpits of Negro churches, especially the 16th Street Baptist Church located at 16th and 8th Avenue North, the largest black church in Birmingham and not far from the main drag of black businesses, is where Civil Rights organizers and ministers elucidated strategies and methods to the parishioners to secure equal rights for the second class blacks of Birmingham.

Dr. J. W. Goodgame was the minister.

The church was bombed in 1958, killing four little girls attending church services.

Arthur D. Shores, a black lawyer, pioneered the fight for civil rights in Birmingham from the beginning of sit-ins at lunch counters in the Sixties, to denial of voting rights for Negroes.

He was a short, dark brown skinned fearless gentleman with quiet demeanor. His home was bombed and many threats made against his life by bigots and racists. Negroes guarded his home on "Bombers Hill," the name given the location on 11th Court North where he lived.

He was truly a crusader in breaking down segregation in Birmingham.

Nancy's Tearoom was located across the street from *The Birmingham World* at 3rd Alley. Everybody raved about the food. I was too poor to experience that kind of gastronomic treat.

The black socialites of Woodlawn and all of Birmingham, had their affairs in the beautiful Masonic Temple ballroom above the drug store or the Elks Rest at 12th Street and 8th Avenue North. I graduated to their affairs when I began attending Miles College in my late teens. The Masonic Temple dance hall was beautiful but had quite a few large beam supports scattered about it. I grew into dancing there in my college years.

The socialites were school teachers, postmen, pressing establishment employees, railroad men and their wives and ordinary workers with adequate means. Word of mouth spread the news of their social activities.

East on 4th Avenue was Bob Williams' huge barbecue place where hundreds of blacks ate, day and night, until the wee hours of the morning. Across the street were the Famous and Champion Theaters. Going eastward to 18th Street was Brock's Drug Store, the other colored drug store and soda fountain. South on 18th was the Knights of Pythias Building which housed three floors of black doctors medical offices. There were no Negro hotels.

Mr. A. G. Gaston, a prominent mortician, established a school of secretarial science at the corner of 17th and 5th Avenue in the 1940s for people of color. It grew and attracted a large number of students, as it was the only kind of school associated with that type profession for Negroes. The Smith and Gaston Mortuary was located at 16th Street and 5th Avenue North. Mr. Smith, with whom he began the mortuary, died and Mr. Gaston expanded it into a very large business.

Kelly Ingram Recreation Park, located at 17th Street and 5th Avenue, was for whites only. In later years we were allowed to walk through the park on our way downtown from Industrial High.

The Birmingham Railway Light and Power Company (B R L and P), at 21st Street and 1st Avenue North, was the tallest building downtown. Public transportation via very convenient streetcars, and power for the entire city including suburbs and mountainous vicinities, were all under its jurisdiction. The streetcar fare was seven cents from east to west, plus two cents for a transfer from downtown to the north or south sides of the city. Transfers were free from downtown to Irondale, after exiting in Woodlawn.

As convenient as streetcars were to get from

here to there, segregation raised its ugly head. Whites boarded and sat on comfortable, straight-back seats for two in the front. Blacks boarded on the opposite side and went to the back and sat on long-hard seats. A movable rod divided the two sides where we sat. It could be adjusted to accom-modate the overflow of white passengers. Blacks couldn't go to the front when the back overflowed.

The same rules applied on the Irondale bus which passed my home, except there was no rod. Everyone boarded at the front, but if whites were standing in the aisles, blacks paid their fare, stepped off and went to the back door to board. The buses got fairly crowded sometimes and we breathed on each other but no confrontations arose.

The First National Bank building on 20th Street, the Bank for Savings and Trust, and the Penny Savings Bank across the street were big financial institutions.

Pizitz Department Store was huge—three sto-ries with a bargain basement—displaying clothes, shoes, garden tools, radios and anything else of which one could think. I was embarrassed one day by a white woman, a sales person, for only observ-ing the beautiful wrist watches in a showcase on the first floor. "You think one of those watches is going to jump out to you?" she said. I looked at her and walked away without giving a reply. I was crushed. Just across from the showcase was a water fountain with a sign above it that read: "White—Colored". That hurt too, even at age fif-teen.

There were several other big stores, Burger-Phillips displaying high class women's and men's clothing, Blach's exclusive men's clothing store, Herman Saks an exclusive men's and women's clothing store and Parisien's all around store for less expensive shoes, clothing, candy, nuts and many other necessities. Rhodes-Carroll, McKelvey-Coates and R. B. Broyles were super furniture stores. S. H. Kress, Woolworth's and J. C. Penney carried a variety of notions, candy, nuts and inexpensive everyday household items. The Alabama and Ritz Theaters, for whites only, were beautiful and located in the middle of downtown.

Hoboing was a visible sign of hard times brought on by the Great Depression. We lived about a block from four railroad tracks and I saw dozens of poor souls, young, old, black and white, riding the Norfolk & Western, going to Norfolk, Virginia, and the Illinois Central to Chicago. The freight trains slowly climbed a steep grade traveling through our community and made it convenient to detrain. Some came to our home which was only a block away. Their standard introduction was "Miss, I'm hungry; do you have any work I can do for some food?" Mother fed many of them cold biscuits, cornbread, neck bones, spare ribs and sweet potatoes from our previous night's dinner. The most ravenous case of thirst and hunger I observed came about one morning. Mother was in the kitchen when one poor soul opened the screen door to the back porch, stepped in and, to his surprise, met her. Before uttering a word, he spotted a large pan under the dripping kitchen faucet, grabbed it before she could say anything and began drinking, ants and all. The ants always made their way into the pan and drowned. Handing the pan to Mother he begged her pardon and humbly asked if there was any work he could do for some food. She prepared a lunch for him from the leftover food stored in the warmer, wrapped it in a piece of newspaper and handed it to him. With her usual sweet smile she told him there was no work for him and wished him a good day. He graciously thanked her and left. I felt sorry for him.

I saw many a lump of coal, large and small, thrown and kicked from the slow-moving gondola cars by youths and young adults. The three mile grade extended to Irondale and leveled off. The coal was collected in hundred pound croker sacks and sold to neighborhood patrons for fifty cents. Daddy bought quite a few.

Detectives began riding the freights and curtailed the activity somewhat, but not altogether. They shot at a few of the persistent outlaws, but none were ever hit or arrested to my knowledge.

Before the word malnutrition, meaning undernourished, came into popular usage in my community, children were referred to as poor or skinny with wasted bodies, mottled skin and pot bellies. I saw quite a few in the community and at school. Many subsisted on syrup and biscuits on a routine basis. Sopping syrup and gravy when there was no meat, milk or other protein foods, was an unhappy fact of life. The depression was devastating. Alaga, Brer Rabbit, Yellow Label and Sorghum were popular brands of syrup. I sopped my share when it was heated and mixed with butter. It was fairly good,but I really didn't prefer it.

We always had plenty of good wholesome food because we raised dozens of chickens which were eaten regularly. They provided lots of eggs, too.

Our garden yielded collard and turnip greens, corn, tomatoes (I ate many cornmealed green fried tomatoes—um, um, good), string beans, cabbage, squash and beets plus fruits and vegetables from Daddy's fruit and vegetable wagon. We had rice, grits, oatmeal, macaroni and cheese, corn flakes, bacon, butter and eggs alternately for breakfast throughout the year. Fried chicken, biscuits and gravy always on Sunday mornings.

Fish was cheap, three pounds of mullet for a quarter was a bargain, except for the dozens of sharp bones encountered. I invariably managed to get one lodged in my throat. It was only a temporary discomfort because there was that piece of crusty corn bread or corn pone to dislodge it, bringing instant relief without a trip to the doctor. Croker was popular but Mother didn't like it. We could occasionally afford the more expensive red snapper or Spanish mackerel. Fried fish was delicious to me.

Fried wild rabbit was very good, too. Mr. Slaughter, a neighbor, loved to go hunting, always bagging enough to give us one. Father bought them for a quarter at our local grocery store. Buckshots frequently were encountered while biting into a piece.

I don't know if there were any ordinances in Birmingham against raising hogs within the city limits. If there were, they were never cited. Mr. Slaughter butchered two annually. Father helped him and vice-versa. He would give us a nice mess of pork tenderloin and liver, we reciprocated.

Rapid sounds, glop, glop, glop, glop emanated from the bucket of slop poured into the hog's trough and very quickly mopped up. All of the leftover scraps from previous meals, plus the gastronomic delights from McGough's Bakery, loaves of day-old bread and cakes returned from grocery stores, were lapped up rapidly. Daddy bought the old bakery goods cheaply by the truckload. They were a bargain for feeding the hogs and us. I retrieved many a loaf when our flour bin was empty. If there was a little greenish mold on the bread or cakes, it was removed. A little undiscovered penicillin from a tiny portion of mold never hurt us. The baked goods were stored in the barn where "Old Sugar" slept, the horse that pulled Daddy's vegetable wagon before he bought the truck. The pound cakes, some filled with raisins, were a super dessert for me, as well as the hogs.

Shorts, a very fine, powdered, pale brown feed made from grains and mixed with water, was lapped up readily by the hogs. The price was five pounds for a quarter. Watermelon rinds, remnants from the hundreds of slices sold at the stand every summer, were a delicacy for them.

The hogs to be butchered were kept in a pen with a specially built wooden floor and were generously fed the best whole-grain corn for fattening.

I wonder how many people have seen a drunken hog? Father and I had such an experience and, I must say, it was a hilarious sight. We heard an unusual amount of intensive squealing and grunting from Susie, the hog, and went to the pen to see what was wrong. Her staggering was baffling. Daddy said "Damn, I bet that corn mash from the still made her drunk. I didn't realize it would affect her."

The mash was the result of an aborted attempt by him to distill some pure whiskey in our dining room from whole-grain corn. Since Susie was on a wooden floor receiving corn for fattening at butchering time, corn was corn, so he poured it into her trough.

We butchered a couple every year, each weighing eight hundred to a thousand pounds. They yielded lots of pork chops, sausage, roasts and lard. Nothing about those hogs was wasted. The small and large intestines were removed, opened and the putrid contents taken away and buried. The intestines, called chitterlings, were then washed three or four times in a large tub of cold water to thoroughly cleanse them. They were then ready to be boiled or battered and fried. They were a delicacy which we enjoyed during hog killing time in December or January every year. Cabbage slaw, hot sauce and corn bread with a plate of chitterlings was always a delightful meal for me. Chitterlings, neck bones, collard and turnip greens, sweet potatoes and corn bread are classified as "soul food." Chitterlings are the godfather of soul food. I don't eat them anymore because of their high cholesterol content. Mother also made stew with the liver and lights, the lungs.

We had plenty of ham as the two hogs Dad butchered yielded four large hindquarters. We didn't have a smokehouse for curing so Father took the long butcher knife he used to pierce the heart, penetrated to the bone making a fairly wide tract and filled it with table salt. They were wrapped in gunny sacks, placed in trunks and stored on the back porch.

After curing, it was a slate color and desalted by soaking in water for a meal. When eaten with biscuits and syrup the salty taste was much more palatable and always tasted good to me. The outer skin and underlying fat, when salted, became bacon. Even the hooves were utilized, after being roasted and boiled, to make a hot tea that was supposed to be good for treating colds and bad coughs.

Although Lux, Camay, Ivory and Palmolive soaps were used for bathing and hand washing, at ten cents a bar and three for a quarter, Mother made her own soap from the fat of the hogs.

Octagon bar soap, brown in color and bland, cost five cents a bar and was used to wash clothes. It served on many occasions the same purposes as the higher quality, sweet-smelling, perfumed soaps.

Red Devil lye was a very powerful, white powder sold in a 4x7 inch can, symbolized by a small elderly lady in a red dress and cap, holding a pitch fork. It was caustic and powerful. When a tablespoonful was added to a bucket of sudsy, medium hot water and a mop inserted, the sloshing action produced a bleached-white floor and hands to match. Added to hog fat in our huge, black iron pot it produced a brown mixture. After solidification it was cut into convenient soap-sized bars. When we were out of store-bought soap we washed our face, hands and bathed with it. It lathered fairly well and did the job. It didn't burn the skin, but felt strange. It was one of Mother's favorites.

Lunch at our home was never a planned affair. I was on my own. A visit to the warmer of the stove was in order. Cold biscuits were the anchor for my variety of good fixings. Two thick slices of a red onion, a ripe tomato or cucumber slices saturated with salt made a superb snack. A heaping teaspoonful of sugar or jelly atop a well-buttered biscuit was also delicious. Sweet pickles were great, but my favorites were a bologna or sausage pattie inside a cold biscuit. Peanut butter was good, too, but very stiff and hard to swallow until I mustered up enough saliva to soften it.

A cold sweet potato was filling and pleasureful, as were left-over spareribs, pork steak and chops or neck bones from the previous night's supper. I never received any static from Mother for cleaning out the warmer.

Blackberry soup was the name I coined for the glass of crushed berries with sugar added I was about to enjoy. While eating my delicious concoction thoughts of cobblers with dumplings, especially during the winter months, jumped for joy in my head. The multitude of scratches that stung so much, especially after a bath, seemed to magically heal. Mother canned many quarts from the five to ten gallons I picked every summer.

On the way home we always stopped at the artesian well for a cold drink. We three, Curtis Canada, Bunch Washington and I, took turns lying on our stomach drinking that bubbling, cold water. What a welcome treat after picking berries for several hours in the heat from a boiling hot sun.

Growing boys like to eat. I was a good example. The depression brought about gastronomical survival inventions. The empty spot in my alimentary canal (stomach and intestines) was always begging to be filled. Running, jumping, falling and rolling around in the grass consumed all the calories I could muster. Food was the answer and money was scarce.

Hunting by blacks for food during the depression was a rewarding pastime, putting questionable delicacies for exotic tastes on their tables.

While elite whites dined on caviar, pheasant and squab at fancy restaurants where blacks couldn't light, blacks dined on opossums, commonly called possums, a mammal with a pouch to carry its young. Thought of as graveyard scavengers that dug into graves and feasted on the dead, they were considered a delicacy. Raccoons, a flesh eating, nocturnal mammal, rabbits, squirrels and various kinds of birds were special treats, too.

When I saw my first opossum, one of several given to Father by a life-long friend and excellent hunter, Mr. Joe Gates, I was dumbfounded by that scowling, rat-looking critter. When told it was edible I said, "No way." Father was reared in rural

Alabama where there were quite a few. His mother prepared them for their family and he developed an extreme liking for them. He instructed Mother how to prepare it. She placed that large, grinning creature with its long hairless tail into a roasting pan, keeping her head turned aside to avoid that awful sight, and surrounded it with lots of sweet potatoes sprinkled heavily with cayenne pepper. I was sick to the stomach observing. As it roasted, she collected more than a half dozen cups of grease from the pan. Finally, she removed that sort of shiny brown, roasted delicacy from the oven and called us to dinner. My first fork full, along with the extremely hot sweet potato, wasn't too bad. There was a tiny streak of lean in it and mixing it with a huge bite of corn bread made it palatable. We ate several during my childhood. I was always happy for Mother to roast one. They were fairly good eating.

The happiest time in my young life in the early thirties was the end of May with the closing of school and the beginning of the watermelon season. The deepening depression had caused Father to stop his fruit and vegetable route. He continued to deliver a few gallons of whiskey to his former huckster route customers via his automobile, until it became scarce due to the federal revenuer's destruction of many illicit stills.

As a carryover from his days of buying and selling fruits and vegetables, the thought flashed through Father's mind of selling watermelons from an ideal spot, the vacant lot adjacent to our home underneath the convenient shade of a large old elm tree on the corner of Georgia Road, a thoroughfare to Atlanta, Georgia, and also heavily traveled by locals, extending to the corner of 62nd Street, which dead-ended into Georgia Road.

Beginning with one hundred plus melons, their rapid disappearance encouraged him to buy more. A profitable income utilizing his expertise of predicting what was on the inside of one from observation, patting, thumping and interpreting the sounds, made his word law. His reputation spread widely for selling good melons.

One day I heard him say, "I wonder who owns this lot. I'd like to buy it and build a stand to protect my melons from the elements." He didn't know about inquiring at the tax assessor's office to find out. He decided to hire Mr. James Bennett, a local carpenter, to do the job. It didn't take him long. The lower part was solid wood, about three feet high with screen wire extending to the ceiling on three sides. The back was all wood from the ground to the roof.

Mr. Whiteside, a white businessman who lived in Anniston, Alabama, 22 miles north of us, occasionally went to downtown Birmingham passing our home en route. One day he stopped, knocked on the door and Father answered. He introduced himself and told Father his mother owned the lot which was filled with two to three hundred watermelons. Father acknowledged his introduction, introduced himself and said he was interested in buying it. Mr. Whiteside said he would ask his mother if she wanted to sell. Two weeks later he stopped and said his mother was interested in selling it for five thousand dollars. Father told him he didn't have that much cash. "I will ask mother if it could be paid in monthly installments." He returned a few days later and said she accepted his offer. A deal was made and Father eventually became the owner of the lot.

Knives, forks, spoons, plates and four chairs were brought from the house. A dishpan of soapy water was kept on one end of the icebox to wash the silverware and plates. They were rinsed in another pan of water and dried. One-fourth of a twenty-five to thirty pound watermelon, when cut, sold for ten cents with half that size going for five. Slices to go were also popular. Some customers became so sophisticated wanting table salt, that we had to bring in a salt shaker and refill it quite often. Some said it made the melon sweeter. That form of socialization was very popular. Watermelon was very filling and enjoyable to the taste. A full bladder resulted, but not hard to remedy.

Father went to the Farmer's Market about fifteen miles from our home where many farmers from nearby Alabama and Georgia towns brought truckloads of melons. A price agreeable to both parties resulted after much bargaining. The farmer brought the load to our stand. He always threw them to Father who handed them to me to stack. Sometimes there were several hundred inside and out front of the stand. Two large lights which burned all night were installed in front and on one side. If anyone ever took any in the lateness of the night, we never knew.

Professor Oliver, a high school principal, came from the north side of Woodlawn to the south side to buy his melons. All were guaranteed. Father told all of his customers they didn't have to bring back half of a green melon for replacement, just tell him. Very few abused the privilege, returning with nothing but praise and bought another melon.

Business was brisk all summer, every year. I became quite a little salesman as the melons were in piles and priced according to size. Proudly, I carried quite a sizable amount of change in my pockets and at night deposited it in a large bowl in our china closet. That made me feel like a big business man.

Father began to buy twenty to twenty-five pounds of spareribs at eight cents a pound for Mother to barbecue. I sat outside with her until 2 or 3 a.m., Sunday mornings to keep her company. She started barbecuing early Saturday during the summer and developed a large clientele.

Those good, old fashioned, barbecued spareribs and pork shoulder, arranged atop a number 3 tin tub ventilated by several holes punched around the side of the tub that was covered with a square piece of window screen, simmered for hours over the hot, charcoal embers. I'm sure Mother had never heard of a barbecue pit. It was located next to our watermelon stand and was a bustling gathering place every Saturday during the hot summer months. Everyone's taste buds would get excited in anticipation of those oh, so good delicacies.

Mr. James Collier always used his pocket knife with a three-inch blade to clean the bones—a strange sight.

Barbecue sandwiches were sold for ten cents each and consisted of four ribs between two slices of bread to which she added her original, red-hot barbecue sauce. It made the taste buds tingle and the sandwich very tasty and delicious.

The sauce consisted of tomato catsup, lemon juice, the pulp of the lemon, cayenne pepper, vinegar and water. The mixture was placed atop the kitchen stove and allowed to simmer an hour or so. The aroma really stimulated my taste buds. I made hot sauce sandwiches after the ribs were gone. They were finger-licking good.

Whenever somebody stopped to buy barbecue, Mother wrapped it in a piece of the old daily newspaper that was kept on top of our kitchen cabinet. One day, a white gentleman bought a small slab of ribs that she wrapped in newspaper. He watched, then pointed out to her that she should use waxed paper. She apologized; he took his ribs, went on his way and never returned.

From that day on she bought large quantities of waxed paper and used it to wrap the sandwiches.

We also sold soft drinks, all flavors: ginger ale, grape, strawberry, cherry, Coca-Cola, orange, cherry cola and chocolate, for five cents per six ounce bottle. Town Hall flavors cost five cents a quart. I was always happy to see summertime come as the stand was a hub for many entertaining relationships.

Now and then Father would take me on his truck to sell fruits and vegetables. I was thrilled. First we would go downtown to 20th Street and 1st Avenue North, not far from the Louisville and Nashville Railroad Station, to a place called The Team Track. There were boxcars of watermelons, bananas, apples and vegetables sold wholesale to hucksters, like him. I was left sitting in the truck and remember the first time I saw him returning with a big stalk of bananas cradled in his arms. I jumped up and let out aloud yell, "Goody, goody, gum drops!" because I liked bananas better than any fruit I had ever eaten. He immediately yelled at me, "What's the matter with you, boy?" I had no answer, as his tone of voice subdued my enthusiasm. I never showed that type of emotion again, even though I went with him off and on.

My next best thrill was stopping in a place called Avondale, at Mrs. Brown's Cafe for lunch. Father bought two barbecued, sliced pork sandwiches with a great tasting barbecue sauce, which soaked the meat and bun. I thought it was the best sandwich I had ever eaten. Over the next few years I was overjoyed being with him and stopping at Mrs. Brown's.

It was interesting to hear his myriad of customers, mainly female, call him "Sweet Oranges." He adopted that moniker after quite a few of his customers jokingly told him how sour his oranges were. "Oh, no, all of my oranges are sweet," he would always reply. "Sweet oranges, sweet oranges," became his clarion call to let them know he was in the neighborhood. Guess I would have become "Little Sweet Oranges" if I had been with him more. Oranges, peaches, bananas and apples were sold by the dozen. Large red and golden apples sold for five cents each.

Early one winter morning, his Ford truck overturned and landed upside down from skidding on icy streetcar tracks. He left home at 5 a.m. to get his fruits and vegetables for his daily route. He also distributed gallon cans of moonshine whiskey to Mrs. Ada Coleman and Henry Eskett. This particular morning he had only a gallon can. Fortunately, he wore a large, leather, fur-collared coat, wasn't hurt, alighted from the truck, grabbed the whiskey, put it underneath his coat and walked three miles home. Luckily no one was around that early in the morning.

When he returned home and knocked on the back door Mother was surprised. I heard the knock, arose and went to the door behind her. She unlatched it and there he stood. "What's the matter, Thomas!"

"The truck turned over. It's out in Avondale."

"Are you hurt?"

"No, I'm O.K." He pulled the gallon of whiskey from under his coat and placed it on the kitchen table. I felt relieved when I saw he was O.K. and returned to bed. I heard Mother ask. "What about the truck?"

"I don't know, guess the police will tow it to

their lot and I'll call Crawford's to go get it and fix it."

We didn't have a phone, so he waited until about 8 a.m. and went to Mr.Worth's home, a couple of doors down the street to call. They said they would go get the truck and he could call that afternoon about repairs. A few days later he called and they told him to come get it. He was in business again, selling booze and huckstering as usual.

As the economy grew tighter, our dogs, old Jack, a male English bulldog, and Spot, a female mongrel, came upon hard times, too. The ten cent soup bone, formerly theirs, became ours exclusively. Mr. Tombrello, the grocer, and Father were good friends and, at his request, saved them for us. There was always enough meat left on the bone to make a delicious pot of beef stew with all kinds of garden vegetables added and some of Mother's great corn bread to top it off.

There was no canned dog food in those days. We fed them leftover biscuits, gravy, chicken, ham, steak and sparerib bones. Luckily, they never had a problem with the chicken bones, which were said to be bad for dogs. They sharpened their teeth on the bones and survived very well.

Old Jack, white in color and built like a fire plug, bowed front and back legs, big, wide turned up nose, well moistened, drooling mouth and deep set, dangerous looking eyes had to be respected. Spot was so designated because of her solid white color, accented by a round, black spot the size of a small orange on her back. They were excellent watch dogs. When visitors came to the swinging gate, Old Jack would rumble against it and roar, almost frightening the life out of them.

Even though the weighted gate closed after exiting, he would open it and go after dogs that walked through the vacant lot next to our home, his territory. He shook quite a few, always by the throat. Daddy doused him and his prey many times with large buckets of water, attempting to make him break his hold after pulling his hind legs and frantic commands failed. Mrs. Betty Humphrey's shaggy dog from a few yards down the alley became a fatality one Saturday night near the watermelon stand. His throat, Old Jack's specialty, was cut from ear to ear.

Our speckled, black and brown cat, Sweet Ditty, was a jewel. She, too, was fed table scraps. I have known her to jump atop the dining room table where Mother had placed a platter of meat, snatch a piece, jump off, only to be apprehended and robbed of her prized meal by Mother. When we were eating she always meowed, purred and rubbed against my pant legs. I would break off pieces of biscuit or corn bread and drop them to her, over the protestations of Mother, who positively said, "Don't throw bread on that floor. If you don't stop, I'm gonna put you outdoors with her." I never stopped. She just gave up.

I was emotionally shaken one day when Ditty, wandered over to Robert Hood's home. I knew the Hood family very well. Mr. and Mrs. Hood were fine working people with a beautiful yellow home, which I could see very well from our back porch. They had two children, both young adults. Robert was a jolly, hyperactive young man, frequently seen with his two big unleashed brown and white bulldogs running up and down Georgia Road. He was very fond of them. They looked dangerous to me. His sister, Mae Lizzie, was a jolly, outgoing young lady.

One day, his dogs jumped on Ditty as she wandered into their backyard, slashing and chewing her head until it had the appearance of hamburger. He undoubtedly stopped the carnage, as she was able to return home. When we saw her, Father decided nothing could be done to make her well. He put her into a croker sack and took her up to the railroad tracks. When a slow freight was passing he threw her onto a gondola car heading for Chattanooga, Tennessee.

That was a sad day in my life. I really missed Ditty.

Little did I realize I would one day receive a lesson in chastisement from Robert's father, who bought watermelons from Father. Old man Hood was a Birmingham Barons baseball fan and often discussed baseball with Father. I was a novice, at nine years of age, but read the sport pages and was knowledgeable about the Barons. Mr. Hood followed the Barons via radio. We didn't have one at that time, so one Friday night while at the stand, he invited Father and me to his home for a baseball broadcast the next day. Daddy didn't go, but said I could and with my uninhibited enthusiasm, Mr. Hood welcomed me. Things went well as we listened to station WAPI when Birmingham put on a rally. The announcer sounded a gong, once for a single, twice for a double, three times for a triple and a rip-roaring, ear-bursting four times for a home run. I was sitting quietly when suddenly Fielding Flue, his real name and a pitcher for the Barons, singled. The announcer banged the bell and two runs scored. I couldn't stand the prosperity, jumped to my feet hollering, "Wooo-weee! Wooo-weee!" until Mr. Hood, in his raspy voice, said, "Sit down, don't carry on like that in my house." I was stunned and sat down, my enthusiasm squelched for the rest of the game. I never went to his home again to listen to a baseball broadcast or for any other reason.

The news of the new dimension to Father's huckstering business spread. He introduced mind altering, narcotic-like, addictive, crystal clear, 135-proof whiskey, made from corn and called various names—hooch, booze, white lightning or fire water. Call it whatever you want, it was powerful as evidenced by the multitude of beautiful, multicolored beads which covered the entire surface when shaken. A beautiful blue flame spiraled upward when a few drops were poured onto the floor and lighted. A burning mouth and inebriation occurred when excessive amounts were ingested.

His new business spread slowly by word of mouth and the neighborhood clientele increased to a goodly number. I knew and respected them all. They were very nice, upstanding people. I never heard any of them swear in our home. There were several railroad employees, steel workers and downtown workers who had charge accounts to pay for their hooch. The railroad men paid off like "Roscoe" every two weeks and came by four to six times weekly after work and weekends to get a shot, half or full pint or a seven-eighth quart. "Roscoe" was the name given to a slot machine instant jackpot payoff. They were found in private white country clubs, even though they were illegal in Birmingham. Uncle Sandy's white friends acquainted him with the word "Roscoe."

The other customers paid as they drank and also became regular enough to ask for and receive credit. Some of them owe Father until this day. Mother had her clientele, three beautiful women. Two were railroad wives and one's husband an ice man. The former charged their drinks. The latter paid on the spot. The railroad wives paid every two weeks. This was a steady income during the depression.

For Mother and me this became a degrading business. Sister was only three and had no feelings about what was going on. As time moved on, unfortunately, Father became his biggest consumer of that mind altering substance. Drinking changed his mild behavior into outrageous cursing, threatening and violent behavior. I never knew when lightning would strike. Our family unit became more and more chaotic. Mother and I were his chief victims. She drank very little and was very mild mannered.

Chapter 3
Childhood Memories

My earliest memory of a childhood incident was when Mother's friend, Mrs. Annie Bell who lived across the street from us, persuaded Mother to go to a Sunday School picnic in our car. Since Mother didn't drive, Mrs. Bell told her she would ask Mr. Bennett, a local carpenter, to drive us. He agreed and we were off to Irondale, three miles away, with picnic baskets full of goodies. Mother and I were in the back seat of our four-door 1930, Buick Sedan and upon arrival at the park, before the car stopped I suddenly pulled the door handle. The door flew open and I fell to the ground on my face. Blood flew everywhere from my nostrils. Needless to say, I cried. Mother was very upset but not too upset to declare me to secrecy that I wouldn't tell Father when he returned from work that evening. I always waited for him to come home so I could climb onto the wagon and get an apple, orange or banana. As soon as he arrived, before climbing up, I excitedly told him about my fall from the car, striking my nose on the ground. He stepped down slowly, after giving me a banana and we went into the house. Mother had heard me tell him about my fall from the car and explained what happened.

She told him that would never happen again.

The streetcar going downtown ran in front of our home and was adequate transportation for her needs. I really got excited as a little tyke when I saw it coming and would begin to jump up and down, loudly announcing to Mother and everyone within hearing distance: "Dee car, dee car," until it arrived and we boarded old Twenty-one. DeeCar became my first nickname, given to me by Mrs. Ada McSpadden, a neighbor who lived about 200 yards from our home across the street, a short distance from where the streetcar stopped. She sat on her front porch every day during the hot summer, fanning, trying to keep cool and heard me holler loudly, "Dee car, dee car," quite a few times so she and her husband, Walter, nicknamed me "DeeCar." They called me that until I left Birmingham at age 23. I don't know if they knew my name was Edwin.

The streetcar ride was a great adventure for me, but even more exciting was the visit to the candy store where Mother bought lots of goodies that eventually caused many visits to the dentist.

Saturday night was the only night of the week I looked forward to. When Daddy did our grocery shopping at Mr.Joe Tombrello's neighborhood store, I was happy when he left and ecstatic when he returned with two nickel boxes of crunchy Cracker Jacks for sister and me.

To double the pleasure was that big surprise, a tin cricket that clicked and made lots of noise. There were always whistles and interesting toys in the box and I was overjoyed with all of them. It was almost like Christmas anticipating what Santa Claus would bring.

The syrup-covered peanuts were the best treat I'd ever eaten. I only wished there were two dozen more, rather than the precious few in that magical box.

Bonding with Father was very brittle. Sometimes he was happy and smiled, other times he drank his 135-proof moonshine and was in an abusive mood, cursing and threatening Mother and me. I was one to shy away from him and tried to do things to make him think well of me. He seemed to be jealous of Mother and me. I came to the conclusion he liked sister better as she did mean things to me, was sassy to Mother and he said nothing.

It was mind boggling when one afternoon he accused Mother of being pregnant by another man when he married her. They were married June 4, 1919, and I was born seven months later, January 9, 1920. I could have been a seven-month gestational infant and he the father, rather than Dallas Green who he said was a one-time boyfriend. He sat in the presence of Mother, my six year old sister and me and counted on his fingers the months since their marriage and my birth. It occurred to me after he blurted out I wasn't a Witt how badly mistaken he was, as I looked exactly like him and heard many neighbors say the same. He stated I had a long chin, while his was short.

I told him on more than one occasion my name was "Edwin Edwin." I didn't want to be a Witt. His drinking, abusive language, physical abuse and threats would pop up at any time. I never felt comfortable, not knowing what to expect, especially goodness, kindness and peace. They were hard to come by. When his finances and supply of whiskey were low, he would take his frustrations out on Mother and me. He never abused sister. She would just stand by and watch the turmoil.

I was especially terrified one Saturday night

when they went a block away to Lang Floyd's house to a weekly fish fry and dance. As soon as they returned home, the slammed front door shuddered and a loud argument began. They rushed through the bedroom and began fighting as soon as they reached the dining room. He grabbed Mother, threw her down and began beating her. I was very frightened. Sister was asleep and never awoke throughout the altercation. I thought he might kill her as the screaming and crying for him to stop rang loudly in my ears. I got up and pulled him off of her. He was very angry at me.

Another Saturday night, I was really frightened when he threw her against the china closet in the dining room. Her left hand went through the glass door and the fifth finger was severely lacerated. She screamed, I jumped from my bed, rushed to her aid and saw blood gushing from the wound. I grabbed a large white towel from the bureau drawer and she wrapped it around her finger, soaking it quickly and thoroughly with blood. It eventually stopped. She did not seek any medical care.

They attended another Lang Floyd Saturday night free-for-all where "Sweet Pertooty" played his guitar and sang. He set the tone for violence as he routinely broke a guitar over his sweetheart's head every Saturday night.

As a child I saw him, with his large guitar slung across his left shoulder. He was a short, mild-mannered man with combed-back glossy, wavy hair, showing his white ivory teeth at the sight of any human being he met. He always smiled and greeted me politely. "How you, Mr. Sweet Pertooty?" I would say.

"Fine young man, how are you?" he would reply. I heard the ladies gloated about him, Mother excluded because Father was so jealous. I hated for them to go to a Lang Floyd party.

When I was between eight and nine years of age I used to hear Father sing, "Ditty, Yitty, Yit, hell's gonna break out in Georgia." He sang it much too often for me. He had no voice for singing, but those words were a loud prelude to the violence soon to be directed towards Mother and was very frightening to me. It wouldn't be long before he would attack her like a linebacker or defensive end on a football team attacks a quarterback. He would throw her down, get on top of her and go for her throat when she tried to rid him of her. She screamed while scuffling, saying, "Stop it, stop it, get up off of me!" His fury engulfed her and me. My mind was a frightened, burning hell because I couldn't stand to see him hurting her. I would always pull him off and that did not ingratiate me with him.

Mother and I developed a very solemn facial disposition towards him every time we saw him drinking a glass of fire-water. I'm sure he read the disapprovals and lumped us as allies against him. We wouldn't have been if the booze hadn't driven him to abusive, threatening and violent behavior. We needed each other's support.

We didn't have to see him drink it. His attitudinal behavior would sooner or later tell on him. Therefore, we always knew the score. His drinking took place daily. He'd sleep off a drunk and begin another immediately on awakening. Those were scary times for me. Furthermore, an uprising of unknown cause could erupt at any time.

Sister told me one day when I wasn't home Father had his 38 Special revolver in his lap while sitting across the room from Mother in her rocking chair about three feet away reading the paper.

He was having one of his wolfing, out-of-touch-with-reality sessions and pulled the trigger. The bullet went across her lap and embedded in the wall. She did nothing.

Another day, Mama told me, he heated her up with a beating and she obtained the 38 Special from the bedroom, chased him out the back door down an alley, shooting at him every step of the way, five times, but missed. He was an exasperating alcoholic.

Alcoholism must be in the genes. His father was an abusive alcoholic who lived in Livingston, Alabama, 105 miles south of Birmingham. According to Aunt Mary—Father's sister—her mother told her he was found dead sitting upright in a chair from poisoned whiskey given him by a daughter in-law.

My sister, Annie Ruth, was mean, hateful and bossy. We fought often, especially when I wouldn't let her test her red fingernail polish on my little finger. She would fly into me at the least provocation, kicking and hitting.

I especially recall one time when Mother was downtown shopping for shoes, clothing and other necessities. She and I decided to make some peanut brittle. We took a pan from the cupboard, put some syrup, peanuts and a little butter into it and placed it atop the heater in the dining room. It was winter and the heater was very hot. She chose to be the cook, stirring the mixture thoroughly. I went to the kitchen, fetched a fork, began stirring in unison and decided to taste it. Sister became angered and told me to wait until it was done. I didn't obey, continuing to taste until she blew a fuse and threw the fork at me. The prongs stuck and became embedded in the skin on the back of my right hand. I screamed and retaliated, grabbing a "Try Me" soft drink bottle and struck her across the forehead. It didn't knock her out, but stunned her momentarily and left a small dent. Shortly afterwards, Mother returned and I showed her the back of my hand with the fork still embedded. She became furious, put her packages down, removed the fork, picked up her little brown strap and gave sister a thrashing. We settled down, the candy cooled and we finally ate it. Mother soundly reprimanded us and told us never to try making candy or anything else when she was not home.

It was very hard to get along with sister. She cursed and spouted off at me and anybody who sparked her fuse. She and Beatrice Duncan were four days apart in age. They had been playmates and classmates from early childhood. For some unknown reason, they became angry with one another and didn't speak for a year. Beatrice lived just across the street from us. Mother and Mrs. Duncan brought them together, encouraging them to start communicating again.

Sister flunked the twelfth junior grade for sassiness. Professor Whatley, her print shop teacher, an old time, very popular teacher at Industrial High, tried to intercede on her behalf, but to no avail. Dorothy Ruth Chatman, a neighbor who had a penchant for taking no foolishness from anyone, was sister's match. When she threatened Annie Ruth, she came to me and said "Ebby", as she always called me, "are you gonna beat her for me?"

"No." Dorothy Ruth had an older sibling, Elizabeth, a rough customer with a short fuse with whom I wanted no entanglement. They had an older brother, Robert, who was bigger than I, but very docile. Things quieted down and there were no further disagreements between them.

Annie Ruth cared for our little brother quite a bit and taught him how to curse. At age two I admonished her for making "Hitty" sound like "Shi—y." He was not toilet trained and smelled kinda bad sometimes, so she composed that little ditty. She paid me no mind. I knew it would be useless to tell my parents, so silence prevented any further problems between her and me on that score.

My earliest introduction to special holidays was Mother's extra emphasis on preparation. I was four years old when she told sister and me about Christmas and Santa Claus.

Christmas Eve was a very busy time in the kitchen, with Mother getting the pastries and cakes prepared. Sister and I assumed the same positions around the kitchen cabinet as we did to eat breakfast and dinner. It was a delight for me seeing Mother filling the sifter from the flour bin and turning the handle round and round over the big yellow bowl, then adding the other ingredients. The mixture was beaten and beaten with roundhouse strokes until fluffy and ready for the pans. Sister and I waited patiently for samples which Mother put in two little pans for us. Our taste buds were secreting saliva by the mouthful in anticipation of that long awaited treat. There was nothing more delicious as that long anticipated hot cake.

She made a large plain cake, a three-layered coconut and a three-layered chocolate one. Coconut milk was my special treat. Mother punched a hole in the end of the coconut with an ice pick, placed it over a glass and I watched it drip slowly. It was sweet and I enjoyed it very much. When she cracked the coconut with a hammer several pieces of varying sizes scattered and we'd be given a chunk. It was delicious. Three sweet potato pies were always on her agenda and the residue from the bowls was cleaned up by sister and me.

Annie Ruth and I were allowed to stay up past our usual bedtime on that special occasion. Christmas was our favorite time. We were so excited, sleep interruptions kept us almost constantly inquiring if Santa had arrived.

After we were sound asleep, Father and Mother took our presents from underneath a big quilt in a small side room and arranged them on the dining room table and floor for that grand and glorious Christmas morning celebration.

Christmas Day had finally come; there suddenly appeared a wagon, two tricycles, a rocking horse, triggered toy guns that sparkled, a train, assorted candies, raisins with bothersome seeds, all kinds of nuts, new shoes, clothing and several games. For Annie Ruth, a doll and buggy, a set of miniature dishes and a jump rope. Mother told us Santa Claus brought them down the chimney. Bedlam broke loose when we began playing with our toys; guns popping and horns blowing—the excitement lasted all day.

Santa had really come to our house.

After the initial glitter that captivated and excited my senses calmed down I dressed and returned to the dining room table where I filled my pockets with raisins and nuts, then to the icebox and fetched a slice of sweet potato pie, a slice of coconut and chocolate cake and chomped them down in short order. That was only the prelude for a growing boy before a hearty breakfast of chicken and dressing, two scrambled eggs and hot biscuits.

I still nurture with deep reverence the close bonding with my maternal Grandmother for the few months I spent with her before she left this life in 1926 for bright mansions above.

I was her first and only grandson. She adored

me. I wish she had lived much longer; my young
life would have been happier and easier living with
her and Mr. Cleveland Mathis, my step-grandfa-
ther. His nickname was "Now." That's what Mother
always called him. I don't know why. He worked
in the repair shop for the Louisville and Nashville
Railroad and was good to me. They lived very well
in a suburb called East Birmingham, about ten
miles from Woodlawn.

Shortly after I was four years old she requested
and received permission to keep me for various
periods of time. Mother had made her aware of
Father's drinking, selling whiskey, emotional and
physical abuse.

There were only two houses near Grandmother's. Mrs. Stroud lived diagonally across the street
and had many, many guineas. I was fascinated by
those funny shaped sort of blue and white speckled birds with white heads. They made lots of very
strange loud noises and were a bit threatening
when I wandered near them. Mrs. Fuchs, the other
neighbor, was elderly and lived on the other side
of a vacant lot separating her home from Grandmother's. There were no children with whom I
could play. The only other building in sight was
about three blocks from Grandmother's back
porch, a crematorium for animals and the stench
in late afternoon was very strange when the wind
blew our way.

My tricycle and other playthings were in
Woodlawn so I entertained myself sitting in the
swing, running and jumping, walking among the
many chickens in the back yard and feeding them.
I also helped her gather the eggs.

The most frightening experience in my young
life took place in the back yard while walking
among the hens, roosters and baby chicks, which
I later learned to call "Biddies." There were many

of them and to me were the most beautiful little things I'd ever seen. They looked like play pretties to me. One day I attempted to pick up one and suddenly with flapping wings mother hen landed atop my head, frapping my face with her bony wings and scratching my head with her feet throughout that surprise attack. I couldn't see and screamed, "Grandmother, grandmother!" jumping up and down, flailing my arms, when she finally rushed from the house to my rescue. The old hen scurried away, all ruffled, as Grandmother looked me over. "Oh, I think you're O.K. I'm sorry she frightened you that way, but you see mother hen was angry because she thought you were going to hurt her little biddie." That somewhat placated my fears as we walked towards the house, scattering chickens in all directions. We retired to the front porch to relax awhile. I never got close to those biddies again. Mother hen's message had registered loud and clear!

I always enjoyed breakfast with Grandmother. We sat at the table, she said grace, and I said my little Bible verse. A large glass of cold milk, fresh from the cows, was a delight. The crowning glory came when she'd announce "Edwin, we're going to the store this morning." I anxiously watched for her to get her shopping bag after breakfast. I began to hop, skip and jump from room to room, filled with the joy of going with her.

Next she got her parasol, as umbrellas were called in those days, pocketbook and told me to get my sun hat. Leaving by way of the back gate, it was a few yards to Vanderbilt Pike, an unpaved, very long thoroughfare with no sidewalks. There were many tall, green trees on either side, except in front of Grandmother's and Mrs. Fuchs' homes. It extended to paved 39th Street where the store was located and in the opposite direction to

Vanderbilt Mines. We never went that way.

The sun was hot, even in the early morn, so Grandmother opened her parasol as we trudged along. She held my little hand whenever a car approached from behind. There weren't many cars in those days. She and "Now" didn't have one. He rode to work with a co-worker who picked him up very early every work day. They rode the streetcar to Woodlawn and downtown.

It was a nice long walk up Vanderbilt Pike, across a bridge over the rather long, wide Cahaba River. People said there were cotton-mouthed water moccasin snakes in there, but that didn't deter some brave people from swimming. The store was about two miles from Grandmother's so I was really ready for some refreshments when we finally arrived. A strong "cheracola" soft drink would almost strangle me. The effervescence excited my nostrils with bubbly, stinging sensations. It was fun. She bought me a long stick of peppermint candy one day, the next a black cow, a thick piece of sticky caramel covered with chocolate, a real cavity producer. Her goodness helped me develop a sweet tooth for which I later paid the price. I looked forward to another special treat every evening at milking time. I patiently watched her milk the two cows when they were brought to the barn from the nice green pasture between Grandmother's house and Mrs.Fuchs'. As soon as she reached the kitchen with a steaming pail of foamy milk, she filled a big glass, added several chunks of ice and handed it to me. It was oooh, sooo good!

Uncle Buck, Raymond Ogletree, was Grandmother's only son. He was living at home with her and stepfather and was my big, grown-up buddy. Sometimes he would take me to his favorite hangout, Mrs. Ada Rye's small grocery store, and buy me a bar of sugar-coated rainbow colored coconut candy. It had three layers; green, red and white. I really liked it. Once he took me bird hunting. We trekked through the woods and suddenly he raised the gun to his shoulder and BANG! A little yellow hammer fell to the ground. I felt sad, but Uncle Buck just picked it up and we traveled on. It began to rain very hard. We found a shelter in an old abandoned barn and he took that opportunity to pull out his harmonica and serenade me. He seemed to enjoy playing while I just sat and listened. It was O.K.

Early in January Grandmother and Grandfather decided to go to Detroit, Michigan, to see her sister, Lela Spurling. I was just a little tyke, all decked out in my neat little knickered suit, Buster Brown shoes and stingy-brimmed hat. I remember well, one very cold, windy day we went for a walk. The hat blew off suddenly, flying, bouncing, rolling down the street with Grandfather in pursuit. He finally ran it down. From that time on, I held onto it and we returned to Aunt Lela's. I was happy when Grandmother began packing to return home because I liked to ride the train. Aunt Lela packed a lunch basket for us with fried chicken, biscuits and cake which I wanted to start eating as soon as we boarded.

We had been home a very short time when Grandmother became ill with pneumonia. I can still remember seeing her propped in bed, on a chair turned upside down and cushioned with pillows trying to breathe. In those days it was called eight-day pneumonia. Mother was in attendance, as were several neighbor women. She died on the eighth day in February, 1926.

That was my first observation of someone ill. The doctor visited her daily. I was in awe of the stethoscope as he inserted the ear pieces into his ears and listened to her chest. They looked like horns to me. Maybe those were the mysterious hooks that sank into my young mind and remained until I could unlock them in adolescence, which ultimately led to my decision to become a doctor. I never asked for, nor received, any explanation as to what he heard listening to her chest.

On Mother's Day, Mama and I always went to Zion City Cemetery 15 miles north of Woodlawn to place flowers on her grave. We rode the streetcar part way, transferring once, then walked several miles uphill to the cemetery. It was always very hot and humid. I didn't mind, Grandmother was in heaven. I loved her.

On our way home we always stopped at Hadely's Drugstore. Mother bought two pints of Melrose delicious vanilla ice cream for twenty-five cents. It was a special price on Mother's Day, two pints for the price of one.

Those sweet treats, candy and ice cream brought about the beginning of many nights of mega-toothaches for me after Grandmother died and I returned home. Pledgets of cotton anointed with turpentine or Sloan's liniment were instilled in the cavity. Sometimes I got relief or just cried myself to sleep. Once in a while Mother would give me a small sip of 135-proof hooch to be held in the area of the cavity and I would get a little relief. Maybe the relief was the systemic, anesthetic-like action that mellowed me out and into the land of Morpheus.

Daddy finally took me to Dr. Guinn, a dentist who had an office halfway between Woodlawn and downtown called Avondale. Unfortunately for me, one time I pointed to the wrong tooth after my jaw had been deadened. At dusk Father overheard me tell Mother my tooth ached. "Son, how could you have a toothache? The dentist took it out...let me see." I opened my mouth and pointed to the carious tooth. "I be damn," Daddy's favorite expression,

"How could that happen?" The next day we returned and the dentist removed the carious one. Oh, what a relief that was. I had no more toothache, hurrah!

At age five Mother took sister and me downtown for our first visit with Santa Claus. She had prompted us to tell him what we wanted him to bring. I remember telling that big fat man, decked out in his red outfit and long white beard, what I wanted for Christmas. We had been told he came down the chimney to bring our toys. I never questioned how he managed that task.

Later, as a little tyke, it was a joy for me to accompany Mother downtown and visit the beautiful department stores. She enjoyed going to the Famous Theater. I was afraid of the dark and didn't want to go in there and sit still. Cowboy movies got my attention, however. Seeing the big, pretty horses and cowboys all dressed up in their colorful attire roping cattle and having gun battles while chasing robbers with fast-drawn guns, the loud bangs and clouds of gun smoke and dust made the action appear real to me. It was appealing, as all little boys like to play cowboys and robbers.

I was seven years old when Santa brought me my first cowboy suit. I put it on immediately and wore it all day until bedtime. I wanted to wear it to bed but that was a no, no. I invented my own cowboy and robber action. With my new cowboy suit I wore a wide-brimmed Texas Ranger hat with a chin strap, so as not to lose it in a wild battle. My brown cotton gloves were no match for the freezing weather. The fringed cuffs from my wrists halfway to my forearms only made me think I was warm, but being a big-time cowboy I just had to carry on.

My first "Gat" was a single cap shooter that had to be reloaded after every pop. Sometimes the single cap would be blown out by the wind when I cocked the hammer. That was disgusting. I'd retrieve the cap, place it in the chamber and fire. Later, the single shot pistol was replaced by an automatic one. A roll of fifty caps was placed inside a lateral area in front of the handle. The caps rotated upwards into the chamber. When the trigger was pulled slowly for one pop, or rapidly for many, that made for real control of how many shots fired.

There was no gentlemen's agreement when we played cops and robbers. I kept my "Gat" loaded with red-headed caps, ten for a penny or fifty for a nickel. They were packed with gunpowder, ready to explode in rapid succession as fast as my forefinger could pull the trigger, smoking the enemy. I kept it by my side in a so-called "scabbage" which I learned later was called a holster. Acting like a real cowboy, I straddled my imaginary horse, an old broomstick that I named "Old Sugar," after the real horse that pulled Father's vegetable and fruit wagon. I'd give the command "Gitty up; gitty up!" running as fast as I could through the field of grass, ringed with gravel and dirt, around the convenient playground next to our home. Echoes of bookety, bookety, bookety, echoed in my head from the sounds of my feet, symbolic of the hooves of the cowboy's horses pounding against the plains in the movies.

The battle started when the first one of us jumped up and ran, that was the robber. The cowboy then took off in hot pursuit. Our roles were often reversed, popping caps until the gat jammed. This necessitated stopping and realigning the roll. When the robber was caught the bang, bang, banging became furious as did the voice of the pursuer, loudly yelling, "You're dead, you're dead!" We'd finally retreat to the shade of the big old elm tree, sit down on one of the huge protruding roots and cool out. Several other battles began with the same routine when we were thoroughly rested. When we were completely exhausted, my playmates went home and I slowly dragged to the icebox in our dining room for a big drink of ice water, then to the back porch for some much needed rest while looking forward to dinner to restore my energy.

I had worked myself down playing and the four o'clock dinner was happily greeted. Candied yams, string beans, chicken and dressing, ambrosia (only at Christmas), potato salad, Mother's rolls, with which she was dissatisfied as usual but good to me, creamed green peas and desserts were outstanding. After dinner, full and feeling fine, I relaxed behind the warm heater for the rest of the evening.

Chapter 4
Early Childhood Memories

With all the in-and-out traffic at 6218 Georgia Road, it wouldn't take a fortune teller to know something illegal was going on and it would just be a matter of time before the police would again drop in to investigate. There was plenty of 135-proof alcohol for sale, some was hidden in a unique stash on the back porch where a panel of the wall had been removed and the flat, seven-eighths quart bottles set inside. When the panel was replaced one could not tell it had ever been disturbed. It was never discovered during subsequent police raids which were staged quite often and very frightening to me. With all of the instability around our home, Mother was devastated. She told Father she was going to take sister and me to Detroit to see her aunts—Lela, Angie and Pearl, whose nickname was "Cook." He agreed and preparations were begun.

Mother got sister and me ready for the 750 mile trip to Detroit. She packed our clothes in suitcases and a big trunk which held enough to last the entire time we were going to be away. Father tied them securely with a rope to the trunk of the car and away we went to the L & N (Louisville &

Nashville) Railroad station baggage room where he asked the baggage man to check the trunk to Detroit. He went into the station and purchased Mother's ticket. My sister and I were allowed to ride free and, at ages 5 and 7, excitedly waited until the train master called for passengers to entrain. I still remember the joyous feeling seeing the long, black, shiny train with its engine huffing and puffing, steam rising from the hoses connecting the cars and underneath the train.

We finally boarded; Mother bought two pillows for twenty cents to rest our little heads during the night. We would arrive in Detroit about 2 p.m. the next day. The coach in which we rode was directly behind the baggage car and had no air conditioning so Mother raised the window for air. A cinder from the coal burning engine flew into my eye causing great pain. She took a little white handkerchief from her purse, rolled one corner to a point and proceeded to remove the culprit. That didn't detract too much from the pleasure of the train ride.

Detroit was quite a place and very exciting to me. There was a large park across the street from Aunt Lela and Uncle Henry's flat. He took me there to play and my first time ever seeing a sliding board. Climbing the steps hurriedly, I became paralyzed with fear looking down and wasn't about to let go, hollering loudly with such fear that Uncle Henry knew I needed immediate help. He tried to coax me down but I refused, so he came up and brought me to safety. Adjusting later after working through my anxiety, I had a ball sliding down many times.

I had the same fear of riding a pony when we visited Bel Isle Park. Mother paid the attendant fifty cents for me to ride and when he placed me atop the pony I began to cry. He took me off and I have never had that frightening experience again.

We stayed in Detroit about a week. We never did much family going. Once in a while we visited Father's sister, Katie Knox, who lived in Avondale. She had three children who were sister's and my ages. We were very fond of them. Their father had several fruit wagons drawn by horses and kept plenty of bananas underneath the kitchen sink. I was always given one or two by cousin Henry, who knew I really loved bananas. They are still my favorite fruit. We occasionally visited Aunt Susie McCain, another of Father's sisters who lived in Westend. Her sons were all much older than sister and me. Sister and I often sat in on adult conversations, remaining quiet of course, because in those days children were to be seen and not heard.

Aunt Mary, Father's oldest sister, lived beyond the railroad tracks about a mile up a moderately steep hill. She had a large orchard of peach trees which were very prolific. The peaches were huge, red and delicious. I couldn't wait until school was out, that's when the peaches were ripe. She was a sweet lady and didn't mind our collecting and eating as many as we wanted. There was also a chestnut tree but the nuts were covered with a hull with many thorny stickers so I was not tempted to pick them. Just below her home was a millet field. I don't know by whom it was planted and cultivated, but we enjoyed eating it. It grows in jointed stalk form resembling sugar cane, but not quite as sweet. When the millet was gone, the field was a diamond for us to play baseball. It was a pasture for someone's cows, too, as evidenced by the dung in which we often stepped and had our feet and baseball anointed. Those were good times.

About a mile away from Aunt Mary's in a wooded area were many blackberry vines, persimmon and hickory nut trees. My cousin James, eleven months my senior, and I would go hickory-nut and persimmon hunting alone, or with his sister, Cora, a real sweetheart, and a group of eight to ten community kids.

After the first frosts blanketed housetops, trees and grass, and the temperature fell below freezing, it was time to begin thinking of gathering hickory nuts and persimmons.

Plums, peaches, apples, pears, grapes, pecans and black walnuts had disappeared and I looked forward to winter's astringent plum-like fruit, persimmons and hickory nuts. They were tucked among miles of thick foliage and serene, dark green trees leading to the top of steep Red Mountain.

Persimmons, when not ripe, were symbolic of soapy water used to wash out mouths of foul-talking little boys. They would turn one's mouth inside out. When orange in color and over-ripe after being saturated with heavy frosts of late November and December, a frigid blast cast them to the ground where they splattered on leaves and grass, mealy, granular and ready for eating.

I always gathered three or four twenty-four pound flour sacks of hickory nuts and ate them all winter long. Sister ate a few, my parents weren't interested. With the old claw hammer and Mother's smoothing iron between my legs I went to work cracking the hard-shelled, tough husked ones, many times stinging my fingers. The soft-shelled, scaly barbs, with sweet meat were easy to crack. The husks burst on their own when they were ripe. I hulled those I knocked to the ground. Persimmons and hickory nuts were a delightfully tasty winter snack.

The woods which yielded the goodies were located in "Cracker Town," so named for poor whites who lived in the area. Old Mountain Jack, a six-foot-two-inch, 220 pounder, made booze which everyone called "canned heat," a variant of 135-proof pure white lightning or corn whiskey. He would get high off of that stuff and heave a holler that could be heard over the entire area of the hill, even to Aunt Mary's. He sounded just like a mountain lion. The revenuers raided the woods and destroyed his stills, but never caught him. Their visits never stopped him. He made a new batch whenever his supply ran out or was destroyed.

Uncle Sandy lived down the hill a block from Aunt Mary's. In the summer he had a backyard full of peach trees, but was very stingy. Once in a blue moon he would go out and fetch us one or two. We didn't like that, but his high fence prohibited us from getting them on our own. I raided peach, plum, apple trees, sometimes going over the fence of our neighbors.

September 1927, was my time to begin school. Mother enrolled me at Patterson Elementary, a Birmingham public school, Grades 1 through 8, in the heart of the black community four blocks from our home.

Mother bought new clothes for me; a pair of shoes, socks, shirts and neckties, and a brown canvas satchel to carry my books, tablets, pencils and crayolas. Books were provided by the Board of Education.

On the first day of school Mother and I went directly to the principal's office and were taken by a monitor to Miss Hess' first grade classroom. I was registered in the junior first grade. There was no preschool or kindergarten in those days. I was fearful of that strange room filled with 36 unfamiliar faces. I felt deserted when I saw mother turn and leave the room, but I had been told I was a big boy now and big boys didn't cry. I was not too happy having to give up my freedom of playing at home to become a quiet tyke in a school room.

I played alone quite a bit, but sometimes Nathaniel, Pete, Harry C. and Blair would come to the vacant lot opposite my home where a huge elm tree provided lots of shade and large protruding roots extending from the tree trunk for us to sit on after playing a game of stickball with a broom stick and tennis ball.

The school was a large, square, sprawling, one-story, brown, wood-framed building, facing busy 64th Street, which was very heavily traveled, and extended five blocks between 1st Avenue South and Georgia Road. Across 64th Street was a large unpaved lot where we played touch football and stickball. There were no basketball hoops. A volleyball net extended from a tree just outside of the third grade classroom door to the limbs of one of several trees lining 64th Street.

My classroom was large and heated by a medium sized pot-bellied, coal-burning heater. There was a small lunch room operated by "Ma Massey," an old settler of Woodlawn. She was a very kind, slightly heavy, stooped, light complexioned lady with beautiful, straight, mixed-gray hair and a jolly, deep belly laugh. Everyone loved her. She lived on the street a block from my home.

The grounds around the building were all dirt, covered with rocks of all sizes. My room was located at the back of the building. A sandbox was easily accessible and close by were two large green leafy trees. There was quite a large play area, even though limited by Mr. Womack's wire fence located on the south side of the building.

On the north side of the school was 3rd Avenue South which was fairly well traveled and lined with many very well kept homes with pretty green grass in the yards. Mr. Beard, who invented the "coupler" which connects railroad cars, lived in a large, brown, old home on 3rd Avenue within ten feet of the second grade classroom. I saw him a few times. He was a large ruddy-complexioned man with thick, bushy, reddish-brown hair. I never spoke with him but often heard my parents say that the railroad company defrauded him of his patent, however, his real financial status was never known.

I was assigned a seat with Taylor Woodruff, who Miss Hess brought to school every day as he lived in East Birmingham near her home. We got along famously; however, after my first year in school I never saw him again.

Miss Hess was a small, kind, round-shouldered lady with gray hair, light complexioned and very nice. Mr. Welton, the principal, was a dark-skinned man and not too healthy looking. His face was drawn and shoulders noticeably rounded. He passed through my room many times. I didn't really get to know him very well as he died the next year.

At 8 a.m. sharp, the principal rang the bell for school to begin. It was line-up time, in a straight line, no pushing or talking. When everyone was at attention and quiet, the bell rang for us to go to our room. We had devotion for ten minutes every day and a Bible verse was to be said by everyone. I always wished I could be first, because "Jesus wept," was everyone's favorite. We sang "Jesus loves me, this I know, for the Bible tells me so," and "Glory, Glory Hallelujah," which I didn't learn until many years later was entitled, *The Battle Hymn of the Republic*. We had no flag saluting ceremony. We had a "little recess," which was fifteen minutes for a snack and play time for grades one and two, and "big recess" for thirty minutes for all students at noon. Hot dogs were a real treat and the biggest seller once a week. Sandwiches, half-pints of milk, a wrapped piece of bakery cake and small bags of potato chips sold for a nickel. I usually brought my lunch, a sandwich and an apple, orange or banana, in a brown paper bag or a piece of newspaper. I sometimes splurged when Mama gave me a nickel or dime. A red, candy-coated apple on a stick was a rare treat. I tried to keep a nickel in reserve to get one whenever they were for sale. They were awfully sweet, very sticky and messy to eat, but I loved them.

I remember my first vaccination, the one for smallpox. No other immunizations were required to enter school. The skin pricks kinda hurt, but I was brave and didn't cry. I strolled around the grounds with my shirt sleeve rolled high above the vaccination, exhibiting my bravery. I had a nickel that day and bought a candied apple, which sort of helped me overcome that painful experience. The vaccination took and I suffered no ill-effects.

School was out at 2 p.m. for Grades 1 and 2 and 3:15 for others. The end of the school day was always welcome unless a big bully had threatened to beat me up after school. I was threatened several times but escaped any attacks.

I was very happy when Miss Hess gave me my first reader. I didn't do a lick of work in class. Guess she thought I was retarded. Upon arriving home I told Mother all the happenings in the classroom had not passed me by. I began to spout the numbers heard recited in class that day, plus the A B C's on which the teacher had drilled the class. Neither Father nor Mother paid much attention to me as I had just started school.

Soon I began to open my new primer where I saw Jane, Tom and Dick, a ball, a cat and a dog. My fantasy as to what they were doing became outwardly vocal and drew Mother's attention. I was reading with so much "oomph" she decided to check out how brilliantly her first-born was doing. I looked at the picture and began to read as she sat beside me, "The boy hit the ball," the interpretation of the picture was correct but the words were figments of my imagination. She took the book and began reading to me, pointing out the words and pronouncing them slowly. After many repetitions of reading with me every evening I began to connect visually, mentally read correctly, and very well. Her kind devotion to my school work motivated me and I became a ready reader, happy to please Mother as well as myself when she began praising my progress.

I moved up in class the next Christmas when I received a new blank pistol and a scabbage (scabbard) in which to carry it. That firearm was very real and shot blank cartridges. The silver colored shells contained real gun powder, very dark in color. The powder was held in place by a wad of grayish-white paper. I had several boxes and when shot, sounded like a real gun. I threw away the old broom and ran on my own, pulling the gat from its scabbage, spinning it round and round until it came into position for me to grasp the trigger, pull it and fire, bringing down the imaginary robber and exclaiming, "You're dead, you're dead!" That I did most of Christmas Day, alternating with trips to the house to replenish the pockets of my cowboy suit with raisins, pecans and almonds, eating a piece of sweet potato pie and a slice of coconut and chocolate cake. After warming my nearly frozen hands and feet, I returned to the battlefield to romp again.

I almost didn't make it out of early childhood after receiving that shiny new blank-pistol. All day I had played cowboy, drawing it from the scabbage, shouting "Bang,bang!" I wore the cowboy suit and hat into the night.

I remember standing in front of Mother, who was visiting with two of her friends, Bessie Jeter and Minnie Moore, just posing with the hammer cocked. For some reason it would release on its own, forceful enough to explode the cartridge. Suddenly, "Bang" it went and she screamed, "Thomas, I can't see! I'll never see again!" I had blinded her temporarily and was frightened stiff, couldn't utter a sound. I felt so sorry for shooting her.

After all the commotion settled and her sight returned, the neighborhood ladies decided it would be nice for the three of them to go down to Mrs. Millie Brewer's Christmas party. After they left, Father was quietly reading the newspaper when I, out of guilt I guess, reenacted how Mother was shot, positioning my left hand a few inches forward to represent the position of her head and with the cocked gun facing it, "Bang," went the gun without my pulling the trigger—that tricky trigger. The full load of gunpowder, paper wadding and all, entered the outer half of my left hand.

"Oh, oh," I cried out. Father threw the paper down and said, "Damn." He left me and rushed to Mrs. Brewer's to get Mother. She was really smoking with anger when she reached the house, immediately rushing to crack my head while fussing furiously all the time. I was crying continuous sobs as my hand was slowly oozing frothy, dark red blood and was very painful.

Father and Mother took me to the garage, got into the car and drove to the home of Dr. Kinkead, a kind white physician who lived about five blocks away. He put a big white bandage over my hand and told Mother to soak it continuously in a warm salt water solution. We returned home and I was in bed for two weeks. Dr. Kinkead came daily to check on my condition. I was a very sick little boy, listless and not eating.

Mother cried all Christmas as she knew of a 22 year old man who lived on the north side of Woodlawn who had received a similar wound and died of blood poisoning.

On about the seventh day when the bandage was removed, the doctor expressed a large amount of paper wadding and gun powder from my hand. It really smelled bad. After expressing that deadly poison, like magic I began to feel better, soon started eating and was on my way to a complete recovery. I carry the scar of that injury to this day.

Mother's troubles, however, were just beginning. The gun powder stained the white of her eyes black, for which she went many months to an eye specialist for scrapings. The discoloration never completely disappeared. We both suffered permanent reminders of the premature buying of a dangerous toy. They say a cat has nine lives. I am sure I used one of mine with that traumatic episode.

As I grew older I couldn't wait for December to come and especially the two week vacation from school. It was the slowest passing month of the year. By this time I had heard my school chums talk about their Christmas trees and asked Mother if we could have one. She said "Yes, if you go up the hill to the woods and cut one." I was thrilled. I fetched our trusty old axe, went several blocks to Oakridge where I chose a tree about five feet tall, cut it down and dragged it home. Father made a stand out of two crossed pieces of wood, fastened them to the bottom of the tree and stood my very first Christmas tree in the living room. We had no lights for the tree, but Mother and I decorated it with peppermint candy canes and silver icicles, which gave it a beautiful glowing appearance. I was so proud of that Christmas tree, I just sat and admired it.

At age nine I was a veteran Santa Claus know-it-all. I knew everything about the mystique of Santa Claus and how he came down the chimney. Older neighborhood kids had told me, "Your papa is the Santa and your mama is the Claus, both of them together make Santa Claus." I kept this a secret from my parents until a year later when I smartly blurted out, "I know who Santa Claus is!" Mama said "O.K. since you know so much, no more Santa Claus for you." It was all over for me! Guess I blew it, Christmas was never the same.

After the near fatal accident of shooting myself, I was anxious to return to my first grade class. I was happy to see Miss Hess and my classmates. I had become acclimated to the school routine and missed my playmates. To my surprise we had a new principal, Mr..J. C. Mickle, due to Mr. James Welton's death. He was a short, dark-complexioned man with a big abdomen, large eyes, wide smile, quietly personable and a supreme disciplinarian.

My first few days back to school were great fun until one day during recess Curtis Smedley walked up and socked me in the chest. Being startled, I socked him back. His brother, Paris, also in our class, saw me hit him and came to little brother's defense. We pushed and shoved each other a couple of times before Miss Patterson, who was on yard duty, separated us and told us to behave before we had a real fight. That was the end of that little fracas. We never had another confrontation.

Chapter 5
Home Remedies

The art of healing and medical practice were home-spun when I was a child. Old remedies had been handed down through the years by our elders and people depended on them rather than go to a doctor. Never a routine physical or immunizations.

It snowed rarely, but thick frosts felt and looked like snow. The temperature sometimes dropped to zero with ice everywhere and often lasted from December through March. Icicles, almost three inches in circumference and eight to ten inches long hung from the roof of my classroom. Taking a book and with a perfect strike, I knocked down dust-laden, germ-infested joy sticks. I ate quite a few, but was never ill. During snowy winters, Mother made so-called ice cream, a bowl of snow, vanilla flavoring and sugar mixed in a large bowl. It sometimes produced a sore throat but it was oh, so good and worth it.

I was fairly healthy throughout childhood; however, I did have colds aplenty during the winter, but not too many sore throats. Mother's favorite concoction for colds and sore throats was a pepper sauce gargle at the onset. The pepper sauce was made from a five-inch long, extremely hot, green pepper. A hole was cut in one end and several placed in an eight-ounce bottle of vinegar. The mixture resulted in an extremely hot solution, and ouch, what a burning sensation. After gargling, the "fleem," as phlegm was called, was cut loose and expectorated. So long to that sore throat, it disappeared like magic. That old saying, "It will cure you or kill you," almost seemed true to me from that treatment.

When I developed a nagging cough extreme enough to cause my chest to be sore, a flannel cloth was saturated with Vick's salve and applied. It felt good as the heat penetrated deeply. A big glop, two fingers worth, from the medium-sized blue jar, stirred up my throat as I swallowed it and subsequently gave welcomed relief.

I never had headaches, even though I was reared in a very dysfunctional family where confusion reigned supreme. I sometimes had stomach aches which were always treated with a teaspoonful of crystal-flaked epsom salts in a little hot water. It was extremely bitter and gave immediate results, but could have been dangerous if one had had appendicitis.

Castor oil, the nastiest medicine known to me and mankind for stomach aches, the common cold and any other complaint, was my nemesis. I get nauseated now just thinking about it. Mother always had to threaten me with a whipping before I'd finally attempt to swallow it. When it hit my tongue I'd gag and vomit anytime I accidentally swallowed some. To add to its awful taste, three drops of turpentine were added to keep it from griping; i.e. bad abdominal cramps. I don't know how I can continue to like orange juice—it is remembered with taking castor oil. Mother had me strip to my shorts one day after it took me more than thirty minutes to attempt swallowing that awful stuff. With strap in hand, the threat was cause enough for me to attempt a small sip. Out it came. She gave up and I was extremely happy.

In my 35 years of practicing pediatrics, I never prescribed a dose of castor oil to any child for any reason.

Senna-leaf tea was given as a system cleanser. The green leaves were boiled, set aside and covered with a saucer to steep. When it settled, a teaspoon of sugar was added. The bittersweet taste was awful but the cathartic results were super.

Calomel was also bad. It was good for anything that ailed you. It caused extreme salivation and abdominal cramping.

Asphidity smelled like stale garlic and was worn around the neck in a little bag until replacement was necessary. A stomach ache always meant you had worms and it was the preventative.

A mixture of sweet, rock-candy pellets placed in a flat quart bottle of 135-proof moonshine was also good for colds. I liked the sweet taste and was happy to get a teaspoonful. I went "night, night," and rested well, even if it didn't cure my cold. Another "cure all" was called herb juice and was another cleanser. It tasted bitter, like black licorice. It did the job well, as my feet and legs will attest. I ran a beaten path to the outhouse, often and quickly, or to the slop jar on cold winter nights.

A good spring tonic was a must in our household. Mother gave sister and me a cleansing solution of fine, yellow powder called "flowers of sulfur" mixed with molasses. It would rid one of the residuals of winter colds and other ailments incurred from cold weather. After swallowing that thick mixture, my throat felt as if a strangler had attacked it. Struggling to get my breath, I went through all kinds of contortions trying to get it down the hatch. Ground egg shells and molasses, given to get rid of worms, was almost as bad.

Sister and I received a yellow liquid which contained sulfur during a polio scare in the early thirties. Mother put two drops of the mixture into each nostril, which quickly stopped up my ears—I couldn't hear. It was a funny feeling but recovery was quick.

Turpentine, a volatile oil, was a bitter tasting liquid given for stomach aches. Three drops atop a teaspoonful of sugar were given to me after eating small green peaches or apples, and did a good job. It was also used on skin lacerations and burned intensely. A drop in a teaspoonful of castor oil was mandatory for colds and constipation.

Many a sore on my feet from glass cuts, while running barefoot, were healed courtesy of Mr. Daisy Johnson, a lifelong friend of my parents. He saw some milkweed growing on the lot adjacent to our home, broke off several pieces and applied the whitish, milk-like secretion to the sores. They healed like magic.

Iodine was the most widely used antiseptic for cuts anywhere. It came in a small, dark brown bottle, but had a big sting when applied with the thin stem attached to the bottle cap and burned like fire for awhile, but soon quieted down. Receiving many applications, it did the job. It is only found in a preparation called Betadine now and used in surgery to sterilize the skin.

Mercurochrome, the forerunner of Merthiolate, a red antiseptic liquid in a bottle similar to iodine, was good in keeping lacerations from becoming infected.

Lacerations of my feet often occurred during

the summer. Iodine or turpentine was applied, then a penny and a piece of fat meat placed over the wound and bandaged with a clean white cloth. The penny always turned green indicating the poison had been removed. It's a wonder I didn't get lock jaw (tetanus), having never received a tetanus shot, as Mother never took me to the doctor.

Rudolph Ferguson, a school chum, was not so fortunate. He stepped on a rusty nail, was not taken to a doctor, developed tetanus and died at age nine.

The best remedy of all for colds was sliced red onion, lemon, honey and a couple of tablespoons of 135-proof moonshine. The mixture was brought to a boil and allowed to simmer for about thirty minutes. When cooled, Mother gave me a table-spoonful. I didn't mind having a cold, crazy about that remedy.

Everyone swore about relief of back pain from applications of Sloan's Liniment, a brown colored liquid with a very powerful smell. His picture was on the trim, two-ounce bottle.

Poultices, saturated cloths with an extract of Jimson weed, applied to inflamed parts of the body brought about localization of pus to the skin surface with automatic extrusion or expression by squeezing, with relief and healing.

Medicated mustard plasters were used extensively for back pain and applied to the lower back. My father used quite a few.

Chapter 6
Adapting To Wordly Woes

Neither Mother nor Father finished high school. They were both literate. Mother's handwriting was beautiful, his awful.

We had no encyclopedias, novels or books in our home. The only magazine was the annual Almanac, sent through the mail to every household. Father subscribed to *The Birmingham News*, one of two quality daily newspapers. He sat in his leather, overstuffed chair in the dining room, also our family room, winter, summer, fall and all, to read the paper, even though our screened back porch and the front porch with its swing and two rocking chairs were very convenient for cooling out and reading in the hot, humid summertime.

My parents were moderate readers. I never heard them discuss hard news except for their extreme sensitivity to the glaring headlines of the white press and radio stations that fired them up enough to read the unproven guilty accusations of crimes which Negroes did not commit. Lynching was an unpunishable act when committed by white men against black men. Blacks who were accused of raping a white woman were lynched or executed in the electric chair at Kilby Prison in

Kilby, Alabama. She only had to accuse him, truthfully or falsely. A saying among Negroes in Alabama was, "The only free persons from sexual incrimination were colored women and white men."

"YOUNG WHITE WOMAN MURDERED BY A NEGRO" was a glaring headline that caught the eye of every black person in Birmingham. Little did I know the accused killer would be a neighbor, Mr. Willie Peterson, who lived just up the hill from me. He was an elderly, very meek and physically disabled miner, suffering from chronic red-ore, miners disease. He was picked up by the police for the murder.

He often passed our house on his way to the streetcar line, the A & P, or Hill Brothers Supermarket, four blocks north. I didn't believe he'd harm a flea, but alas, one day, on his way to First Avenue North he supposedly fit the description of the murderer given to the detectives by the victim's brother. The newspaper flashed the headline, "Suspect Picked Up In The Ann Ward Murder." Her brother picked him from a police lineup.

The story goes, one of the victim's brothers, a lawyer, and his girlfriend were picnicking at East Lake Park near a wealthy, all-white suburb of the same name. He was angry with his girlfriend and intended to kill her. He pulled a gun and shot his sister accidentally, killing her instantly, then killed his girlfriend. Before the latter died, she repeated over and over, "Mus I tell it, mus I tell it, mus I tell it?"

That version circulated throughout the Negro community which was shocked hearing and reading the news of Mr. Peterson's arrest. At his trial the accuser shot him several times. He recovered and later was sentenced to die in the electric chair at Kilby Prison in Kilby, Alabama. The assassin was acquitted of any wrong doing. Mr. Peterson died in prison of his debilitating lung disease.

His death was symbolic of a lynching and genuinely believed by all who knew him that he was an innocent man.

It was disheartening for me to see a disabled neighbor accused of a crime I didn't believe he could have committed. He and his wife lived in their own comfortable home directly across the street from Mr. Macon's small grocery store where I stopped many times to buy a piece of penny candy on my way to Aunt Mary's, a little over a block away, to play with my cousins. I spoke to them many times as they sat on their front porch in a swing. He was soft spoken and polite in returning my greeting.

Uncle Sandy, who lived around the corner, worked with him in the ore mines at Huffman, Alabama, twenty-two miles north of Woodlawn. I heard him express, in utter disdain, his disbelief in that awful accusation.

I believe until this day that he was innocent.

The Scottsboro boys were eight young blacks hoboing through Alabama. Scottsboro is about one hundred miles north of Birmingham, population 6,000, where they were apprehended and accused of raping two young white women hoboing with two white male companions.

Shortly after their arrest they were transferred to Jefferson County Jail in Birmingham for safekeeping. It wouldn't have been uncommon in those days for blacks to be abducted from jail, with or without the knowledge of the sheriff, and lynched by a white mob. The lynchers were never apprehended and prosecuted by local authorities.

Attorney Clarence Darrow, a renowned New York criminal lawyer, and his team represented them. Money was raised in Negro churches and some influential whites contributed to their defense fund. He represented them out of the goodness of his heart because he believed, along with thousands of others, that the boys were framed. The boys stated they had an altercation with the two male companions, but did not attack the girls. The case was tried in Birmingham. Proceedings were so powerfully hot they were broadcast daily over WKBC, a leading radio station. A group of our neighbors came to our watermelon stand every day to listen to the court proceedings.

The case went on for years with appeal after appeal, after they were sentenced to die in the electric chair at Kilby Prison in Alabama. They were never electrocuted and two were eventually freed. The others languished in prison for years. I don't know what finally happened to them. The first Negro newspaper during my early childhood was *The Birmingham Times*, a weekly publication. One day Pete Hardy, a playmate, said "Egg (as he called me), a man is coming to the Knights of Phythias Hall Sunday looking for some boys to sell newspapers." My ears perked up.

"How much are we going to make?"

"I don't know, we are supposed to meet him at 9 a.m."

"O.K. I'll be there."

Several of us turned up, all about nine years old. He told us it was a colored newspaper, selling for five cents per copy and we could keep half from every one we sold. He gave each of us twenty-five papers.

Away I went on my first paper route, stopping at the neat, white home of Mr. and Mrs. Zack Mitchell. Unfortunately for me, they had just painted the front porch and had newspapers covering it. I didn't have any better sense than to trample on them, which raised the ire of Mrs. Mitchell, who answered the door and said, "Don't you see I have just freshly painted my porch?" Standing there frozen in silence, finally I asked her if she wanted to buy a *Birmingham Times* newspaper. She said, "No," without asking me what type of paper it was. I was crushed with my first unpleasant encounter as a salesman, hastily turned around and left.

I sold only ten papers after knocking on about fifty doors, earning a total of fifty cents. The man waited three hours until we returned. No one else was any more successful than I. I didn't return the next week as Mother put her foot down and told me not to bother our neighbors again.

Father read the sports pages completely as he followed the Birmingham Black Barons in their heyday of the twenties and thirties, and the White Barons who were members of the eight team Southern Association. He also read the front page of the paper as well as its inner pages.

I liked Dick Tracy, Maggie and Jiggs, Gasoline Alley, Toots and Gasper, Olive Oil and J. Wellington Wimpy, in the *Birmingham News*, published daily. Barney Google and his horse, Sparkplug, appeared in the *Birmingham Post*, the other evening newspaper. Mr. Moot Felton subscribed to it and I went across the street to their home every day to read it. I never saw Annie Ruth read the paper. She dug swing music on the radio. Mother had no particular preference, reading whatever she found interesting, mainly department store sales and discussing them with Father when struck with the desire to go shopping.

Mother and Daddy read the Almanac, especially the weather predictions for each month of the year, when to plant gardens and specific prophesies of coming life's happenings. Reading it apprised them of the prophesy that if the ground hog saw his shadow the second Tuesday of February, there were going to be six weeks of very cold weather and mild weather if it were cloudy at 10 a.m., his official time to appear.

In the neighborhood I heard this political axiom, "The Republicans freed us, I am a Republican." The only politician of whom my parents made reference was Congressman Oscar De Priest of Chicago.

Politics was not a subject for discussion in our home. I never heard my parents say they were going to vote and no political preference was ever expressed. They knew better because they were prohibited. For many years, states (five as late as 1962) used the poll tax as a means of discouraging blacks from registering in order to exercise their right to vote. The Supreme Court upheld the state rights to do so.

In 1964, the 24th amendment to the Constitution was ratified, nullifying all state laws requiring a poll tax as a condition to vote in any federal or other election. A few states, until 1966, when the Board of Elections 383 U.S. 663, ruled that a state violates the 14th Amendment whenever it makes the affluence of the voter or payment of a fee, an electoral standard.

The poll tax in Alabama was $2.50 annually. It was accumulative until one attempted to register to vote. Blacks had waited so many years to attempt to vote the fee was prohibitive, so they didn't give any thoughts of registering. The nerve to try to vote was frightening, as the registrars were racist whites who didn't think blacks had sense enough to vote intelligently in a sophisticated, segregated society.

At age 21 I attempted to vote and went to the registrar's office in Gate City, about three miles from my home, all hyped up that this would be my chance to exercise my newly acquired right as an adult and a big-time sophomore in college.

At age 21, the voting age, I put myself in double jeopardy deciding to walk a mile and a half to the Gate City at 77th Street and Georgia Road registration and polling place. Gate City began at 65th Street, where the colored section of Woodlawn ended. There were many well built homes, some in need of painting, trees in the front and back yards and small well kept lawns. Paved Georgia Road on the way to Atlanta, Georgia, went straight through. Numerous cars traveled the highway and the segregated Birmingham Electric Company's public transportation buses were convenient. A small, neat public school for whites only was at 68th Street. North to 77th Street and West was Brown Springs, inhabited by blacks. Their children had to walk three miles to Patterson School, which I attended.

On a few occasions when father sent me to the only supermarket at 71st Street to buy some hog feed, three to five white youths sometimes hollered, "Do you have any wind in your heels?" That meant to get moving in a hurry. I never hesitated. When they passed by our watermelon stand on their way to Woodlawn, maybe to shop or to the theater, I discouraged my pals from bothering them, explaining, they weren't bothering us. "You scared!" I often heard. Negative transference wasn't a part of my conscience. One night Feber Milford, a large evil friend who didn't like whites especially and everybody else in particular, threw a large rock and struck a young white boy who was accompanied by his adult brother. His head was very bloody.

Feber ran as the brother came to the stand where I was sitting. "Who threw that rock?" Father entered the scene as I denied any guilt. He went into the house, returned with a wet rag and applied it. The bleeding stopped. They went on their way. Nothing of that sort ever happened again. I was really frightened. Feber was killed in prison by an inmate. He was in and out of prison for robbery and aggravated assault.

The area resembled a small, country business village with a small grocery store and auto mechanic business across the street from an old corner lot filling station at 77th Street. West of the filling station, a few yards away, was an old wooden building with medium sized windows on either side of an open door. Two wooden steps covered by an overhang led to a sagging, deteriorating porch. Entering a small room cluttered with old, well worn furniture and pictures adorning the walls, I got my first glimpse of an elderly, small, gray haired, wrinkled, bespectacled, tobacco-chewing, white man, the registrar, sitting behind an old beaten-up desk, covered with papers, who would soon fulfill my expectations of his being another race hater. Suddenly a blast from the past blurted indignantly, "What do you want, boy?"

"I'd like to register to vote, Sir."

He reached into his desk drawer, came out with a book which contained the Constitution of the United States and said "Read this."

I said, "Yes, Sir," took the book and read for him. His motive was to assuage his hatred for blacks, to see if I could pronounce words like constitution, representatives, president and other words which he thought were too difficult. If I had stumbled, he would have said, "You can't read, therefore, I deny you the right to register to vote."

After I finished reading the assigned passages perfectly, he took the book and said. "Now, tell me what you read."

Well, I really didn't remember what I'd read very well and answered, "You didn't tell me I had to explain what I read."

"I deny you the right to register to vote. If you don't like what I've done, go to the judge of the circuit court of Alabama. If it is alright with him, it will be alright with me."

I left without saying a word, but was thoroughly crushed inside despite not really being surprised. I didn't go to court and finally got the right to register to vote after the Civil Rights Bill passed in 1964.

That was the end of a very difficult period in American History.

In the mid-20s, I heard my first cousin, Robert Washington, talk about the hush, hush speaking engagements he conducted in small towns around Alabama. The subject of the speeches was the overthrow of the U. S. government. It was obviously a communist movement and Father and Mother were afraid for him, because the K.K.K. was on the lookout for such group members, would beat them unmercifully and run them out of town.

My parents were afraid to think of such a movement and didn't want to entertain any thoughts of becoming involved.

All of my cousin's movements were very clandestine, as was his talking about his activities. His involvement with the communist movement came to a sudden end one night after he was caught speaking to a group of blacks in a small Birmingham suburb. He was abducted by a band of white men, who took him into the woods, beat his clothing into his skin and told him to leave town. He heeded their advice that time, after many warnings, and went to Detroit, Michigan, where he got a job at Chrysler Motor Company, settled down, married and became the father of four daughters.

My family never went to a theater. The Famous and Champion theaters downtown were for blacks. There were two parks, Tuxedo in far away Ensley and Cliffwood in farther away Zion City.

We got our first radio in 1930, a table model Echophone, and I was thrilled. It was hot, hot, hot, having been stolen by Sam Sims, the delivery man for McKelvey-Coates, a large furniture store downtown. Daddy gave him a quart of booze for it. He was one of Father's regular whiskey customers.

WAPI and WBRC, the national network radio stations in Birmingham, were entertaining with music and news of what was happening in the world. WKBC and WJLD were independent stations with local news and music.

Walter Winchell, a syndicated columnist, came on every Sunday evening at six with, "Good evening ladies and gentlemen and all the ships at sea." He gave news briefs in rapid-fire fashion. I never failed to listen. Amos and Andy, black-faced white comedians who demeaned Negro intelligence, came on once a week. Paul Whiteman's orchestra, the Kate Smith hour, big band music beginning at 10:30 p.m. from the Meadowland Ballroom in Cedar Grove, New Jersey, were very entertaining. The Waldorf Astoria in New York City, the Roosevelt Hotel in New Orleans and the Coconut Grove in Los Angeles also featured big bands. All were super entertainment. Sister, Father and Mother were in the dining room, too, where we congregated every night, but were not interested in those programs. Father and I listened to sportscasts. He was not especially interested in football, but I listened to the Rose Bowl game from Pasadena, California, and college football games. I enjoyed them all.

When the Ringling Brothers, Barnum & Bailey Circus came to town, our school granted us a half day to attend. My first experience was thrilling. Father took Mama, Annie Ruth and me. I had never seen a live elephant, tiger or monkey, nor a picture of them in my schoolbooks. I fell in love with the animal exhibitions and the clowns with painted faces and brightly colored, funny clothes. After my first taste of cotton candy, I couldn't get enough. A big bag of popcorn and a large hot dog with all the trimmings made my day. A ride on the ferris wheel was frightening, especially when my chair stopped on top and began to rock. I never wanted that ride again. The ride on the canopied caterpillar was great fun, up and down, up and down, with good speed, and thrilling. I could have gone again and again, but Father said "No." Going to the circus was very enjoyable.

The following September, I was promoted to the junior second grade.

Miss Mamie Durr, the teacher, was a short, dark lady, the meanest one I encountered in all my school years. Strict discipline was the rule every day. I did my work as best I could. Any infraction of her rules brought about a reprimand and a quick strapping of the palms of one's hands.

I was glad to go to the second senior grade to Miss Adele Patterson's room. A tall, light complexioned, slightly heavy, sweet lady, was stern and insisted on excellent work, thus, extracting the best effort out of each student without the use of an ever-threatening strap.

My writing skills soon began to improve. She had us doing ovals and push-and-pulls, which had to be in perfect perpendicular order. I finally got the hang of it and did very well. We played games to develop eye and body coordination. When she said, "Birds fly!" we raised our arms and remained standing. If she said, "Horses fly!" and you raised your arms you had to sit down.

This exercise continued until everyone was seated. We played other games of this nature to develop our physical coordination skills.

Miss Lewis, my junior third grade teacher, was a wisp of a woman not five feet tall and awfully strict. She didn't weigh 75 pounds soaking wet. One day she stood Robert Eaton, a heavy-set eight-year-old with very large, hanging jaws, in front of the class for misbehaving. As he began to drool—what a funny sight—a few snickers began, then laughter. "Stop that laughing!" Miss Lewis commanded. I joined the funsters, as did Nathaniel Felton who lived across the street from me. "Come here, make a fist and place it on my desk," she demanded. I had never experienced that type of discipline.

"Yes Ma'am," I said, and did so reluctantly. She took a long ruler from her desk drawer, came forth and started striking the back of my hand. After a few hard swats she said, "Put the other one down." My hand was really hurting, so why do it to the other one? I put it down after making a fist and she immediately gave me another bang, bang, bang, bang. "Now go take your seat and no more laughing." Tears welled in my eyes. I didn't cry, but it was hard to resist.

Nathaniel was next and received the same treatment. The backs of my hands were red and swollen at 3 p.m. when I arrived home. I couldn't wait to show and tell Mother what Miss Lewis had done to me. "What did you do?"

"Nuthin'."

"Oh, yes you did. She wouldn't whip you for nothing. I'm going to give you a good whipping for being bad in school. I don't send you down there to cut up."

"Oh no, Mama, please don't!"

"Yes, I am," she snapped. I really thought she would become incensed with Miss Lewis for hurting her dear son in such a severe fashion, feeling too much damage had already been done. She got her reliable leather strap and warmed me up pretty good. She didn't say she'd go to the school and get that teacher straight, nor consult the principal. I was disappointed. She agreed with the teacher and that settled it.

Nathaniel's stepmother, who was a rural school teacher, came to school and read the riot act to Miss Lewis. He quit school after the sixth grade, went to work delivering groceries, later dealt drugs in New York and died there as a young adult.

Miss Bragg, my senior third grade teacher, was a medium-height, heavy-set, happy-go-lucky but no-nonsense lady with a smile and a heavy laugh to match. I liked her very much and really learned to read and do arithmetic. I had no difficulties in her room.

My fourth grade teacher for both semesters was Miss Leola Washington, a very tall, sweet, lovely lady, with a gentle smile. She taught arithmetic, reading, spelling, history, geography, art, music and penmanship. I received a solid academic foundation from her teaching.

At this grade level, we began receiving a report card monthly. It was taken home, reviewed by both parents, signed by one and returned. Grades were "E" for excellent, "S" for satisfactory, "P" for poor and "F" for failure. Mother always signed it after showing it to Father. My grades were good and all was well.

There was no library at school and I never visited the public library in Woodlawn. All of our books were furnished by the Board of Education. We bought tablets, drawing paper, crayolas and pencils.

Our teachers taught music from a prescribed school district song book. Miss McCarroll, the school district music supervisor, visited all rooms monthly. I can see her very fair-complexioned face, thin lips softly puckering up to blow her little harp, tuning us to the correct pitch. That was always a big thrill for the class.

Physical education was fifteen minutes of daily exercise on the school grounds. We had no gym. I played ball with my peers on a vacant lot across the street from the school. We chose sides, up to nine on each team. Bats or broomsticks brought from home, balls from the principal's office, a volleyball and net were the extent of our equipment. The net was stretched from Miss Bragg's third grade door to a tree about fifteen to twenty feet from the street. I sometimes banged away at the volleyball but preferred baseball.

I became aware of the "hooky cop," Miss McQueen, a small, bespectacled, brown-skinned, pleasant-faced lady, of the Jefferson County Juvenile Services. I was afraid of her even though I didn't know what playing "hooky" meant and never entertained the idea of finding out. My parents would have taken care of me. I saw her from my fourth grade classroom window as she alighted from her car carrying an armful of papers on her way to the principal's office. I wondered for whom she was looking.

I went into a slump in the fifth grade. Miss Mae Ola Alford, my teacher, was short with a wide grin, not too good looking and all business.

I played too much and picked up the bad habit of shooting spit balls. It seemed funny at the time, to everyone except the victims. I graduated to a wire, U-shaped staple shooter and shot Francis Smith behind his bald head, he cried. I threw it into my desk and never practiced that type of behavior again. I didn't receive a reprimand, as he was a quiet boy and didn't tell the teacher.

I did act out just enough to get a "P" in conduct. Mother was always interested in my report card. She was upset with it and warned me to behave myself and not bring home another one. I knew that meant a whipping as she always said, "I send you to school to learn and not to misbehave."

When the second month rolled around, I thought I had done better. As Miss Alford fingered through the report cards and finally came to mine, a nervous feeling came over me. I took it, not really wanting to look at the conduct mark which was at the top, preceded only by days present, absent or tardy. Another big fat "P" stood out like a sore thumb. I felt a need to become invisible, slowly and silently walking away, frightened almost to death. I knew I had a reckoning coming from Mother because of my continuing misbehavior. Upon arriving home, I put my books on the table, greeted her sweetly, "Howdy, Mama," because I knew she was going to become very sour with me. I knew better than delay taking it from between the pages of the book, so I slowly pulled it out and said, "Mama, here's my report card." She hadn't forgotten the "P" and was anxious to see it. I had erased the "P" and replaced it with an "S" for satisfactory, in pencil.

She immediately noticed the erasure and asked me, "What have you done to your conduct mark?"

"Nuthin', Mama."

"Oh yes, you have erased and changed your grade."

"Oh, no Mama."

"Yes, you have."

She told Father, who was sitting nearby. He didn't seem overly bothered, but said, "Let me see it. I be damn, he certainly has erased what's been there. Did you erase your report card?"

"Yes sir, I did."

"Why did you do it?"

"I was afraid you all would whip me for getting another "P"

"Whip his ass, Virginia."

Mama got the strap and was giving me a good licking as I cried, "Oh, Mama, Mama, I'll never do that again," hollering and jumping around. "Oh, Mama, please, I promise I won't."

She finally stopped and said, "You'd better not do that again."

"No, Mama, no, I won't do that again."

"I'm gonna see Miss Alford Monday morning and have her to give you a whipping, too, if you don't behave yourself." All weekend I tried to be good to allay Mother's anger towards me.

Monday, bright and early, she accompanied me to school. I was very sad, wondering what Miss Alford would think of me for doing such an awful thing. Mother said, "Good morning, Miss Alford, I'm Mrs. Witt; Edwin's mother."

"I'm so glad to meet you, Mrs. Witt."

I was far behind Mother as I could be without raising her ire and showing my guilt. Out comes the report card all signed by Mother. Miss Alford made me feel a little better when she told Mother my work was good but my behavior was not. "He talks and plays with Herman Williams all the time.

I think I'll change his seat and hope that will help."

"That's why I'm here, Miss Alford, to check on his conduct grade." She showed her the card and said, "I found what looks like an erasure and the mark written in pencil. I'm sorry he did it."

"Didn't know he'd do such a thing," was Miss Alford's reply.

"It won't happen again, I guarantee you. I took care of him."

"Thanks for coming, Mrs. Witt."

"Thank you, Miss Alford." Mother looked at me and left. I felt terrible.

Mother's going to the school helped and my next three grades in conduct were satisfactory, including the final grade for the year, an "S".

I don't think my school ever ran out of bullies. I saw so many bluffs, heard so much cursing, so many other threats on the way home from school and lunch time was no exception to disagreements and fights. I was afraid of Moses Hicks, a plump, always grinning room-mate as he balled his fists and said, "I'm gonna git you this evening." I dodged his wrath.

I had my second and last altercation after school with Marshall Canada, who was a year my junior and lived around the corner from me. We often shot marbles for keeps. Arguments were frequent, especially when one was losing. Sometimes when a marble was on the ring line, a heated discussion would crop up—was it in or out? Careful scrutiny came into play and an overlay of anger finally culminated in a fight. I called him "Ance." For some unknown reason he said it after every shot.

I had forgotten the argument with Marshall, but when he saw me at school the next day he threateningly said, "I'm gonna git you this evening."

I didn't say anything because I knew that meant trouble. He had a brother, Curtis, whom they called Keddy. His siblings couldn't say Curtis at an early age, so Keddy stuck. He was larger than I, but only three weeks older. Marshall knew he and Keddy could whip me but he couldn't do it alone. True to his word, when we left school, he picked up a rock and I ran until I was far enough ahead of him to pick up one or two. We had a crowd of onlookers as fights always drew an audience. He threw at me, missing, and I threw at him. Neither rock struck the intended target.

Fortunately, or unfortunately that particular afternoon, Miss Aileen Simpson, the home economics teacher who lived in our community, was on her way home and saw Marshall and me having the rock battle. We stopped, but she reported us to Mr. Mickle the next morning. He sent for us and had us explain our troubles. We didn't satisfy him, so he got that famous strap and went to work on me. I jumped all over his small office hollering, "Oh, Mr. Mickle, I won't do that again." Marbles in my pockets flew all over the place.

He stopped and said, "Now, pick up those marbles." I was so relieved after that flailing, I picked them up quickly and stood at attention. "Now go to your room."

I said, "Yes, sir, Mr. Mickle," and sheepishly walked away. Marshall had observed my licking with that stick, which was about the same size as a shovel handle, with a hole in the end where about six leather strips were inserted. I left him there to get his flogging and hurriedly returned to my room.

I was never referred to the principal's office again for misbehavior. I sometimes went on errands for one of my teachers and always tiptoed in and out quietly.

Chapter 7
Bootlegging, Raids And Arrests

I heard Mother call policemen "Bulls." I guess that's why they looked so threatening and awesome to me. Others called them "the Fuzz," "the Heat," or just plain "Cops." Our home was always at risk for a raid because of prohibition and Father's selling whiskey as an occupation. A bootlegger was looked upon with disdain by the law-abiding people of our community. We suffered the indignity of police searches and arrests on many occasions.

My realization that selling whiskey was against the law came in the late 1920s when Officer C. M. Robertson and his partner raided our home. It was the initial and largest confiscation of whiskey during my childhood and a very frightening experience. I witnessed many more raids and arrests.

In the late twenties, Officer Robertson and his partner were informed by a neighbor, "Black Will," Willie Farr by name, that there was a whiskey stash concealed beneath the ground in our barn. The ground was covered with sawdust which could be pushed aside for retrieval of the hooch. The five-gallon cans in which it was delivered were stored in a corner of the barn which once housed the horses Father used to deliver his fruits and vegetables. Black Will didn't know about the large quantity of booze, but one night when Father went to get a bottle from the stash, he was walking down the alley behind the barn on his way home and heard the sound of bottles clinking. As he listened in the dark, he knew he had made a solid discovery and reported it to the policemen.

A week or so later, Officer Robertson and his partner came by, knocked on the front door. Father answered and they said, "Where's that whiskey, boy?"

"I don't have any, sir."

"Open the door, we're going to find it." They entered the front room, proceeded through the shotgun, three-room home, out the back door and to the barn. To their surprise, there were 13 five-gallon cans of moonshine. The stopper was removed from one of the cans and the aroma saturated Officer Robertson's nostrils. "This smells like some good stuff, boy. You are under arrest. We're going to take you in."

"All right, sir."

Officer Robertson's partner went to the patrol car, drove it down the driveway, parallel to our home and to a gate which opened to the area where the barn was located. They loaded the car with their cache and Daddy, and went to the ice house three blocks away which served as their headquarters. The whiskey was poured down the sewer, according to them.

Sergeant Stewart, officer in charge of the Woodlawn Station, was a friend of Father's and interceded on his behalf with Officer Robertson and his partner. They agreed to report only finding five gallons to the judge. The judge fined Father $53 total and released him. Officer Robertson became a friend to Father later and never bothered him again.

He came by our home alone occasionally for a gulp or two of the 135-proof moonshine.

The steady stream of traffic in and out of our home was extremely upsetting to me, because I wondered what my peers and our neighbors thought about me. I felt sure our family values were lowered in their thinking. It gave me a feeling of guilt.

Any afternoon at our home could have been reserved for an afternoon police officer's roll call. Cars 5, 39 and 42 patrolled the area from Avondale, six miles away, to East Lake, 15 miles in the opposite direction and all territory in between. A visit to the inner sanctum of 6218 for a shot or two of moonshine was in order. Some could consume the hard stuff with one gulp without frowning, others mellowed out the flavor with a few sips at a time. They were on their own, in full view of a large audience of bus riders on the regular Birmingham Electric Company route and dozens of citizens traveling the highway to Atlanta. That didn't matter to them. They were the law and did as they pleased.

There was not a disrespectful officer of the dozens I learned to know over the years. They called Father "Tom," and me, "Little Tom." Mother was never involved. A smile of acceptance was all that was necessary. No morality or any kind of judgment entered my mind, as I was pleased they would not raid our home and place Daddy under arrest. He was not so lucky with the deputy sheriffs who worked for Jefferson County. Frisky Adams and Happy Dobbs were real menaces. They arrested him many times. Father's attorney was able to get his fine reduced to court costs, amounting to $53. The crowning point with the deputy sheriffs came one Saturday afternoon when a tall, tomato-faced, tough deputy named Kilpatrick seemingly followed Father home, just after he had paid a fifty-three dollar fine for a previous arrest. A pint of whiskey was found and an appearance bond prepared. Fortunately for Daddy, he knew Mr. Patrick, a veteran elderly officer, who dropped by occasionally with his morning partner to get a little nip. Deputy Kilpatrick was a lodge brother of Mr. Patrick's and was compromised by that relationship and got Father off, again just paying court costs. This arrest plus his just having been caught and convicted could have meant incarceration and at least six months on the county road cleaning streets in the heat and high humidity of Birmingham in the summertime.

Despite the embarrassing sight of four to six Birmingham policemen visiting our home, life went on.

One never saw policemen in that setting without some kind of disturbance. Feelings of impending danger and problems that could arise at anytime stuck in the back of my mind. Did the neighbors think father was a stool pigeon, apprising the officers of neighbor's improprieties? Could he have the officers raid their homes for any reason? I felt quite guilty when I faced my peers at school, church and gatherings on the steps of the Knights of Phythias Hall, adjacent to our baseball diamond, which we frequented before and after baseball games. Not all of the officers were so friendly. There was no fixed time when a new set might come by to raid our home.

A significant raid occurred one hot Sunday around 8 p.m. when two uniformed officers entered clandestinely through an unlocked front door. They could "smell the rat," an old saying about a suspected illegal activity. Something fishy had to be happening with the constant traffic seen going in and out of our house everyday.

Officer J. M. Ellis, six-foot-three, straight as a West Point Cadet, very handsome and business-like, and his partner, J. M. Major, a very country-talking southerner with a big pot belly, strolled in and asked, "Preacher, where's the whiskey?"

"I don't know what you're talking about, sir."

"Oh, yes, you do," replied Mr. Ellis. They walked through the house to the kitchen, looked behind the stove and there on a shelf was a gallon jug, about one-third full of charred whiskey siphoned from a ten gallon underground keg, golden brown, with a heavenly aroma and tasty and mellow as a sweet yellow meated watermelon. I had the pleasure of tasting both.

"What's this?" asked Mr. Major.

"Just something I have around here for colds."

"You can't fool me, preacher." Negroes were either "boy," "preacher," or "nigger," to all white folks in Alabama. Mr. Ellis was non-committal and just observed, standing tall with his forty-five, bone-handled, notched gun hanging neatly from his side. Each notch represented a victim from shots fired from that silver barreled weapon. Mr. Major's gun looked dangerous as it hung sloppily from his waist, the holster leaning outward and the trigger slanted forward. Mr. Major fetched the gallon jug and said "Let's go, preacher." Father and they went to the car and headed for the Woodlawn Police Headquarters.

A funny thing happened on the way to the station. In a car just ahead of the officers was Seth Ball, a friend of Father's who lived on a hill across the railroad tracks about two miles away. He drove a delivery truck for Louis Pizitz, a large department store. Mr. Major and Mr. Ellis were traffic cops who rode motorcycles but sometimes rode in a patrol car. This Sunday night they were in a 1936 Plymouth. They were known to the youngsters in our community as the "Plymouth Men." Everyone was afraid of them. No one was out after 9 p.m. They had a sling shot and shot at animals and humans for fun.

"Hey, Rod," as Mr. Ellis called his partner, "look at the tag on that nigger's car. It's from Georgia."

"Tom, do you know that boy?"

"Yes sir, he lives on the hill up from me."

"Let's stop him," Mr. Major said.

"No, we've got Tom in here and he'll think Tom tipped us off. Let's let him go."

Seth Ball went on his way without knowing he was almost arrested for having an out of state license plate. It only cost three dollars and Alabama's cost much more with its ad valorem tax, a tax proportionate to the value of the car.

When they arrived at the police station, Father saw a familiar face in desk sergeant Stewart, who visited our home often to get himself a nip. He was afraid to say anything to the officers as they were known to be rough and tough, taking nothing from anyone. Father was released on his own recognizance and fined $28, including $3 court costs.

A strange thing happened from that arrest— an additional vice for Father from an unsuspected source. One bright and sunny July afternoon, what should we see but two motorcycle officers enter the lot parallel to our home. We were all sitting on the screened back porch. I immediately thought this meant trouble for Father. He is going to be arrested again for possessing illicit liquor. We looked at each other nervously. The officers who

arrested him a month before stopped their motorcycles and slowly approached the house. Daddy
descended the steps of the back porch to meet
them.

"Tumm," as Mr. Ellis called Father, "we came
by to talk to you."

"Yes, sir."

Mr. Major alighted his motorcycle and joined
his partner. "Howdy, Preacher."

"How you, Mr. Major?"

The three of them went in to the house to the
dining room. They seated themselves. Father didn't
want to become too presumptuous and stood,
thinking another raid was imminent. Mother, sister and I were very nervous, not saying a word,
just praying they wouldn't find any whiskey. Father's secret stash where he kept his moonshine
was on the back porch behind a panel of the wall
where we were seated.

I overheard Mr. Ellis say, "Tumm, do you know
how to make beer?"

Father swallowed and answered, "No, sir."

"Well, we like beer and would like you to make
a batch for us. We'd like to show you how."

"If you say so and show me how, I will be happy
to make some for you."

"Well, here's how it's done. Get a five gallon
can of Pabst Blue Ribbon malt, five pounds of
sugar, four Fleishman Yeast cakes, a five gallon
churn and some bottles."

Daddy went to the store and bought the ingredients. We had two five-gallon churns left after we
got rid of the two cows that strayed onto our prop-
erty. Mr. Ellis and Mr. Major worked the three to
eleven shift and true to their word, came by the
next afternoon. It was summertime and all doors
were open. Daddy went to the back door and in-

vited them in. Mr. Ellis greeted him. "Tumm, how's the cat a'hopping?" his favorite salutation for the few years we had known him.

Daddy replied with an old slavery hand-me-down expression passed on from the past. "Fair to middlin', Mr. Jim." He had assembled the ingredients suggested by Mr. Ellis and placed them on the kitchen table, which was quite small, with Mother's dishpan empty and clean setting beside them.

Mr. Ellis rolled up the sleeves of his khaki uniform, washed his hands and went to work. He opened the can of Pabst Blue Ribbon malt, which had the appearance of a very dark thick paste. It looked good enough to eat. Subsequently, I got a chance to taste that very, very bitter stuff.

It was placed in the dishpan. Sugar, yeast and hot water were added to liquefy the mixture. It was poured into the churn where more hot water was added and covered tightly with a cloth, then placed behind the kitchen stove in order to receive the necessary heat. The mixture was allowed to ferment and after about five days was strained and ready to be poured into the bottles.

A bottle capper was also purchased. The beer was poured into the bottles through a funnel, placed on a bottle holding device, capped and placed in a big barrel filled with ice and covered with a quilt to keep them cold.

They came by everyday to sample the brew and get a "snort," as a shot of moonshine was called by Mr. Ellis. Both took a single or double. Mr. Ellis always paid, his partner didn't.

The only flaw of the beer was that the yeast settled thickly on the bottom and sides of the bottles. Upon pouring carefully, only a little got into the glass. Mr. Ellis, on tasting a sample of the first batch, said, "Tumm, this is fine beer. Couldn't have made it better myself."

Well, Father began selling beer to his whiskey buying customers for ten cents a bottle.

Washing the emptied bottles in a number three wash tub filled with soapy water was my job. A thin bristled brush was used to remove the yellowish-white and very sticky residue and a second tub of clean water to rinse them.

I sneaked a few bottles to taste. It was so bitter, I added a little sugar—it spewed everywhere, even through my nostrils. I didn't like the sensation and never tried it again.

Burris Grocery was a ritzy store located only three blocks from our home, but their prices were too fancy for us and most blacks. It was patronized by "the folks," well-to-do whites. Their delivery man, with his helper standing on the running board, chug, chug, chugging up Georgia Road, horn honking, "Oogie, oggie, oogie," got the attention of the neighborhood. With all the noise that truck made, I thought of it as a fire engine.

The driver and his assistant stopped by our home regularly for a drink of Father's 135-proof whiskey. As they approached our driveway the helper waved wildly, signaling a left turn off Georgia Road into our driveway. Two city police officers who happened to be in the neighborhood, stopped by to investigate the attraction. To their delight they found hundreds of bottles of cold, home brew and several bottles of 135-proof moonshine. Father was arrested and allowed to sign a recognizance bond.

The driver of the truck was a real loud-mouthed redhead. I heard him tell Father one day as he took a sip of that throat-scorching hooch, "Tom, I can smell the feet of that nigger who planted the corn this liquor was made from." Father said nothing as the rest of the hooch was consumed. A big laugh erupted at the end by the purveyor of indifference to the feelings of Negroes in the South during my childhood.

When the policemen brazenly brought out that huge orange barrel of home brew and fastened it to the front of their patrol car it caused a neighborhood circus. The Birmingham Electric Company's No. 21 Irondale bus on Highway 78 ran in front of our house loaded with many of our neighbors. The stream of cars passing by slowed to see what the commotion was about and people on the bus peered from the windows to get a glimpse of the action. It was very embarrassing to me.

The slickest maneuver I ever saw, to this point in my 12 years of life, was in the Municipal Court room in downtown Birmingham. Father was there for disposition of his case. I don't know which of Father's officer friends introduced him to "Sikes," Mr. Arnold Jakes, who became a regular visitor to our home to wet his whistle with the 135-proof moonshine. He was hunchbacked, less than five feet tall, keen features and had a pleasant personality. His father was chief of detectives. He, too, stopped by occasionally for a nip. Sikes was unemployed, living with his parents. A pearl-handled, holstered gun was strapped to his hip as if he were an officer of the law. Being a regular visitor to police headquarters was routine for him. He knew the judges, policemen and clerks well. When Father was arrested he contacted Mr. Jakes, who told him he knew the court clerk and would try to get the subpoena if Father knew someone to make the arrangement with the arresting officers. Daddy said he knew officer Jim Ellis. "O.K. call him."

Father called Mr. Ellis, who said he knew the

officers well and would get them to have the case nol-prossed if someone could get to the clerk and get the subpoena as it was now in the hands of the court.

Mr. Ellis contacted Mr. Jakes after Daddy told him Mr. Jakes knew the clerk and could arrange to get the subpoena secreted to him before being presented to the judge. One of the arresting officers was to be in court in case the arrangement fell through.

Father and I went downtown on that torridly hot August afternoon and took our seats in the gallery, awaiting the action. Well who appeared in court but little Sikes, his coat draped over his left shoulder, casually idling up to the right side of the clerk. In the blink of an eye, as the clerk came to Father's bond and clandestinely slipped it to Little Sikes, who swept it up in rapid motion and stuffed it underneath his coat. On his way out he spotted Father and me and casually turned his head to the right, signaling us to join him outside. As we hurriedly approached him he said, "I got it, Tom."

"Thanks, Mr. Jakes. What do I owe you?"

"The clerk likes cigars, give me $5 and I'll buy him a box."

That was the smoothest case of stealthiness I believe anyone will ever see.

Several weeks later Mr. Sanders and his partner, the arresting officers, stopped by. Mr. Sanders said, "Tom, you didn't have to pay a fine, did ya?"

"No, sir."

They never raided our home again, thanks to Father's friends.

Our good friend. Mr. Ellis, lost his life tragically one Sunday morning while working for a friend. He and his partner followed a trail of green beans from a burglarized grocery store leading to a garage, which closed as they arrived. Mr. Ellis said, "Open that damn door and come outta there." In response, he received six slugs of lead into his upper torso and died that afternoon. Upon hearing of his death, our family was saddened.

His partner, Mr. Major, stopped by to see Father sporadically after his retirement and eventually stopped altogether.

When prohibition ended in 1932, the state of Alabama opened liquor stores and sold many brands of whiskey and gin. Father continued to sell illicit moonshine but began to buy and sell "sealed whiskey," a name given to state, store-legalized booze.

I was barely 16 years old when he started sending me downtown to buy three or four quarts. The legal age was 21. I went every Saturday night and sometimes during the week if his supply ran low.

When I entered the store, I pulled my hat down so near my eyes I could hardly see, lowered my voice and spoke rapidly in order for the clerk not to look up and possibly see that I was a minor. It worked.

It was always my luck to board a streetcar when five, six or more neighbors were aboard. Many times I wished I could have shriveled to the size of a pretzel. There I was with an armful of whiskey, sure that everyone knew what it was and for whom and what purpose. It was always extremely embarrassing. I'd speak to them every time. There was no way I could hide, I just had to face the degradation.

The in-and-out-going traffic at our home was like Grand Central Station in New York City. What could the attraction be? Anyone's suspicion would be aroused, especially the deputy sheriffs of

Jefferson County and the local Birmingham police officers who passed our home routinely, every day. I became concerned every time I saw two white, well-dressed men entering Georgia Road from 62nd Street or coming eastward on Highway 78, thinking they might be city detectives or deputy sheriffs in plain clothes on their way to raid our home.

Deputies Frisky Adams and Happy Dobbs were nemeses. They arrested Daddy a half-dozen times. It seemed every time they needed to make an arrest, they'd come to our home and find a pint or more.

It was really quite ironic. We enjoyed hearing Happy Dobbs on the radio, singing country and western music. He was very good, but after he arrested Father, dislike reigned supreme for him in our household, so no more Happy Dobbs on our radio.

One Saturday afternoon they drove up in a county car and Officer Adams slowly walked to the back porch, knocked and Father answered. "What you got today, Tom"

"Nothing, Mr. Adams."

"Well, we'll see." Both officers searched the house, going room to room. They came up empty. Father seemed home-free. He had placed 18 pints of whiskey underneath the mattress of my one year old baby brother's bed, one place they hadn't looked. Mickey, as I nicknamed him, was standing in bed, looking at Mr. Adams, who turned and said, "Tom, that's a nice looking yellow baby you got there."

"Thank you, sir." He was very light-brown skinned.

Everything was hunky-dory until Mr. Adams moved the baby aside, raised the mattress and said, "Well, Tom, I got you again."

Father dropped his head and answered slowly, "Yes sir, Mr. Adams." They went into the dining room where Mr. Adams made out the bond for a court appearance which Father signed, collected the booze and left. Again, Father had to go to court and we were saddened once more. He was fined $50 and court costs of $3; fortunately, no jail sentence was attached.

A highlight of every year's school ending was a concert given by the first, second and third grades one night, another night for fourth, fifth and sixth; and lastly, grades seven and eight.

My most memorable one was in grade seven. Five classmates and I had a singing and dancing routine. We wore straw hats, white pants, carried canes and a ukulele and strutted our stuff in rhythm to Miss Simpson's piano music. Richard Macon was next to me. The feedback we received from a few wisenheimers in the audience, old time eighth graders was, "Tell those two on the end to remove those boards from their backs," we moved so stiffly. I'm not much better today, but I must say we had lots of fun and thought we were the greatest.

The love bug hit me in the second grade, inflicting my heart with romantic notions. Dorothy Walker, a very fair-skinned lassie, was the apple of my eye. I would slip behind her and kiss her cheek. She turned red as a beet and would run away.

My romantic notions extended to writing her a love letter, my first, that consisted of two sentences, "I love you. Do you love me?" I never received an answer. Her best friend Dorothy Truss, was infatuated with me and expressed her sentiments by writing notes to me, "I love you. Do you love me?" I never answered her; I only liked her friend.

I was quiet until Edna Stevens and I exchanged longer love letters in the fourth grade, passed to each other by our peers when the teacher wasn't looking. I overstepped my bounds before Christmas vacation when I asked her a nasty question. She never wrote me again and our romance ended.

I upped my academic tempo in Miss Rummage's sixth grade class for the junior and senior semesters. She was a beautiful, shapely, no-nonsense teacher. A part of every pupil's desire, whether the son or daughter of a school teacher, postman, Sunday school superintendent, college graduate or bootlegger, was to be an excellent student. Honor roll recognition came into prominence for the first time for me. I wasn't too outstanding in the fourth and fifth grades. Whose names would be displayed on that fancy scroll, highlighted by colorful chalk, in a special corner of the blackboard for everyone to see? The coveted position of being number "1" was every student's goal. I persevered, as did Grover Price, Richard Macon, Ethelyn Lindsay, Marie Jordan, Otillia Talley and Lois Dansby to gain that coveted position, number "1." I succeeded.

The very interesting process of debating was introduced in our junior sixth grade class, in addition to percentages, fractions, English composition, spelling, geography, art and history. Debates were held monthly.

Miss Rummage appointed two pupils to present each side of the question. Marie Jordan and I were paired against Ethelyn Lindsay and Grover Price. The next debaters were judges. The subject chosen for us was: "Which are the more productive states, the northeastern or the north central states?" She explained the art of rebuttal.

Fortunately, my partner and I were success-ful. We acted as judges later in the semester.

Miss Revis, a short, portly, quiet, sweet lady was my junior seventh grade teacher. I maintained my number "1" standing on the honor roll and continued working to the best of my ability. I thought I was proficient enough to be chosen a judge until Miss Rummage sent for Grover and Richard to judge a debate. I was very disappointed.

Later I became infatuated with Louise McGee, a veteran lover in the eighth grade. She made a complete fool out of me. We wrote each other let-ters, but never had any physical contact. She was going with 15-year-old Junius McClure from a dysfunctional family on Oakridge Hill. He went to see her and told me at lunchtime of their physical relationships on Sundays. Louise lived across the branch from the school.The joke about our rela-tionship was conning me into bringing her lunch money. I, the infatuated fool, went into Mother's change bowl and lifted thirty-five cents daily. She gave it to him. It was Mother's hard-earned cash from the watermelon stand, soft drinks and bar-becue sales.

Well, the school year ended. Louise moved with her family to the south side of Birmingham. I heard through the grapevine she became an alcoholic and a prostitute, became ill and died. He had an arrest record, became an alcoholic, chain smoker, derelict and died at an early age. Later I associ-ated with girls, but only platonically.

I witnessed many frightening happenings dur-ing childhood. Early one morning about 2 a.m., a man who regularly stole chickens from commu-nity chicken houses came to our home. Daddy answered a knock at the back door. After letting him in, another loud knock followed. Two city policemen saw him cross Georgia Road with a large croker sack on his back. They didn't know its contents, whiskey or what. He, on occasion, stopped at our house. Father bought chickens at twenty-five cents each or a thirty-five cent glass of whiskey. Instead of continuing into the alley behind our barn, he took a frightening chance dashing to our house. He threw the sack underneath sister's and my bed. Mother could see the sack protruding from her very close vantage point in bed less than two feet away. A grinning Birmingham police officer and his partner entered the house. The chicken thief was seated at our dining room table. One officer said, "Boy, what did you have on your back?"

"Nothing."

As fate would have it, the officer knew Father sold whiskey, but had never raided us, and turned his attention to the icebox, which tickled his fancy. He opened the door and behold, there was a pint of moonshine. He asked what it was, got no answer, compromised for $10 and looked no further. The chicken thief heaved a sigh of relief, unaware of the deal between Father and the policeman. He came into the bedroom, picked up his sack and left. The officer became a friend of Father's and no further raids took place.

Daddy had one whiskey delivery stop at John Jones' home on the south side of Birmingham. He was a heavy-set, graying,deep voiced man and bought two to three gallons weekly. His 14-year-old son, Tommy, had a billy goat, wagon and harness. I was fascinated seeing him hitch the goat to the little green farm wagon and ride around the neighborhood. He took me riding sometimes and I was thrilled. I worried Father so much about getting me a billy goat and wagon, one day he did just that. I was only eight years old. The goat had long curved horns and was larger than me. My wagon was also green and large enough to seat me comfortably. Daddy harnessed and hitched the goat to the wagon, I'd get in, pull on the reins, say, "gitty-up, gitty-up" and away we'd go. One day the goat, stubborn as he could be and hard for me to control, decided to take me underneath a neighbor's house about a block from home, where we got stuck in the pilings. I was terrified. I finally succeeded in getting out of the wagon and began trying to pull the goat and wagon free. Being unsuccessful I decided I'd better go home and have Mama come help me. She came, extricated the goat and wagon, I got in and rode up the alley home, unhitched him, put him in his pen and put the wagon under the house.

I made many trips along my famous route with the goat and wagon until one day, after Mother had washed our clothes and hung them on the line, he reared up against them. She had run him away several times with physical and vocal gestures, until she was fed up, fetched her broom, swung at him and struck one of his long horns dislodging it at the root. It was very painful, he moaned and bellowed continuously. Father was on his vegetable route. I was very sad to the point of wanting to cry, but could do nothing. I was angry at Mother and forgave her reluctantly. I didn't want to see my goat suffer, but didn't know what to do to help him. Mother was very remorseful because she hated to see the goat suffer and knew how much I loved him and the wagon.

When Father arrived about 4 p.m. and was apprised of the situation, he began to search for a solution to the dilemma. By nightfall he decided to kill the goat and barbecue him. I was petrified, losing my goat and the fun rides in the wagon. There was nothing I could do but take the decision so dreadful to hear. Daddy contacted his brother-in-law, Griffin Kidd, who said he would kill the goat the next day. I was devastated when Daddy took him to his house on Oakridge Hill the next afternoon.

Well, the hour of reckoning came. Mr. Kidd took a long sharp butcher knife, grabbed the goat and slit his throat. I turned and ran towards the steep steps leading to Aunt Mary's back porch when I heard him bellow loudly. I felt so sorry for him. That was the end of his life and the pleasure of having him pull my wagon was gone forever. The bellowing stopped as he lay bleeding profusely. I slowly and sadly went into the house. After about an hour I returned to the yard. They were barbecuing my poor goat. The smoke was spiraling skyward as the meat slowly cooked.

When the feast began at about 4 that afternoon, I didn't eat, just couldn't bring myself to eat my dear goat. Everyone there, including Aunt Mary's five children, my parents, Aunt Mary and her husband, Griffin Kidd, seemed to enjoy the feast. I never got another goat. The wagon and harness remained under our house and deteriorated over the ensuing years.

Chapter 8
Neighborhood Fun And Games
(Boys Will Be Boys)

My peers and I entertained ourselves with a variety of games, some we created and others were handed down from one generation of children to the next. There were no swimming pools or parks for blacks. The closest pool to my community was East Lake Park, about five miles away, with a very explicit sign, "Whites Only." There was a branch of contaminated water about three feet deep running through our neighborhood where some children swam, and into which neighbors frequently threw dead animals and other debris. This was a common sight at our swimming hole. Mother would have died if she thought I tried to learn to swim in that polluted water. I knew better. I cannot swim to this day. It's where a peer, Nathaniel Felton, learned to swim, saving his life at Pearl Harbor when his ship was bombed by the Japanese and declaration of war by the United States.

Hop scotch was played mainly by girls, but I participated in a few games. It really tested one's agility.

Playing jacks, five in number, with a small rubber ball was fun. I picked up many splinters on the side of my hand scooping them up.

I often played with a thing we called a Zooner made from a piece of flat wood about five inches long, two inches wide, one-fourth inch thick and whittled into a cylindrical shape. A string was put through a hole at one end and tied to make a loop. Swinging it around and around splitting the wind, making a zoom, zoom, zoom, zooming sound was entertaining to me.

Jump rope was very fashionable. Hot peas was a favorite way to get rid of the slow jumpers who could jump seemingly for hours. My partner and I whirled the rope as hard and fast as we could to get rid of them. When the jumper failed to clear the rope, he or she was eliminated and waited his or her next turn, after eliminating all others.

Shooting marbles was a great pastime. "I first go ya," was my outcry when I saw one of my friends coming and vice versa. That meant I'd shoot first. We played for keeps. The old winning spirit is in-born, I'm sure.

All colors of marbles, at two for a penny, could be bought at the grocery store. Finding them in the street or winning them from an opponent was super. There was no limit as to how many could play. Playmates were always on the loose, looking for some kind of action.

The ring was drawn with a stick. A marble was placed on opposite ends and in between if more than two played. "Taw," the line from which one shot was five feet away. "Skunking," was when an opponent didn't get a chance to shoot because the shooter got lucky, knocking a marble from the ring on his first shot, earning the right to continue shooting until he cleared the ring.

Girls didn't shoot marbles. Too much stoop-ing and bending for dress-wearers. My sister hung around watching us play. I didn't like that and would try to shoo her away because some of the boys called me "bruddun," meaning they'd like being my brother-in-law.

Bull's eye was more difficult. A large circular ring was drawn and the marbles placed in a small circle in the center. The player had to knock one or maybe two marbles clear of the larger circle. We'd play for hours.

Overalls were my daily attire when not in school. I wore out the right knee of many pairs of pants and the toes of my shoes sliding along to get into position to shoot.

Playing checkers was a thought-provoking game and very competitive. We made our 24 man boards, bottle tops were the checkers. There were many rules to observe, jumping backwards as well as forwards. Flying kings were controversial, some liked to play whereby you could only jump one man at a time instead of going all over the board. After jumping over one man, if a vacant space existed between two succeeding checkers it was dead meat. The same execution was in order all over the opponent's area.

We played "Rise and Fly," where the loser was replaced by a waiting player. It was a fun game.

A game called "Bourger" would make you wish you were a saint and not a sinner for using profanity. An agreement was entered whereby each participant locked fifth fingers to become a member. If a curse word were uttered, the closest peer could strike the swearer in the middle of his back with as much might as his fists could produce. The stroke could shorten one's breath. I slipped, as did others, once in a while but tried to be on guard and not use bad language ever. Quick thinking was in order by saying "Bourger," immediately, to nullify being stunned from a heavy blow.

Spinning tops was another game very popular among boys. The top was flung from a string wrapped around it, beginning above the sharp point. It spun around and around, finally tumbling over as it slowed down. We'd rewind and spin again, over and over, becoming expert at performing intricate maneuvers such as picking it up above the point with the string and flinging it into the air, catching it in the palm of my hand, as it continued spinning. It was fun.

"Knulling" was played with two spinners. One spun his top and the opponent tried to hit it with the sharp point of his inflicting a dent. A few hits and many misses at damaging each other's tops was the norm for that type competition.

I got a pair of roller skates every year for Christmas. Skidding, slipping, sliding, bruising my elbows, knees and tearing holes in my pants was a daily occurrence. I skated most of the year as there was very little snow. There was plenty of company, a real enjoyment for all of us. I never became an expert because I couldn't eliminate the negatives. Older adolescents jumped over barrels, did eagle splits and skated very fast down 77th Street and Newman's hills, the epitome of a super skater.

Roller skates cost $2.50 a pair. Some had aluminum wheels, the cheaper ones were wooden and called "chariot wheels," el cheapos. I wore out many pairs of skates. My last pair, at age 12, almost cost my life. I was preparing to get up from the curb, not looking to my left as a speeding automobile blazed by and just missed me. I took off the skates, walked to our back yard, placed them under the steps of the back porch where they stayed until they rusted away. I never got another pair.

The strong winds of March always meant kite flying time. I made dozens of two and three-stick ones. I made a flour paste to glue them together, robbing myself of many of Mother's good biscuits. Sometimes I used sharp thorns for stabilization. I bought a few kits at a nickel apiece, when I had the nickel. They were more colorful. A ball of cord cost five cents. I flew them very high and far away. If the string broke, some treetop or telephone line would be the final inaccessible resting place. I lost quite a few.

Pitching horseshoes was real fun. We used old discarded ones thrown away by animal owners. Two two-foot iron rods were driven into the ground twenty-five feet apart. A ringer, which meant pitching the horseshoe around the stake, was five points and three points if it landed partially around the stake and could be dislodged by striking it with another shoe. One point was awarded the player closest to the stake and two points if the shoe landed on its side, propped against the stake. Twenty-five points was game. I really liked trains and often found one under the Christmas tree. I'd wind the engine after attaching it to four cars, putting them on the light aluminum tracks and watching the action as it ran around and around. I wore out and wrecked many.

The pride and joy of childhood toy trains was the one I built using a 15 ounce syrup can for the fire box, into which a hole was cut on top to accommodate a bottomless snuff box, the chimney. A flat piece of wood one-half inch in diameter and three feet long anchored my choo-choo. Six smaller tin cans were the boxcars, coupled by a piece of strong twine through a hole punched in the bottom of each can and stabilized by tying them to a nail at the ends of each anchor. I stuffed the fire box with newspaper, wood chips and chunks of hard coal for fuel and lighted it. A black cloud of smoke spiraled upwards, symbolic of that emanating from the smoke stack of the many trains seen daily passing my house. I was thrilled with my invention and joyfully pulled it with a strong piece of twine, around and around the large vacant lot adjacent to my home. It was more durable than those Santa brought me.

I really liked my yo-yo. It cost a nickel. Making it spin on the string, which we referred to as walking the dog, was really fun. Splitting the string at the end and letting it spin when thrown down before giving it a jerk to return was great fun.

Once I had a purple-colored one that I dearly loved. It came up missing and I wondered where I lost it. One day, Nay, as Nathaniel Felton was called, came across the street to our watermelon stand with a yo-yo, speckled with small nuggets resembling diamonds. It was pretty as he spun it up and down and sideways. On closer observation, I noticed that it looked just like my missing one. "That's my yo-yo."

"Whatta you mean?"

"You stole my yo-yo and I want it back."

"This is my yo-yo."

All of a sudden he grabbed and flipped me into outer space. I was stunned as I struck the ground, flat on my back. Our friends laughed. I got up and went after him. I was only six days older and about the same size. We tugged around briefly before Father came out of the stand to see what was happening. "Daddy, he stole my yo-yo."

"No, I didn't, Mr. Witt."

"Well Edwin, he says it's his. Let that be the end of it." Nay kept the yo-yo. It was messed up by the holes and I didn't want it anymore.

I forgot about it over the years and our friendship remained mutual.

Baseball was my game. I weighed only 90 pounds, wasn't very fast or muscular, so football was out of my league. Some of my peers were bigger and rougher, and I didn't want to get a broken bone any place, including my neck.

There was no basketball court or hoops over garage doors, or even a basketball to dribble.

We made baseballs by removing the covering of a golf ball and wrapping the rubber inside with cord string. I knew it was the right size when I could hold it in the palm of my hand and grip it with my thumb, index and middle fingers. It would go as far as a professional baseball when struck with a bat. We preserved our home-made balls by wrapping them with adhesive tape, giving them added life. However, we'd finally wear away the tape and retape.

Our bats and gloves were old hand-me-downs that neighbors were given by their employers. Some bats were handleless, others frayed, but we made use of them anyway.

We chose sides and played on a makeshift diamond adjacent to my home when we were small. Later we graduated to a larger diamond a block away, adjacent to the Knights of Phythias Hall.

Mr. Otis Heard and Mr. Allen Slaughter sometimes wouldn't give us our balls when they landed in their front yard or garden. We were very angry at them for being so mean.

We chose sides of up to nine players, depending on the number present. As to which side batted first, one player would throw a bat to the opposing team's representative. They would go hand over hand up the handle, the one reaching the top was declared the winner unless the opponent could get hold of enough to throw it five feet over his shoulder.

When we graduated to the larger diamond, my peers and I would get together a group of nine players and challenge the boys who lived on 64th and 65th Streets. We lived from 60th to 62nd Street and called ourselves the 62nd Street Tigers and them, the 64th Street Raggety Roaches. We played double and triple headers under the broiling hot sun, with very high humidity.

I pitched every fourth day and played right field other days. The pitcher always wore the glove of poorest quality, a worn piece of leather with fingers, but no padding. After throwing bad pitches to my catcher, Pete Hardy, he'd return the ball harder to me than I threw it to him. The sting really woke me up.

Being a poor hitter, I'd try to pitch well. Pitchers weren't supposed to be good batters.

My most devastating game pitching against the Raggety Roaches was a day with the score tied nine to nine in the ninth inning. The count was three balls and two strikes on James Williams. Pete called for a breaking ball, down and away. I shook him off until finally he called for a hard one down the pike (the middle of the plate). I had decided after James fouled off several pitches, it was going to be him or me, meaning he'd hit the ball out for a home run or I'd strike him out. Well, he hit the next pitch faraway, up and over the two story lodge hall. I looked up as the ball flew over the hall, dropped my head as his teammates exploded with joyful laughter, put that piece of glove in my hip pocket and briskly walked up the alley home. I prepared myself a plate of food, sat down and ate. Everyone else had eaten. At the conclusion I retired to the watermelon stand, relaxed on the bench, knowing that there would be another day and, hopefully, a winning one.

The most spectacular play I made as a pitcher was when Falling Dad, as James Jackson was called, catcher for the 64th Street Raggety Roaches, hit a pitch weakly between home plate and the mound. I broke towards the plate and about halfway fell completely flat in my haste to get the ball, grabbed it and threw towards first base. The first baseman stretched as far as he could and fell, reaching for the errant throw. Falling Dad was streaking towards first base as Sam scooped the ball from the dirt, touched the bag an eyelash in distance before Falling Dad arrived. I jumped up, dusted myself, looked at Sam who had begun to scramble up, blowing dust from his face. I ran over to him grinning, "Man, that was some play." We embraced, as everybody showed their approval with big smiles and shouting, "Way to go, Babe." That was my greatest day on the mound.

Stilts, two six-foot 2 x 4s with four-inch wide blocks of wood nailed midway inside upon which to stand, were very popular with the Felton brothers, Pete and Gordon Hardy and me. Guess I wanted to feel like I was on top of the world, over ten feet tall. We had a good time trying to walk, jumping off frequently to keep from falling. The fun was in the attempt. It was hard to stay up very long, but that didn't deter us.

One of the most dangerous missile launchers my peers and I made was a slingshot. It was a woefully traumatic weapon, wounding and maiming any animal or fowl that crossed our paths. I don't know who invented it, but I copied that injurious weapon. Birds sitting in trees were our primary targets. I don't remember crippling or killing any, but shot at quite a few.

Those little glass objects atop telegraph poles were good targets, shooting at them for long periods of time, just to hear the wires zing when struck. I don't know how much damage was done, prayerfully none. Window panes were broken, dogs and cats frightened, and needlessly, a few children lost eyes when unlucky enough to be hit.

I played golf before I knew anything about the game. Some peer would bring an old golf ball and a worn-out club, given to a domestic. We dug four holes, three by three and fashioned them like bases on a ball diamond. We had never seen a golf game since there were no recreation or park facilities in our neighborhood, and made our own rules. We hit the ball towards the hole, the one who put it in all four holes with the least number of strokes was the winner. The player was jubilant when lucky enough to knock it in with a single shot. Hole-in-one wasn't in our vocabulary at that time.

Never having the joy of owning a bicycle, several of my friends did, and I bugged them for a ride every once in a while. The hardest fall I ever received was from Haywood Fagan's bike, who lived across the street from me. I always asked him to let me ride, against Mother's vehement warnings. One day as my parents sat on the back porch, I came up Georgia Road flying, made a left turn into the gravel driveway parallel to our house. The bicycle slid around, throwing me to the ground. I was stunned for a time, my mouth dry as a powder house. The palms of both hands were full of gravel and covered with blood. I thought Mother would come to my rescue but she didn't. After a few minutes I regained my composure, got up slowly and walked even slower to the back porch. She greeted me with "I wish it had killed you." She didn't mean it literally but was angry because she had warned me, in vain, about bugging Haywood. I washed my hands with soap and water, dried them; what a burning sensation. I never asked him again.

My childhood friends and I invented our own walkie-talkies. We came upon the idea of talking to one another by taking two large tin cans, cutting a hole in the bottom and connecting them with a seven foot piece of string tied to a small match stick at the bottom of the cans. We talked into the open ends, a good imitation of the modern day walkie-talkies and provided endless hours of fun and games for us.

It was 12 noon in mid-July, the sky was clear as the sun made its way westward. The temperature was 100 degrees plus and the humidity seemed higher as beads of perspiration extended from my scalp, to my neck, chest and back with the slightest amount of activity.

"Edwin," Mother called out to me, "I need some eggs. Go up to Mrs. Walker's and get me a dozen." Mrs. Mattie Walker, an elderly gray-haired widow, had plenty of chickens and dozens of large, fresh eggs which she sold for fifteen cents a dozen.

"Yes, ma'am, do you want me to go now?"

"Wait until it gets a little cooler, it's so hot outside."

About two hours later, "Mama, are you ready for me to go get the eggs?"

"All right, here's the money." She gave me fifteen cents with the warning, "Be careful when you cross the railroad tracks. Look both ways to see if a train is coming."

I picked up my hat and skipped out the door calling out, "Yes ma'am. I'll be careful." We lived below two railroad lines, four tracks at the foot of a hill which the hill toppers called The Bottom.

I discovered a real source of amusement on

my way, along the dirt path, up the hill and across the tracks where the Brownings, their three sons, Mrs. Mattie Walker, a widow, her brother, Mr. James Kingston, and the King's three sons and three daughters lived. This route was a convenient passageway separating their homes and a wooded area past the homes of their neighbors and beyond.

Approaching Mrs. Walker's home, I heard a strange, seemingly muted voice singing. I paused for a moment, looked around and saw Mr. James Kingston sitting on a bench under a tall pine tree holding what appeared to be a little black boy on his right knee. He had his right hand behind the little fellow's back. I could clearly hear the youngster sing, "I'm so glad Daddy don't know where I is; Oh, Lordy, Lord, I'm so glad Daddy don"t know where I is."

Drawing nearer I could see it was a dummy made of wood, jet black, with life-like roving eyes, large red lips, decked out in a white suit and cap with S.B. embroidered in front. It stood for Snow Ball. He was very nosy and sassy.

Mr. Kingston, a bachelor, was a kind-hearted mulatto gentleman with big eyes, pigeon toed, bowed legs, shy and not very tall. He discovered that cool, green grass-covered area among the vast forest of pine trees where he enjoyed relaxing and entertaining the neighborhood children and himself. It was across the street from his home, so I named the park Kingston's Kingdom. When Snow Ball saw me he blurted, "Hey man, who's that kid?"

"That's Mr. Witt's son."

"What's his name?"

"I don't know, but his father sells watermelons down in the bottom on Georgia Road."

"My name is Edwin."

Snowball looked at Mr. Kingston, "See, you don't know everything, you always call me a dummy, now who's the dummy?"

"If you be good, I'll take you down there and we'll get a slice of watermelon to eat and bring a whole one home."

"Hooray, hooray, I'm ready," replied Snow Ball.

Richard and Archie Browning, Ethel Mae King, her younger sister Eloise and brother Edward, who visited the park often as they lived close by, were sitting on the grass listening to Snow Ball. I was baffled as to how that dummy could talk. I finally asked the kids, "How does Snow Ball do that?"

They answered in unison, "We don't know." Mr. Kingston halfheartedly laughed and continued to converse with Snowball, letting us stew and listen in bewilderment as to how that dummy could sing and talk. I noticed that Mr. Kingston always kept his right hand behind Snowball's back and his lips moved slightly.

Some time later I was told that Mr. Kingston threw his voice into the dummy to make it talk. That was the key which unlocked a baffling mystery for me. I never tried to talk to that dummy.

At that time, I had never heard of ventriloquism and don't know if Mr. Kingston had. He never explained to us how he got the idea for that unique bit of entertainment.

I always enjoyed going to Kingston's Kingdom, especially the swings. He threw a rope over the very tall, sturdy limb of a pine tree, tied the ends, found a flat piece of wood, placed it in the loop for a seat and it was ready for action. I immediately jumped onto the seat and began to move my feet back and forth but couldn't get up enough speed while seated, so I stood up and one of my peers gave me a few shoves while I pumped with all my might. Soon I began soaring higher and higher. Oh, what a thrill.

Sometimes two of us stood pumping back and forth reaching heights which caused the rope to buckle and almost dump us. We never thought of the danger of the limb breaking and spilling us.

I returned whenever Mother gave me permission. Crossing the railroad tracks could be very dangerous for an early school-aged child like me. Sister never went, she was too small.

The main source of Father's whiskey supply was Emmett and Thomas Beyers. They were first class whiskey distributors. He bought twenty to seventy-five gallons every three to six months at $5 per gallon.

Emmett was a high stakes poker player and occasionally came by to receive a loan against future deliveries.

They had a very amicable relationship. I went with Father on several occasions to Mr. Beyers' home, 15 miles away in Zion City, to inquire about an order. Sometimes whiskey became scarce, as the revenuers raided and destroyed many stills in the wooded suburbs of Birmingham.

I named another of Father's whiskey sources "Nervy," because he would park his car about a third of a block past our watermelon stand and streak with a gallon can underneath his arm in broad daylight. That was a frightening sight to see. We lived on a very heavily traveled street, frequently patrolled by City policemen and Jefferson County deputy sheriffs.

Once the cops were so hot after Father, he asked Joe Green, who was married to Daddy's niece, Juanita, if he could store a few gallons in his basement. The house was built on a hill. As a matter of fact, it was located up from our home, across four railroad tracks. Fifty to sixty-five gallons were always stored there. It was presumed the cops had no suspicions of this hideout. Joe became a real culprit. He loved corn whiskey as a hog loves corn and stole some, refilling the cans with water. The whiskey was 135-proof, so a little watering down wasn't too easily detected. Daddy finally discovered what he was doing and stopped stashing it there, but not before my debacle the Sunday night Aunt Mary married Griffin Kidd.

Mother was aware of the stash and sent my cousin Bunch Washington, eleven months my senior, and me to get a gallon of that powerful stuff for the guests. He decided we should sample the spirit-giver before taking it to the guests, stopping by the old-fashioned deep well and taking several swigs. I held up fairly well under the first onslaught. The party became livelier with the disappearance of gallon No. 1, so Mother dispatched us to go for another one, which we did gladly.

On returning we duplicated the previous procedure. I was really looped after this episode. We delivered the goods to the guests, ate and mingled with the crowd until they finished the second gallon. It became our honor to oblige the guests once again, getting another cache of this make-you-feel-good liquid, making this trip a floater. Imbibing another big swig, I was on cloud nine, talking loudly and staggering. Unfortunately for me, Mother met us at the door and immediately diagnosed the cause of my unsteadiness from the strong odor of alcohol on my breath. She bopped my head ,"What is wrong with you?"

"Nothing." I settled down in the bedroom and slept until Mother was ready to go home.

That was my first and last drunken episode during childhood.

There's an old saying, "Monkey see, monkey do."

Father never smoked cigarettes but often felt like a big shot and sent me six blocks to buy some Virginia Cheroot cigars, two for a nickel. Sometimes he laid a lighted one on the kitchen cabinet on his way to the front of the house. I'd pick it up and take a puff. I didn't know how to inhale but got enough nicotine in my bloodstream to get a buzz I didn't like.

It was the same with Brown Mule chewing tobacco. He would leave a plug on the cabinet and I'd bite a little chaw, sweet tasting but oh, so powerful. I didn't have any better sense than to swallow the ambeer, as the juice was called. My head began spinning and I had to lie down for a good spell to regain my equilibrium.

I smoked corn silk, the dried tassel of an ear of corn, without my parents knowledge. It wouldn't burn until dry when it made the best imitation of tobacco. Rolling it in a piece of brown paper preferably, or newspaper, and dampening it with a copious amount of saliva, it resembled the real thing. After lighting one end and puffing the other, the hot smoke felt like someone had slit my tongue with a very sharp razor blade. Not willing to take many puffs, it was just the principle of the thing. I felt grownup and thought I looked as chic as an adult.

There was a tall tree which grew thumb-sized pods about nine inches long, and when dried looked like cigars to me. They were pithy inside. Cutting off both ends, lighting one and puffing on the other, smoke as seen from a lighted cigar billowed upwards and gave me the feeling I was smoking the real thing.

Neither of my parents ever saw me trying to

smoke one of those make believe cigars or cigarettes, all for the betterment of my well being.

Halloween was a hazardous time in our neighborhood, when thirty to forty of us youngsters dressed in ragged, weird outfits, masks, brooms and sticks took dead aim on our neighbors' darkened front porches. Bam, bam, bam, a dozen fists banged on their doors as we goblins shouted, "Trick or treat," when the door opened. Many times we got nothing, but rarely did any dirty tricks to them.

An occasional corner street light was a good target for rock throwers, sometimes successfully, and our community was in total darkness for days.

The best was yet to come as Patterson School, which we attended, was really going to get it. I threw my share of rocks and laughed when I heard the windows breaking. I don't know if I struck the target, it was pitch dark.

I finally quit the gang when Clifford May set Mr. Turner's large stack of hay afire. It was the biggest fire I'd ever seen and very scary. At the outset we laughed with glee until the fire grew higher and higher, spreading wider and wider, then we became very frightened and quiet.

I had seen the deaf mute man pass our house twice daily on his way to cut the tall grass on the hillside by the railroad tracks, hauling it in a wheel barrow to Mr. Turner's and stacking it. The stack was twenty-five to fifty feet high. He would be soaking wet with perspiration, as it was very hot and humid in mid-summer. I felt sorry for him.

Mr. Turner worked for the railroad and owned two cows. Mrs. Turner sold milk and butter and Mother often sent me to get a quart pitcher of buttermilk for ten cents and sometimes a cake of butter for a dime.

When the fire erupted, Mr. Turner came from his house with a pearl-handled 32 Special pistol in his hand. "Who set my hay on fire?" he shouted. A few of the crowd had split, but the enormity of the blaze froze most of us in our tracks. He looked at me and repeated, "Who set my hay on fire? Do you know who did it?"

"No sir, Mr. Turner, I didn't do it."

The spell from the fire lifted from around me and I slowly walked away knowing who set it, and felt saddened because I knew how the hay got there. I was afraid to tell him because the culprit, Clifford May, was a mean, freckled-faced dude who didn't mind kicking rear ends.

I went home, told Mother what happened and who did it. "I'll say it again, you'd better stop going around with those bad kids." Despite the warning, we greased the streetcar tracks with lard and soap and got a charge as it slipped and spun, trying to go forward.

Father somehow became involved with a bookie shop downtown where bets on horses and baseball games could be placed. Magazines, local and out of town newspapers were the main business. The fellow who worked there was a very nice Syrian gentleman, known to me as Mr. Charlie. He called me Little Witt and was always nice to me. Daddy bet on baseball teams, a fifty cents or dollar parlay consisting of two,three or four teams. He won a few times and since I was a baseball enthusiast and impressionable, I decided to take fifty cents or a dollar from Mother's kitty which she openly placed in the china closet. That was stealing, pure and simple.

My days for gambling on baseball parlays came to an end when one day sister saw me place two quarters inside my hat band as I was getting ready to take

Father's bets downtown and told him. He asked me what I had in my hat. I said, "Nothing." He had me remove it. Upon lowering the band out fell two quarters and an immediate hard slap to my left cheek hurt very much and was most embarrassing. He kept the quarters and gave me a severe tongue lashing. I went to town very sad. Learning a valuable lesson, I never did that again. I graduated to another form of thievery when I withdrew the few dollars I had in a savings account at the Industrial Savings Bank for school children. The savings were placed into the account by the school weekly, ten cents up. There was about $15, so Mother thought. Barefooted as a river duck in the heart of winter, I sludged through the snow with cardboard bottoms in my shoes. Mother, who was very protective of us, could stand that cruel fate no longer and told me to go to the bank, withdraw the money so she could take me to town and buy a long overdue pair of shoes. Knowing I didn't have any money left, having withdrawn it in small increments while betting on baseball parlays and losing, I put her off as long as I could with one excuse after another. Finally she demanded the bank book. When she saw the balance was zero, she almost died and lighted on me like a duck on a June bug. I lived down that mistake and never did anything like that again.

I got the gambling bug so bad upon seeing an advertisement in a newspaper where one could send away for the name of a horse that was sure to win. After winning, you would pay the tipster five dollars by return mail. Without anyone's knowledge, I sent for the information. In those days, my preteen years, messages were sent through Western Union or Postal Telegraph. One day a postal telegraph messenger delivered a letter which Father accepted. Paying a delivery fee of fifty cents, he wanted to know from whom the message came and who or-

dered it. I confessed. He was confused and surprised, as here was the name of a horse, Clientele,
running in the fifth race at a track in New York the
following day. He never bet on horses, even though
Mr. Benny Hudson, a regular moonshine customer,
did. He stopped by frequently and often talked about
his winnings and losses. Mr. Hudson often remarked
to Daddy who he knew bet on baseball, "I know
nothing about them baseballs." Father never caught
the horse racing fever but scraped up the $5 none-
theless and sent me to the betting parlor that accepted his baseball bets. Well, the next day, when I
placed Father's baseball bet I was informed the
horse ran out of the money. Father was fit to be
tied when I told him the bad news. That ended his
horse race betting days.

I wasn't through yet. The urge to bet horses sur-
faced one day when I scanned the race entries in the
daily Birmingham Post and saw a horse named Black
Helen. I bet fifty cents, she won and paid $7. That
money was chewed up in a hurry as I tried to stretch
my luck. Without a job or any cash, I was finished
without the knowledge of knowing horses could be
bet to run second or third (place or show).

The vice officers were aware of gambling ven-
tures at news stands and visited them frequently.
I can see Mr. Charlie now, shaking his head of
black, moderately long hair, signaling me to keep
walking and wait until things cooled off. I'd walk
around downtown, looking in the windows of
Blach's and Burger-Phillips, two very exclusive
clothing stores.

I'd return to Mr. Charlie's if he didn't shake
his head, go in, place Father's bets, walk two blocks
to the streetcar line, board one and go home.

Chapter 9
The Sparks that became a Flame

My inspiration to become a doctor was undoubtedly sparked at age six when I saw Dr. P. S. Moten
enter my sick grandmother's bedroom with his little black bag. I watched him listen to her chest
with the ear pieces of the stethoscope in his ears.
They looked like horns to me.

My curiosity about those horns was buried
deeply into my subconscious mind.

Later, when I saw doctors entering the homes
of sick neighbors carrying their little black bags, I
wondered if they had some horns like Dr. Moten
which could help them find out what was wrong
and order some medicine so they could get well. I
was mystified and my interest grew more intense
as I grew older.

I remember hearing our grocer, an Italian who'd
been in our neighborhood many, many years, tell
a neighbor of ours that even if I didn't become a
physician I could be a school teacher. I had told
him I wanted to be a doctor. He called me "Heaven"
because of his Italian accent and couldn't say
Edwin. Hundreds of conversations and interactions
occurred between him, his four children, wife and

me. We bought most of our groceries from him until two supermarkets opened on First Avenue North where we shopped sometimes. His son, Joe, was on the baseball team and played center field opposite me in right field.

Dr. Saunders Walker, retired chairperson of the English Department at the Tuskegee Institute, Alabama, which was founded by Booker T. Washington was very fond of me. He taught English at Industrial High and sponsored an after-school club called The Lexicographers. One had to bring a new word each meeting, pronounce and spell it correctly and give its meaning. There were twenty members. It was very, very fascinating. One Sunday he was the main speaker at our 11 o'clock church service. As he spoke so eloquently of this member of our church, an adolescent who was going places in life and was a super human being, no one knew exactly of whom he was speaking. Foreheads began to wrinkle with certainty that he was referring to the superintendent of our Sunday school's son, Grover Price, Jr., who by the way was my seat mate, baseball teammate and best friend. When he called my name and had me stand, you could hear a pin drop. The silence was deafening. That really made me feel good and inspired me to continue working hard and achieving.

I remember Doctor Walter Brown going to see neighbors. He was a short, fine looking gentleman with a super smile and gold inlays glowing from his molars. Dr. Edward Ballard also called on patients in our neighborhood. Both doctors came from across town. Dr. Broughton, who delivered me at home, lived about two blocks away and Mother took me to see him in his small office located across the driveway from his home. His professional demeanor and the smell of alcohol saturated cotton balls used to cleanse the skin before an injection were motivating factors for me to become a physician. I also saw him many times making house calls. Dr. K. J. Kinkead, a white physician who lived on the edge of the Negro neighborhood, was a tall stately gentleman who treated Negro patients at their homes and his office downtown. The only negative thing about visiting his office were chairs in the hallway for the people of color. Whites sat inside.

Woodlawn was blessed when Dr. G. A Martin, a general practitioner, came to live with his parents and became one of my biggest inspirations. His father was my pastor.

He was born in Selma, Alabama, 105 miles south of Birmingham. His mulatto skin and black straight hair inherited from his mother, got him into the University of Virginia Medical School at Richmond in 1924. Negroes at that time could only attend Meharry Medical College in Nashville, Tennessee, and Howard University College of Medicine in Washington, D.C.

Dr. Martin had no automobile and made house calls on foot. His office was a room in his parents home. I saw him from time to time visiting neighbors with his large medical bag full of healing magic. Everyone sang his praises as being a good doctor.

He became friends with Father after finding out from one his friends that he sold whiskey. Dr. Martin drank very heavily. I saw him belt down many glasses without flinching of the 135-proof clear as crystal whiskey, and held it well.

I imagine the Great Depression frustrated him immensely and he assuaged his frustrations by altering his sensorium, so as not to face reality head on. His patients had very little money.

An arrested case of tuberculosis, he smoked incessantly, especially strong Chesterfields, and coached me as to how to make some extra money making cigarettes and selling them to Father's whiskey customers and himself. Daddy bought me a cigarette rolling machine to make my unsophisticated product, but a reasonable facsimile. I didn't get rich with that venture, selling them for one cent each.

He also encouraged me to study medicine, a seed that was planted at age six. "Edwin, I would like to see you become a doctor." That was highly inspirational to me. I never forgot his encouragement.

I shall always remember hearing Father and his sister, Mary, tell of the time Dr. Martin saved my five-year-old cousin Thomas Washington's life. Nothing had worked prescribed by a previous doctor. Father and Dr. Martin were personal friends and when Daddy stopped by to see Aunt Mary, he found her in a state of despair. Daddy said he told her he would ask his friend, Dr. Martin, to come see Thomas and fortunately he agreed. When he examined Thomas and made his diagnosis of pneumonia, he told her how gravely ill Thomas was and that he would go to the drug store and personally order some medication, as special permission had to come from the pharmacist to the drug wholesaler. He trudged to Fadley's Drug Store, told Dr. Fadley (pharmacists were called doctor in those days) that he wanted some pneumococcal pneumonia serum. The pharmacists' eyes widened as he blurted "Where did you learn that type of knowledge, George?" Guess he thought all Negroes were dumb and didn't know about the finer arts of anything, especially medicine. He ignored the pharmacist calling him by his first name and after receiving the serum the same afternoon, said thanks and proceeded to Aunt Mary's and injected Thomas with it.

Aunt Mary told Father that Thomas soon began to "come back this way" after he received that shot, thanks to him and Dr. Martin. Thomas recovered from his very serious illness and I was thrilled.

After I heard Father and Aunt Mary sing his praises, my brain cells sparkled with thoughts of becoming a doctor just like him.

Mrs. Susie Felton lived across the street from us. She was a rural elementary school teacher, very outgoing, outspoken and an inspiration for my ambition to become a doctor. I visited her home hundreds of times because she had two step sons whom she reared from early childhood after the death of their mother. One stepson was six days younger, the other two years older. She had known me since the first day I entered school and long before. Her observations of me were many, some from across the street and many from interpersonal contact. She knew how I was ticking socially, psychologically and academically. Her stepsons didn't do too well in school, a subject she didn't discuss with me, but I knew because we went to the same school.

As I grew older my ambition to become a doctor became deeper. I told her I wanted to become a doctor. This was all well and good, but she never lost sight of the fact that we were in the midst of the Great Depression and my father wasn't gainfully employed. She knew of the bootleg situation at our home because she could see the daily in and out traffic. The watermelon stand during the summer made no fortune. She encouraged me in my aspiration of becoming a doctor by telling me on many occasions of a young man from Pittsburgh, Pennsylvania, whose financial plight was similar to mine and who finally got the chance to work and pay his way through medical school and became a very successful doctor. I imagine she saw the same potential in me and encouraged me to continue to do well in school and somehow, some way, with the help of the good Lord, I could one day reach my goal. I can see her now on her front porch, just she and I, vividly talking about this aspect of my life.

Little did she know that one day I would become a doctor and come to her rescue. She had been a diabetic for years, but I knew nothing about it until one day I was called to her home. I approached the same front porch where so long ago we discussed my becoming a doctor. Upon examining her, I discovered a large abscess in her right arm pit complicating her sugar diabetes. It was the largest one I had ever seen. She had lost control of her diabetes through inadequate insulin injections and dietary indiscretion. I took my scalpel and excised it, from which flowed a large amount of yellowish material.

I placed drains into the incision to keep it open so it could continue to drain, adjusted her insulin dosage and emphasized the importance of adhering to her diet. The lesion drained completely, her armpit receded to its normal size and all was well. She was a very happy lady. I never received another call from her, but never forgot her encouragement and solace for my future on that fateful afternoon when she told me about the young man in Pittsburgh whose position in life paralleled mine.

My senior 7th grade teacher was Miss Lucille Clark, home grown so to speak, as she was born in Woodlawn about five blocks from the school and ten blocks from my home. We attended the same church. She was short, bespectacled, nice looking and very strict. To be on the honor roll, one had to be a good student and have perfect attendance.

Father was an avid baseball fan of the Birmingham White Barons and asked Mother to write a note to Miss Clark excusing me at noon on the first day of the 1931 Dixie Series.

Each year the Southern League champion and the Texas League champion participated in the Dixie Series, the best of seven. Houston won the Texas League championship and had a famous pair of pitchers, The Dean Brothers, Jerome (Dizzy) and Paul (Daffy). Before the game started, Dizzy, a gangly six-foot-three, free spirited individual with a two day growth of beard, visited with Father and me in the "colored" bleachers and gave us a baseball. We kept that ball for many years and played catch with it numerous times.

Dizzy pitched and lost the first game of the series and his brother, Daffy, pitched and won the second. Houston lost the series in seven games.

The next month when my name appeared first on the honor roll, one of my classmates, Indiana Andrews, a bright round-faced girl, reminded Miss Clark that I had been absent a half day. She undoubtedly thought I was keeping her off the honor roll. Miss Clark suddenly remembered my absence, promptly went to the blackboard and erased my name. A thunderous applause erupted and I was saddened.

She quieted the class and immediately rewrote my name. A few seconds later I arose, turned to the class and said "I hope you don't feel constipated." They were stunned, as was Miss Clark.

She eventually removed my name for the remainder of that month. It reappeared the next month, Number 1. Needless to say, I was happy.

Children of all ages gave nicknames to their peers. We created names for some who had long heads, mal-shaped derrieres, hunched backs, poor quality hair, odd shaped haircuts on boys, large feet, lack of ability to do one's work, freckles, large eyes, flat foreheads, knocked knees, overweight, speech impediments, buck teeth, large ears or any conspicuous characteristic. My head was kind of long and pointed in the back. For that reason I was called Egghead, not realizing that in future years an egghead meant the height of intelligentsia. At that time it was highly insulting to me and I was angered every time someone called me Egghead or Egg.

Chapter 10
Religion And Communal Socialization

The church was the gathering place for spiritual, social, cultural activities and fellowship. Jackson Street Baptist was the church of my parents choosing. There were other churches of different persuasions where many of our friends attended. Old Ship AME Zion (African Methodist Episcopal), Allen's Chapel CME (Colored Methodist Episcopal) and Mt. Moriah Methodist.

When I was a young child my parents attended church regularly. Father liked to tell how I reacted at the sight of the church with me in his arms. I would freeze as a prelude to my acting-out behavior. Crying and restlessness necessitated my having to be taken in to the foyer. That happening became a little old and one Sunday he gave me a good spanking, which mellowed my attitude.

Just as mother enrolled sister and me in public school at age six, our Sunday School attendance began concomitably. She didn't attend church with us, but made sure after breakfast every Sunday, we were neatly dressed and on our way to Sabbath School and Church.

Finding herself trapped in a sin bin of a bootlegging, alcoholic, verbally threatening, physically abusive husband, Mother didn't attend church except on Easter Sunday, when she accompanied us. Not an Easter parader herself, she made it doubly important for sister and me to attend. It was a religious celebration of the resurrection of our Lord and saviour, Jesus Christ, more than a parade of frocks and frills.

Easter Sunday was usually in late March or early April, and rain, hail and high winds often penetrated those Easter outfits and chilled our bones. I remember well hearing of a devastating tornado in Helena, Alabama, a few miles from Birmingham. We felt the blustery, cold tail end of it.

However, this particular Easter Sunday was beautiful. Sister was dressed in a cute little fancy dress, a colorful bonnet and a patent leather pocketbook with a shoulder strap and patent leather shoes to match. I was sharp in my pair of Hanover shoes, knickered suit, curly hair parted down the middle and shiny, greased face for the three p.m. Easter service. I strutted onto the stage, rendered my age appropriate recitation and felt good from the loud, enthusiastic applause. At age 12 I graduated to the pageant and participated in a dialogue with my peers.

When Sister and I returned home from Sunday School and church, Mother had prepared two dozen boiled eggs, colored them, placed a few in a straw basket and the remainder in a large bowl with many colorful jelly beans and placed the basket on the dining room table. Oh what a delightful surprise that was. Those colorful candy eggs with a soft white filling were always a special treat.

Mother's Easter Sunday dinner climaxed the day. This song I'd like to dedicate to her:

In my heart,
In my heart,

Lord, I want to be a Christian, like Jesus
In my heart.

Once a year a one-week revival service was held. Hard hitting ministers from churches throughout the city were invited to preach. Reverend R. L. Hall from Zion City, Reverend C. C. Burk were true gospel missionaries and set my soul on fire. I sat on the mourners bench with the other candidates for baptism. Mrs. Ginny Fagan, a devout Christian who lived across the street from us, prayed for me, as did others, and wanted me to join the church. Father didn't think I was old enough to know what religion meant and wouldn't consent to my joining and being baptized. The sisters in the amen corner and the deacons on the opposite side sang and prayed for us. I sat on the mourner's bench five years. Mrs. Fagan couldn't convince Father that I had found Jesus and religion and should become a member of the church. The song, *I Cried and I Cried All Night Long Until I Found the Lord* had meaning for me for I cried many nights while on the mourner's bench. The spirit of the Lord touched me and I wanted to confess my faith and love for my Lord and Savior, Jesus Christ.

Father finally consented to my joining and being baptized. I was immersed in a stream of water called The Branch. My flowing robe was a white sheet wrapped around me and a white towel covered my head. Mother accompanied me to the ceremony. I was baptized by our Pastor, Rev. J. A. Martin.

Jackson Street Church, a block from my home, was a large stuccoed building with six steps leading up to the doors on either side of the foyer. Three long rows of pews made a very large seating area. The pulpit was elevated a few feet with steps on either side, spiraling upward to the large choir stand. Dr. J. H. Eason from Selma, Alabama, was pastor. He was a medium-sized, dark-complexioned man with a raspy voice and wore a long frocked, black coat and dark trousers.

Father at this juncture was into his bootleg business and became a backslider, one who ceases going to church. He retained his inactive affiliation at Jackson Street.

The strict doctrine of the Baptist religion—no smoking, dancing, drinking or womanizing—must have cooked his goose. It was widely known that Mr. Witt sold whiskey. The in and out traffic of people at our house spoke for itself. If a person of that type showed up at church the preacher would point him or her out. If he didn't, one of the deacons or deaconesses would. That was reason enough for such an infamous person to stay away.

I am sure the reason Mother didn't attend church was the shame she felt from the neighbor's knowledge of Father selling whiskey, a cardinal sin in the Baptist church. I don't think he cared. That never dampened my enthusiasm for Sunday school and church.

Everything was going well at Jackson Street between the minister and his parishioners until one of the old members, Mr. Hutcherson, died. He had attended church regularly until he became ill and didn't attend for a long time. Dr. Eason refused to preach his funeral and many parishioners became angered, called a meeting at the church and decided to leave and form a new one. I can see Mother now, preparing a basket of fried chicken, a large bowl of potato salad and a wholesome pound cake which she bought to take to the organizing meeting at the Knights of Phythias Hall, one block away. She was joined by Father's sister,

Mary Washington, who lived three miles up Oak Ridge Hill. She came to our house with her basket of goodies.

"Cook," as she called Mother, "come on, let's go." She sometimes called her "Ginny," nickname for Virginia, Mother's given name. I joined them and we were on our way to the meeting to organize a new church which was named First Baptist.

The members who left Jackson Street Church rented a double tenant house across from the lodge hall, removed the partition and held church services. Reverend J. A. Martin of Selma, Alabama, was called as pastor and remained about seven years before falling into disfavor with the deacons who padlocked it.

Rev. J. F. Brooks from Milledgeville, Georgia, replaced Rev. Martin, but was ousted because a parishioner saw him leaving an Alabama State Liquor Store. Rev. James Mardis succeeded Rev. Brooks and was let go for womanizing. First Baptist Church of Woodlawn, our church, had problems keeping a minister.

The worst tragedy in our church kingdom occurred in 1932 when one of the members was slain by her estranged husband in the small lobby while Sabbath school was in session. It was Women's Day, a big annual event, and many people were in attendance. I was in my classroom where our Sabbath school lesson was being discussed when suddenly a loud bam, bam, rang out. Bedlam broke loose. Everyone began screaming and scrambling to get out the back door. I dashed up some steps, ran through a small classroom, out the back door, up the alley home screaming, "Mama, Mama, somebody got shot at the church."

She hugged me, "I'm glad you are all right." She rushed to the church and saw Mrs. Susie

Johnson lying in the lobby. Returning home, she told us it was Modis Johnson's mother and people were saying that Slim, her estranged husband, shot her. I knew both of them well, as Slim was one of Father's bootleg customers.

I didn't return to church for any of the later services, I was too frightened. The entire community was shocked and greatly saddened by that tragedy.

The next Sunday, services were normal and I returned to my usual Sunday school class followed by church services.

I always looked forward to the annual Sunday school picnic at Pleasant Hill Park in Zion City, about fifteen or twenty miles away. We played ball, had sack races, pitched horseshoes and drank all of the ice cold water from the artesian well our stomachs could hold. I would drink until I could barely get up to run and play.

Mother always prepared a picnic basket full of goodies. I couldn't wait to eat the potted meat and pressed ham sandwiches, potato salad, fried chicken and pound cake. When I saw her spreading the big white tablecloth on the grass underneath a big shade tree I knew dinner time had arrived. After the feast, I stretched out on the grass and relaxed until we were ready to go home. The trip home was uneventful as everyone was all played out, but not too tired to notice the girls. I became romantically inclined, to no avail, as I stood next to Rosalyn Johnson. Her big sister had her eyes on me and crushed my intentions.

When the truck returned to the church, everyone jumped off and headed for home. I was happy, but tired, and when darkness fell I was glad to get into bed with a mouthful of my favorite bubble gum. The wallpaper behind my bed was a good place to store that wad for future chewing and bubble blowing pleasure. I couldn't afford to throw it away as I didn't know from whence the next penny would come. When removed, it sometimes included a chunk of wallpaper which really angered Mother. I never stopped decorating the wallpaper despite her warnings. When I forgot to stick it to the wall it wound up in my hair. Mother got even with me by getting the scissors, removing hair, gum and all. The bald spot made me a candidate for a football flat, a skinned head from Father's clippers. I didn't appreciate it one bit.

I finally got the point, put it into a piece of waxed paper and chewed it the next day. Those mammy-made hair cuts, as we called them, looked like a bowl had been placed on top of my head and the hair cut around the edges. I hated them.

I loved to chew gum and church was no exception. The ushers and usherettes cast their special attention in all directions and always spotted me chewing, came quietly and collected it as I reluctantly let go. I didn't appreciate that but could do nothing but give up my three-day-old, stale wad of bubble gum.

I became very active in the church after baptism. I sang in the junior choir, appeared in Easter and Christmas pageants, attended Sabbath school, eleven and seven o'clock services, and Baptist Young Peoples Union (BYPU) scriptures at 6 p.m.

Tom Thumb weddings were popular for fund raising. I married every girl in Woodlawn, really 17. The weddings were performed at local churches as well as our own. I wore out the popular song *The One Rose*, crooning it to death.

The Twelve Tribes of Israel was a very popular biblical play. Arthur Moss and I were gate keepers for the weary souls who gathered at the pearly gates to enter heaven. Each candidate had to give the password, a quotation from the Bible. I was amused when we put on the play at 35th Street Baptist Church. Brother Pumphrey, an imbibing deacon, said he was going to sit in the back of the church with his flashlight and Bible to see if the quotes from those entering heaven were correct. Arthur and I never turned anyone away. Guess the good brother was satisfied.

Chapter 11
Unforgettable Superstitions

My parents and neighbors espoused this old die-hard saying: "Negroes had all the signs and white folks had all the money." That was quite obvious to me. From early childhood, superstitions were a way of life and people lived by those omens and self-fulfilling prophesies, good or bad. I still live by many of them which were firmly planted in my mind during childhood.

Our elders were skeptical as to how their lives would be affected by an unforeseen event over which they had no control. Old wive's tales interpretations were sometimes frightening to me as I frequently dreamed of some of the things to which they related.

There was a Spiritualist Church one block from my home. Mother Parker, a slim, dark brown, viable appearing lady was pastor. I was afraid of her, as I heard people say she had the spirits of deceased parishioners communicate with active members in a darkened room of the church. She walked one block up 62nd Street to the bus line. I would immediately cross the street to avoid meeting and coming close to her. People of the community called her a two-headed person and I was afraid she would put a hex on me.

One day, Mother found two dimes in a cement flower urn atop a pillar on our front porch as she was loosening the dirt and felt a strange sensation go up her right arm. Immediately she swore someone placed them there to voodoo her. I was afraid for her and wondered what ill effects might occur.

I stayed clear of someone sweeping the floor because if the broom brushed my foot I just knew I was going to be arrested; therefore, to avoid that misfortune, I would immediately take the broom and spit on it.

I was always on my toes in order to avoid the many superstitions that surrounded me. Even dreaming was a hazard. Seeing a snake in my dreams meant I had an enemy of whom I had better be aware. If I killed it, everything would be A-OK.

New Year's Eve was intriguing to me because Father and Mr. Tombrello, our grocer, had a pact between them. If a woman were the first person to visit your home after midnight on New Year's Eve, bad luck would be your destiny for the year. Father and I went to Mr. Tombrello's just after the bells stopped ringing at midnight. He would buy an article for cash and Mr. Tombrello would have good luck all year. Mr.Tombrello, in turn, came to our home a block away, sit down and talk for awhile, buy a pint of whiskey and leave. It didn't matter to Father if a dozen women came after Mr.Tombrello left, good luck would be his the rest of the year.

One New Year's Eve, before Father and I could leave for Mr. Tombrello's, Henry Duncan and Rosa Kidd, neighbors, were out celebrating and decided to stop. That was a definite no, no. He was very superstitious and believed beyond any reasonable doubt that it was bad luck for a female to enter his home first thing on New Year's morning. Before they were seated Father lighted into them saying, "What the hell you doing coming by here? Don't you know it's bad luck for a woman to come to your house first thing on New Year's morning?" They were so shocked, they just turned around and left.

Father always had his 38 Special when he and I went to Aunt Mary's house New Year's Eve, just before midnight so she would have good luck for the new year. He would fire three or four rounds into the air, never thinking of the potential dangers they posed.

Fortune tellers were very popular when I was a child. The oldsters believed in them and spread the news.

One Saturday night, per family custom, we went shopping without locking the front door. Upon returning it was wide open. The first place Father went hurriedly was to the bedroom to look in Mother's face powder box under the chiffonier. Blurting upon retrieving the little box, "I be damned, somebody's done been in here, my eighty-five dollars is gone."

"Wonder who coulda' come in here," was Mother's reply.

"I don't know, eighty-five dollars is gone."

Sunday morning while telling a neighbor about his misfortune, she expressed her sorrow and suggested he go to a fortune teller in East Birmingham. He got into his car and went to the home of a big fat woman who welcomed him. He told her of his misfortune and desire to find out who had done this awful act.

"Place a five dollar bill in the palm of my hand

and I'll tell ya who took your money."

Father reluctantly took a five dollar bill from his pocket and placed it in her hand. She took his hand, putting it over the five dollar bill in her hand, looked up into space and came down with the answer, "One of your friends took your money."

"Which one?"

"Put five more dollars in my hand and I'll tell ya."

He said he gave her a nasty look, turned around and briskly left, returning home on fire, cursing that big fat woman with unmentionables every mile of the way.

With a name like Wingate Moten, one wouldn't think of a magician, fortune teller or spell binder. He confused me with three numbers sent to father that settled in the residue after the burning of an octagon shaped black piece of substance, an eighth of an inch thick. There were twelve to a box. After lighting one, the sweet odor of incense emanated. Three distinct numbers, like 512, could be seen in the ashes. That number was lucky and supposedly would match the bond market total sales seen in the daily newspaper which determined the clearing house gambling game winner.

Daddy had written that mystical man in Wetumpka, Alabama, not far from Birmingham, sending five dollars for a winning combination. He never won anything from that venture and never wrote him again.

I was always shaken up by incidents like stubbing the big toe of my left foot or quivering of my left eye, which meant bad luck.

It's bad luck to tell your previous night's dreams before the sun rises, or while in bed.

If you speak of some unpleasantry that you don't want to happen, immediately knock on wood and it won't happen.

If you dream of something that is out of season, trouble will be coming that is out of reason.

The first twelve days of January represent the weather for each month of the year. I watched the twelve days but could never remember how the coming months were supposed to be.

It is bad luck to open an umbrella in the house.

A broken mirror, not disposed of, is bad luck.

If your ears itch, someone is talking about you.

If your nose itches, company is coming in the house.

If a man comes to your house the first thing Monday morning, have him come in, sit down and you will have good luck all week.

It is bad luck all week for a woman to be the first person to come to your house Monday morning.

If you dream of eggs, it is bad luck if you break the yolks.

If you wash and hang clothes on the line the last day of the year, someone in your family will die. I watched Mrs. Sarah Griffith do that, she died soon after.

To cut your fingernails or toenails on Sunday is a sin.

A howling dog after the sun goes down anytime before sunrise means someone in the neighborhood is going to die. I saw it come true many times in my neighborhood.

If a rooster crows after the sun goes down, someone in the community is going to die. I heard Jackson Street Baptist Church bell toll many times to prove it.

Don't throw away loose hair, make sure it is well contained. If birds find it and build a nest, you will have headaches the rest of your life.

If you walk underneath a ladder, it is bad luck.

If your shoestring comes untied, you are going to visit an unfamiliar place.

If you sneeze at the dinner table with your mouth full of food, you're going to have bad luck.

If a black cat crosses your path to the left, it is a sign of bad luck. If you turn around and back up past the point where it crossed you will nullify the bad luck. If it crosses to the right, that's O.K.

Myths and superstitions cross racial lines, too. One night a strange thing happened. Two of Father's police friends, on their way to our house for a little nip of moonshine, had their caps turned backwards. I chuckled because I had never seen anything like that. As they drove forward to the watermelon stand where Father and I were sitting, they laughed heartily while telling him about the black cat that crossed the street in front of them as they turned into our driveway. Father laughed, too, as they alighted from the patrol car and went into the house for a drink.

Whenever you are in the dark of night walking the streets, if you suddenly feel a warm sensation surrounding you, that indicates the presence of a ghost. I had that sensation quite a few times as I frighteningly walked the pitch dark streets of Woodlawn but never saw a ghost.

In the dark of night, Aunt Mary saw two beady eyes between her house and that of Mr. Coar's, a distance of fifty feet.

Bunch, my first cousin, said he had seen several headless persons as he crossed two sets of railroad tracks on his way to our home in the dark of night. They just suddenly disappeared.

Hog's head and black-eyed peas on New Year's day meant good luck for the whole year.

If you eat fish on New Year's day, your luck

will swim away that year.

If you have chicken on New Year's day, your luck will fly away all year.

If two people say the same word at the same time, in order to prevent bad luck, one or both have to expectorate on their fingers and touch the other's back. The one who touches first won't have bad luck.

Singing at the table is bad luck. If you sit on a bed and sing, it's bad luck.

Putting your hat on the bed is bad luck. Two hats on one's head brings the wearer bad luck.

If you leave your bed covers pulled back, you are opening up your casket and death might follow.

If a pregnant woman is frightened by an animal or an anomalous person and makes fun of them, her baby will take on their characteristics. Mother saw a horse with peculiar eyes while she was carrying me and was frightened. At birth my eyes rolled around and around for a short while.

It is bad luck to clasp your hands behind your head while sitting in a chair.

If you wear down the heels of your shoes, your luck is behind you.

January's wintry blasts caused everyone's mind to focus on the second Tuesday in February when the groundhog exited from hibernation. If he saw his shadow, six weeks of dreadfully cold weather were ahead.

If you follow a rainbow to its end, you will find a pot of gold. I tried once and the end of the rainbow came no closer.

If it rains while the sun is shining, take a straight pin, put it into the ground, get down on your knees, place your ear to the pin, listen and you can hear the devil beating his wife.

If you dream about muddy water, you're going to have bad luck. If you dream about clear water, you can look forward to having good luck.

If you sing or hum while eating, it is bad luck.

If you sew something you are wearing it is bad luck unless you place a match or a toothpick in your mouth.

If someone steps on your foot while your feet are crossed, it is bad luck. If you arise, get a pinch of table salt, throw it over your left shoulder bad luck is prevented.

If your right hand itches, you are going to get some money. If your left hand itches, you are going to lose some.

If the sole of either foot itches you are going to take a trip out of town.

If your right eyelid twitches or the eyeball jumps, it is good luck. If your left eyelid twitches or the eyeball jumps something or someone is going to make you very angry.

Wearing a hat in the house is bad luck.

If you take the left hind leg of a rabbit and carry it in your left hip pocket, that will bring good luck.

If a stray cat takes up residence at your home, you are going to have good luck.

The treatment for mumps is to apply sardine grease to the involved jaw or both, if both are involved. Wrap a clean white rag around your head and tie it underneath the chin. The mumps won't go down on you and cause enlargement of the testicles in a male or ovaries in females with resultant impaired walking and sterilization. I loved sardines and still do. I had mumps on both sides at age seven years, with no complications.

When you dream of a raging fire, big trouble looms ahead. If you put it out, trouble will be averted.

There was one interesting but frightening experiment I was afraid to try: Take a hair from the mane of a horse, put it into a jar of water and a snake would emerge after one week. I wasn't interested in seeing it come to fruition. Happily, I never tried it because I am deathly afraid of snakes.

When one sees a whirlwind, there will be a fight between two or more individuals at that site.

If you see a snake in your dreams, beware of an enemy. If you kill the snake the threat of danger will be averted.

I believe I worried unnecessarily many years of my life in hearsay watching my so-called lifeline, located in the middle of the palm of the hand and extending towards the fifth finger. This imprint, by father time, is supposed to be the predictor of one's life span, short, long or in between. Mine extended slowly about three-quarters across and I was afraid of only living a short life. As I grew, it extended longer and longer, towards my fifth finger. If watching lengthened it, I could prophesy for myself, a long, long, life.

Two dollar bills were known as the bad luck currency when I was growing up. Any person who received one tore off a corner to prevent misfortune. I saw many from which all the corners were missing. The only bad luck I could see from owning one during the depression, was not to have one.

Mr. Jason, a cross-eyed grocer, lived two blocks from my home and became a standing joke among my peers that he'd mistake a $2 bill turned upside down for a five. Some of them hustled all the twos they could find as a good luck charm, however, I never heard of anyone actually being rewarded by Mr. Jason's handicap.

When I was a child, I heard that the combination of eating watermelon, bananas or collard greens and drinking alcohol produced excruciating chest pain from indigestion and sudden death. Ingesting baking soda after eating watermelon could be fatal. They didn't know about acute coronary artery heart disease, which was the killer. The first death happened one night to Mr. Walter Pulliam, a nice man whom I knew very well. He lived about four blocks from my home. I was sitting in front of our watermelon stand when I suddenly heard a very loud yell and thought someone was being assaulted. The screaming stopped. I ran down the street, towards the commotion and met a neighbor who told me Mr. Pulliam had died of acute indigestion after having eaten cabbage for dinner while in an inebriated state.

Buddy Herron drank some whiskey one night after having eaten watermelon and died suddenly. He lived a block and a half from me. His death was attributed to acute indigestion.

Those sudden deaths were undoubtedly due to acute coronary artery heart disease, possibly caused by the high fat content of their diets of pork chops, chitterlings, liver, sausage, lard in biscuits and that used for frying. Eggs and the skin of fried chicken were eaten in large quantities and were real poison.

If a cat sleeps in the bed with a newborn infant, it will suffocate it by sucking its breath. If you see someone or yourself naked in a dream, that's a sign someone in your family is going to die.

As a child, I was interested in Ripley's "Believe it or Not" Comic Corner in *The Birmingham News*, afternoon newspaper. The oddities made me ambivalent. Having heard so many superstitions, -isms and prophesies from my parents, Uncle

Sandy, Aunt Mary and numerous neighbors made me forever cognizant whenever some strange phenomenon occurred.

The person whose knuckles crackle many times when pressed together is a big liar.

Dog days, it'll rain forty days and nights from July 10 to August 20.

If bitten by a dog, whether it is out of control or not, but salivating profusely, the victim will go mad. A playful gesture in August of 1942 towards a paper customer's son in the company of his dog got me snagged leaving a one and one-half inch scar on my left mid-thigh. The doctor applied a white liquid. Mother and I were afraid I might go mad. No one reported the dog. The scar is still visible.

Persons who write large are extravagant.

You will develop a blister on the tip of your tongue if you tell many lies.

If you point at the name on a gravestone, it is bad luck.

Take a coin, point it at a new moon and kiss it for good luck.

Carrying a buckeye from a buckeye tree in your left hip pocket will always bring good luck. They are similar in size and color to a chestnut. I found mine in the woods and carried it on my person for years.

Chapter 12
Normal And Abnormal Societal Interactions

Well, life rumbled on and seemingly I just couldn't escape traumatic emotional encounters.

Pedophiles have always been among the adult population. I had two episodes of becoming a victim during my childhood and adolescent years. The first dastard offender was "Pick," a delivery man for Melrose Ice Cream Company. Every day between noon and one o'clock he parked behind our watermelon stand. As payment for watching the truck he removed two or three five gallon cans containing remnants from his route and gave the remaining contents to me. It was delicious. All was well until one day he propositioned me in very graphic demeaning language, "If you sucked a 'dego' for a rotten banana, what would you suck me off for?" Nothing was the answer he wanted and we'd go from there. I told him I wouldn't do anything like that, becoming so very insulted and never spoke to him again. He continued parking there. I never told my parents, as hell would have broken loose.

The next episode was a newspaper office manager for *The Birmingham Post*. When I came across a magazine or newspaper which contained a contest of any sort I'd enter. I came across one sponsored by Sally Myles Salt Company whereby one had to write slogans from pictures depicting her. I got the bright idea from viewing our neighbor's newspaper, as we only took *The Birmingham News* to go to the office and get back copies. After greeting the manager politely, I told him what I wanted. He was a short, slightly stocky, bespectacled, white man.

"I'll go to the back and see how many I can find."

After about five minutes he peeped from behind the door where I could see him and said, "Come on back." When I arrived in the back room, he had positioned himself in a static pose with his genitalia erect and ready for oral copulation. I was shocked, never having been exposed to that type behavior. "Wanna help me?" he asked.

As I stood speechless, I finally came to my senses enough to tell him, "No." I didn't know what to do. Cursing him out would probably have led to my being beaten and getting killed, as the life of a black living in Birmingham wasn't worth a dime. If you were killed by another black or a white person, everything was all right with the law. A good lie by the defense would suffice.

Leaving very upset and never telling anyone about that awful happening ended my newspaper contest days.

There was always some activity in the community with which one could become involved. Chiefly among them, at that point in time, was the formation of gospel quartet groups.

Having ups and downs, as all youths do, and never running out of ideas and visions of success, Michael Clemens, Clyde Creary, Bob Jones, Henry Henson and I formed a singing group, a lead singer, tenor, baritone and bass. Since there were five of us for four places, I was assigned the embarrassing role of extra man. I attended practices at the home of Michael Clemons, the spokesperson for the group. They would humm la, humm la and melded their voices to good old spirituals like *Down By The Riverside*, *The Old Rugged Cross*, and *Just A Closer Walk With Thee*. They sang Sunday afternoons at neighborhood churches. The embarrassing part for me was sitting in the front row alone. The old amen corner sisters and deacons clapped and sang along with them. The quartet received loud applause and accolades while I sat lamenting the fact I was not signing with them, just excess baggage. I stuck with my role and continued following them during the two or three years they performed until finally outgrowing their devotion to singing. That embarrassing lesson endured by me revealed the strength of one's wanting and the need to belong.

I joined another quartet as the baritone singer, according to me, we were known as the Travelers Junior. The Travelers Senior were four adult young men who sang all over town and were fairly good but they weren't in the class with a group called The Pullman Jubilee Singers, composed of four railroad company employees. They had class and were great. Willie Gray, our leader, found much wrong most of the time with my baritone singing. I stuck it out until the breakup of the group.

I learned my lesson, being at the wrong place at the right time. As a preteen, Poly Pimp, his brother Dick Wooley and I played Annie Russell and Ethel Lee Rudolph a game of stick ball, using a tennis ball and a broom handle for a bat. We gave them first at bat. The afternoon was getting late when we started and it took a long time to get them out. With no intention of giving us our turn at bat, they ran for home. We picked up rocks and threw at them.

Ethel Lee made it into her house quickly and escaped the barrage. Annie Bessie dashed about twenty-five yards to her home, where her mother was sitting on the front porch. I threw a piece of coke, a burned out remnant of hard coal, at her, the brothers threw good sized chunks of slag used by the city to fill pot holes in the street. Dick and his brother were larger and stronger than I. A piece of slag struck Mrs. Russell in her right eye. She jumped up screaming. Mr. Russell rushed out. "Who threw that rock? It hit my wife in the eye and she might lose her eyesight."

"Egg (referring to me) did it," they exclaimed in unison.

"They did it, Mr. Russell," I replied.

He believed them and said to me, "I'm gonna go up to your father's house and tell him."

"I didn't do it, Dick Wooley did it."

Turning around quickly, hobbling on his crippled legs and pigeon toes, up the alley he went with me in close pursuit. I wanted to reach my parents ahead of him and tell them my side of the story in order not to get a whipping. Arriving ahead of him, I rapidly exclaimed to Mother, "Dick Wooley hit Mrs. Russell in the eye and he and Poly Pimp said I did it."

At that moment he arrived, "Mrs. Witt, your boy hit my wife in the eye with a rock."

She turned to me and asked what happened. "Annie Bessie and Ethel Lee wouldn't give us our inning and ran home and we threw at them. Dick threw a big piece of slag and I threw a small piece of coke," luckily I thought, because no one could throw it very far, it was so light.

Mother said "I told you about hanging around with those bad boys. I'm gonna whip you good." Turning to Mr. Russell she said, "Take her to Dr. Broughton (our neighborhood doctor) and I'll pay the bill."

He left and Mother immediately got her leather strap and whipped me to the point I pleaded with her through my hard crying, "Mama, please don't hit me again." She stopped, as guilt gripped her. I heard her say through the years she vowed to never whip me like that again. That was the worst whipping of my life, no blood but plenty of hurt. Mrs. Russell recovered. Mother paid the bill and I never associated with Poly Pimp and Dick Wooley again.

Chapter 13
Looking Forward To High School

Miss Roland, my eighth grade teacher for the junior and senior semesters, was a very small, thin lady with high cheek bones, a very good teacher and real tough. My greatest triumph that year came from an arithmetic lesson. Over the years I had my cousin, James Washington, help me with the very tough problems. That didn't happen very often but I had heard of the difficulty in solving problem number "5" of that lesson so I asked him to come by and help me. He agreed. It was past 6:30 p.m. and dark. Becoming more and more anxious, and no James. At 7 p.m. I began trying to solve it myself, getting nowhere. For our convenience, the answers to the problems were in the back of the book. I knew the answer but the solution continued to elude me. I became so exasperated that I began to whimper and was on the verge of crying, but never gave up. About 8 p.m., one and a half hours after first tackling number "5", my efforts proved fruitful. I was elated.

The next morning, my classmates were asking one another, "Do you have number '5'?" All said, "No." I remained silent. One classmate's mother, a teacher, always helped her but couldn't solve it.

Richard Macon, a math whiz, couldn't solve it. Well, the bell rang, we went into the classroom and took our seats. When the lesson began Miss Roland asked, "Who would like to take number '1'?" Hands flew up, the same for two, three and four until she asked for a volunteer for number "5," no hands. After a short pause, raising mine to the surprise of all, I went to the board, applied my solution and explained it. It was so difficult, everyone observed in amazement. When Miss Roand asked if they understood it, silence prevailed. I really felt like a champion that day.

The very next day she asked me to explain the solution again. I obliged. Needless to say, they were still angry with me. It wore off in a few days except in their subconscious minds. When honor roll time arrived, which was monthly, my name was number one. In order for me not to get a swollen head, Miss Roland gave me only a satisfactory grade the next month after having received an "E" for excellent previously. I was furious.

Shortly thereafter I got what I thought was my revenge.

Being a very good speller, she let me mark the spelling tablets. One day there was a match between the eighth juniors and seniors. Still angry, I reversed the "ie" in believe, left an "n" out of beginning and put my head on my desk, a vindictive thirteen-year-old brat. She knew the problem and ignored me. It worked well.

I finally did myself in. Whenever Miss Roland left the room, for whatever reason, she appointed a monitor to report all misconduct. Tony Nims was chosen. For some unknown reason, I arose from my seat and exclaimed, "You can put my name down if you want to." She obliged.

When Miss Roland returned and saw my name,

without asking what I had done, she went to the honor roll and erased my name, to the delight of all. They received such a charge she immediately rewrote it, to their dismay I remained number "1".

The time arrived for graduation. As salutatorian of the class, I gave my predictions of the future fields of endeavors for my classmates Some were predicted to become school teachers, one a principal, a minister, postman and even a senator. I didn't have any trouble predicting what I wanted to become in life because it was my early lifelong ambition to become a doctor.

Graduation exercises were held June 3, 1933, at Jackson Street Baptist Church, a short distance from the school. I received my certificate with thirty-six other classmates.

I now began looking forward to entering Industrial High School in September. There were no junior highs in those days.

Miss Roland left Patterson School at the end of the 1933 school year and joined the faculty at Industrial High and taught history. I was not surprised in 1934 when she died of tuberculosis. Having seen gaunt tuberculosis individuals in my neighborhood, she had the peachy smooth skin and wasted size for it.

Chapter 14
High School

During the school year of 1899, some Negro citizens of Birmingham called an historic mass meeting. The purpose was to establish a tax-supported high school for Negroes. There was no high school for blacks in Birmingham.

One morning of September 1900, in a room on the second floor of the Cameron Elementary School building, located on the southwest corner of Avenue H and Fourteenth Street North, the first Negro high school was opened with 18 students. The end of the first term saw an enrollment of 45 students.

Arthur Harold Parker was appointed by school superintendent, Dr. J. Herbert Phillips, as principal and only teacher at the new school. The third year Miss Orlean D. Kennedy became the second teacher.

In 1904, the first senior class of 15 graduated.

In 1910, the school was moved to a three story frame building on Eighth Avenue between Eleventh and Twelfth Streets. The site was then known as Lane Auditorium. Formal classes began in industrial training and the school became known as

Industrial High.

In the summer of 1914, the city building inspector condemned the Lane Building and the board purchased the United Presbyterian School on the corner of Eighth Avenue and Ninth Street, which became the new home of Industrial High when I matriculated there in September 1933.

Industrial High was located five miles north of downtown Birmingham in a section called Smithfield and was the only high school for Negroes during the 1920s and 30s. It was a single story, dark yellow, smooth stucco building located on Eighth Avenue North, a very busy thoroughfare going east and west between John and Joseph Streets, one block square. The rear extended from Eighth to Ninth Avenues. Adolescents from North and South Woodlawn, Avondale, Kingston, North Birmingham, Ensley and Elyton attended. Streetcars were our transportation.

It was surrounded by many ritzy, large single and two story homes where mail carriers, school teachers, doctors, lawyers and other well-to-do Negroes lived. Going up the hill northward was Enon Ridge, where other wealthy Negroes resided.

It was inspiring to me as I couldn't help comparing them to the simple neighborhood from whence I came. There were 3,000 students and 150 teachers.

The five white public high schools were Phillips, Ensley, West End, Ramsay Tech and a big one, Woodlawn High, located less than one mile from my home to which I could have walked, but the ugly head of segregation reigned supreme and forced me to ride the streetcar three hours daily to and from Industrial. I bought a book of fifty streetcar tickets, issued only to students, for one dollar and a quarter, a real bargain. The book lasted one month.

Boys were required to wear khaki pants, any type shirt and tie in Grades 9 through 11. The twelfth year boys could wear khaki, black or dark blue trousers. Girls wore blue dresses during the ninth, tenth and eleventh grades and white or blue in the twelfth.

The curriculum consisted of departments of Science (general science, biology, chemistry and physics), English (grammar and composition), American and English Literature, Spanish, Business, Mathematics (algebra, geometry and statistics) and History (civics, Negro, European and American).

Industrial arts for boys consisted of band, printing, tailoring, mechanical drawing, shoe repair, carpentry and auto mechanics. Girls had home economics, cooking and sewing. A few took printing, but none went to band while I was there.

The main objective was to encourage us to prepare for higher education.

We had to buy our books and supplies. Most were second, third, fourth and fifth hand as evidenced by their condition. If not bought from one's peers, they were purchased new or used from the school. I was a little intimidated about going to high school, getting up early and having to travel by streetcar fifteen miles across town.

My cousin, James Washington, was a year ahead of me and well acquainted with high school activities. I was all ears when he told me how he had learned to cast out nines, the highlight of his introduction to mathematics in the ninth grade. The word mathematics was baffling to me until he told me it was advanced arithmetic. Having always been good in arithmetic, I came to the conclusion I'd do well. I received an "A" the first semester.

He boasted about the campus. "What is that?" I asked.

"That's what you call the school grounds now that you are in high school."

It was huge, with a paved basketball court. The rest was just plain dirt. I was in awe of the enormity of the so-called campus.

There was a large lunch room but I had very little money to spend there. I brought my sandwich and a piece of fruit most of the time and ate it in the dining room. I had a treat some days, one-fourth of a pineapple pie for a nickel, my favorite, when I had one.

Across Eighth Avenue were several black businesses. P.D. Davis' Confectionery sold hamburgers with the most distinctive sauce I had ever tasted. I bought one after school whenever I could save a dime. His store was always crowded after school, teacher monitors kept us from leaving the grounds at lunch time.

On one corner of the school, a blind man sat, selling peanuts for a penny per brown bag. He used the honor system for payment. I always felt sorry for him, concerned if any students took advantage of his handicap. On the next corner, a sighted gentleman whose son was my biology teacher, also sold peanuts. I patronized both of them depending on the route I took to the streetcar line.

Dr. A. H. Parker was still principal. He was a well dressed, short, heavy set, bespectacled, very fair complexioned gentleman with graying, wavy hair. I thought he was white. His large office was at the front entrance of the building. Miss Gibbs, a vivacious, light brown, very pleasant young lady, was office manager. Miss Kennedy, an elderly, sweet lady with a very large abdomen, was the girls assistant principal and co-teacher with Dr. Parker when the school opened.

I didn't see Dr. Parker very much, only two or three times weekly during assembly in the large auditorium when he gave a few remarks regarding pertinent school business. The student body program, arranged by the teachers, followed. He retired in June 1937. It became Parker High in 1938, the year he died. He was very well thought of throughout the city and was the first black buried in exclusively white Elmwood Cemetery.

Mr. W. B. Johnson, assistant principal, was the driving force behind the school and took care of disciplinary matters. He was a plainly dressed man, stocky, medium tall, brown skinned, almost completely bald, non-smiling and strictly business. You could hear him cough all over the building, seemingly a half block away, a victim of mustard gas poisoning while serving in the Army during World War I in France. The cough sounded very serious to me and I tried to stay my distance, afraid of tuberculosis.

He swayed from side to side as he walked up and down the halls, heavy with authority. I had been told by other students when sent to his office with a note from a teacher for disrupting class he had a standard theme, "Go home and git your mama, go home and git your mama," before he or she could say, "Mr. Johnson, I didn't do anything." The effort was to no avail. I was never sent to him knowing Mother would give me a good lashing for having to travel to Smithfield, across town.

Some who were told to go get their mother went into the neighborhood and found a friendly lady, gave her twenty-five cents to falsely act in that capacity. When she returned with the pupil, Mr. Johnson discussed the complaint and readmitted the pupil without knowing the difference. The offenses weren't that great was the reason for his mild disposition and a warning to never let that happen again. A teacher was assigned each period of the day to assist him in disposing of other, more serious matters.

Industrial's football team was known as The Thundering Herd. I didn't go to many games as they were played at Legion Field, a few miles away and I only had one streetcar ticket to school and one for home—no stopping in between. I don't know how much thunder they created on the gridiron, but I do know how much thunder the pupils from East Lake, Woodlawn, Kingston and Avondale created on our way to and from school.

We had a "Special streetcar," so labeled for one to two hundred pupils who crowded it twice daily. The noise attracted the attention of people the entire ten mile journey, even through downtown. Gaiety, loud laughing and general bedlam reigned. Fights between the Woodlawn and Kingston Outlaws occasionally erupted.

I was lucky enough to ride "Number 27" going to Ensley some times when adult riders were waiting. The motor man wouldn't stop to pick up a bunch of kids who would crowd out the regular passengers. Whenever a group of us were on the regular streetcar, it was noisy, too. The same thing happened in the afternoon going home.

We were jammed into the "Special" like sardines. One day I asked Mabel Duff for the break, meaning to become my girlfriend. "I'll let you know." Her reply was positive. She was a quiet, freckle-faced, light complexioned, sandy-haired teenager. I never went to her home, neither her mother nor mine would have gone for that type affair. That early romance faded with time.

I rode the "Special" most of my four years at

Industrial. The fare, at five cents a day, was a bargain. We rode the regular streetcar for the same amount but in much more comfort.

My studiousness received a big boost from Miss Mabel Moore, my ninth grade civics teacher. Big Business was the name given her by students whom she had taught over the years. She was a very pleasant, bespectacled, smiling, tall, slightly heavy, very well dressed lady.

We were required to prepare notebooks for her class, a new addition to my high school experience. Somehow I fostered the idea of cutting letters from newspaper headlines and pasting them onto the outside of my notebook, stating the title. She thought that was outstanding, so much so, she took it to Miss Vivian Bell, an English teacher, who was equally ecstatic over the originality. Both expressed supreme satisfaction with my work. I received an "A" in her class.

For some unknown reason, I liked to carry a sharp pocket knife on my person. I had never been threatened by anyone, just prophylactic protection, I guess. One day Miss Moore caught me thrusting it at my seat mate, confiscated it and I never carried one again.

The second boost to my successful orientation came when Mrs. Juanita Smedley, a beautiful, shapely, brown-skinned woman whom I adored, exempted Richard Macon, Grover Price and me from taking the final science exam. I was overwhelmed by her personality, she was so charming. Some teenagers became stuck on some of their teachers.

Miss Peters, my civics teacher for the senior ninth grade, was less than enthusiastic about me. She named Grover Price, Richard Macon and me the three musketeers. We were wiggly, early teenaged devils attempting to imitate the Mills Brothers and performed in her class. I was plump and baw-bawed into my fists, as the bass, not the boom, boom, boom I should have. We never made another appearance, thank heaven. To compensate for her characterization of us, we named her Miss Keg Eye, for the larger than normal eyes over which she wore glasses. She was really rough. Passing her class with a satisfactory grade was an accomplishment, as I looked forward to the tenth grade.

A semester of classics, dealing with poetry and writings of famous authors, such as Henry W. Longfellow's, *Excelsior*, which we had to recite, was impressive.

Treasure Island was thoroughly enjoyed and interestingly imparted to us during our first year. It was written by Robert Louis Stevenson, who was also famous for *Dr.Jekyll and Mr. Hyde.*

The Library was moderate in size and full of reference books, encyclopedias and periodicals. I visited it occasionally to prepare assignments. Miss Veronica Pearce, a very nice lady, was the librarian.

My only knowledge of Negro history before my introduction to the course as a tenth grader, was that slavery once existed. George Washington Carver was a former slave who made over two hundred products from peanuts. Booker T. Washington founded Tuskegee Institute in Tuskegee, Alabama, about which I knew nothing. Langston Hughes was a renowned poet and Paul Robeson, a noted baritone singer, labeled a communist and exiled to Russia in later years.

Black students today, and a majority of whites, know very little about Negroes in medicine, education, politics, inventions and numerous other fields of endeavor.

After all of the racial unrest, demonstrations and riots of the fifties, sixties and seventies, a preoccupation with "Blackness" invaded the minds of many Negroes and became the buzz word for honor and unity against the indifference of whites toward Negro's civil rights. Negroes at white colleges and universities formed black power organizations. This led to demands for Afro-American Studies departments, many have come to fruition.

Carter G. Woodson, born in 1875 in New Canton, Buckingham County, Virginia, was author of the text, *The Negro In Our History*. It was the central text for the Black movement in the 1960s and today is widely used in universities.

He received his Bachelors Degree in Literature at Brea College in Kentucky in 1903; a Bachelors Degree of Arts and Masters Degree of Arts from the University of Chicago in 1907 and a PhD in 1912 from Harvard University. He became Professor of History and Dean of the School of Arts and Sciences at Harvard in 1920.

He was the recipient of the Joel E. Spingarn Gold Medal awarded annually at the N.A.A.C.P. meeting for the highest or noblest achievement by an American Negro.

In 1926 the first Negro History week celebration was established by Dr.Woodson. In 1976 the entire month of February was dedicated to Negro History and is observed annually.

He died in 1950.

Booker T. Washington was born in Virginia in 1856 in a one room, dirt floor shack. When he was five years old his slave master put him to work. He graduated from Hampton School, Virginia, in 1875. In 1879 General James Armstrong, principal of Hampton, asked Booker to return to Hampton upon receiving a letter from a group of citizens in Tuskegee, Alabama, 105 miles south of Birmingham, that needed a principal. Booker reached Tuskegee in June 1881. In 1900 he started the National Negro Business League and wrote his famous book, *Up From Slavery*.

In 1904 he established Tuskegee Institute as an agricultural and trade school. It later became a four year liberal arts college. He died in 1915, some say, from over work.

My wife and I visited his beautiful two story, red brick home in 1987, built by students. It had beautiful indoor plumbing with a white enamel bath tub, bowl and toilet.

The course taught in high school included other outstanding Negroes: Mary McLeod Bethune, who established Bethune-Cookman College in Daytona Beach, Florida; Crispus Attucks, the first black killed in the Civil War; Melvin Beard of Birmingham, invented the train car coupler; William L. Dawson of Illinois; the second black congressman; Frederick Douglas, an orator, debated Abraham Lincoln, our sixteenth President; John Brown, fought at Harper's Ferry, West Virginia; Harriet B. Tubman, writer.

Paul Lawrence Dunbar was an outstanding poet and novelist, born in 1872 and died in 1906.

Benjamin Banneker, 1735-1806, published the first almanac in America and also was an amateur mathematician and astronomer.

I belonged to a teenaged neighborhood social club, The Casanovas, with ten members. We really thought we were hot stuff. We met and played cards every Tuesday night from 7:30 p.m. until whenever. The Camel Caravan with Benny Goodman's orchestra aired at 8 p.m. and all deliberations were placed on hold until we thrilled to the sounds of his band. At 8:30 the business of the club reconvened. After the meeting a fine buffet dinner was served by the mother of the host, no alcohol allowed. We smoked Camel cigarettes behind our parents backs. A single cigarette cost a penny, a pack twenty cents. Each of us had a few pennies from time to time. My Whist partner, Bernard Morgan, worked for a confectionery shop as delivery boy and always had cigarettes. He was generous in supplying us when we didn't have a few of our own. There was keen competition between us, sometimes playing until after midnight. My partner and I were known as the White House. There was the Dog House, etc. It really was good, wholesome, innocent fun, no money involved. We had very little anyway.

There were many silver teas on Sunday afternoons to raise money for the club to buy soft drinks, candy, nuts and snacks. Guess that's why I don't like tea receptions to this day.

Monday morning found us returning to the same old routine, scurrying off to school. None of the students drove cars to school. Daddy had a car, but I knew better than to ask him to teach me to drive and he never offered.

It was the second year of high school that shed more light on my becoming a doctor. Mr. S. W. Sullivan, the biology teacher, was an embalmer and taught his course with an introduction to anatomy and physiology of the human body. Plant and animal biology were also taught. The first medical term I learned was arteriosclerosis, hardening of the arteries. Having experienced this process in his mortuary science work, he made anatomical and physiological references during the class, thus the seed which had been planted earlier in my life was further nurtured in my subconscious.

After having been active in debating in elementary school, giving speeches and appearing in many Easter and Christmas pageants at church, I was well prepared to continue appearing in plays, reciting poems and speaking during auditorium assemblies. There was one comical moment during a stage appearance when I was speaking very well, until I saw my eighth grade teacher, Miss Sidney Roland, slumped in her seat, mouth wide open. Blood rushed to my head and my mind went blank.

The sponsoring teacher had told me to carry the speech in my inside coat pocket and if I forgot, just take it out and read it. I stood there, speechless, frozen, face flushed and scared stiff. A mild murmur among the several hundred pupils began. The rumblings grew louder and louder and finally burst into a crescendo of pure laughter. My faculties returning, I finally blurted "And also, that's all." That did it, they almost raised the roof.

I appeared once more in a play with Juanita Ellis, a petite, pretty young lady whom I was to smooch. The kiss was so loud, the laughter which resulted shook the walls of the auditorium.

After overcoming my fears of the word mathematics, entering my freshman year in high school by easily learning how to cast out nines and factor binominals, algebra in the tenth grade I thought would also be easy. Well, it was, as I was cocky enough to challenge the teacher, Mr. Richard Davis. He was the first person I saw play music on a carpenter's saw with a violin bow at an assembly, and very well. I was baffled and impressed, the likes of which I haven't experienced again.

Our friendship was shaken the day I explained the solution to an algebraic problem and he said, "Edwin, your answer is wrong."

"Why, Mr. Davis?"

"Because I said you are wrong."

I sat down, but later that afternoon saw a neighbor, Johnny Harris, Chairman of the math department, and told him how I was wronged and explained my solution. Several days later Mr. Harris told me I was right. No conference was held between the three of us. Mr. Harris said he had told Mr. Davis I was right, a soft victory for me. No confrontation resulted. I never told my parents and didn't get the big head. I made an"A" for the semester.

I switched to band after a non-productive year in tailoring. Always wanting to be a musician, I chose the clarinet. What an unsanitary experience, playing the school's horn which many others had used. We were encouraged to buy our own reeds which cost ten cents each. Sometimes forgetting the reed or not having a dime to buy one, I attempted to play the school's horn, dirty reed and all. No telling who had used it or what type health problem they may have had. The reed, after being used, looked dirty and had a very unpleasant odor, to put it mildly. That really discouraged me. I never made the band but carried the music stands to the auditorium and set them up for the members. They always played at the beginning and end of the auditorium period, after which I collected the stands and returned them to the band room.

I enjoyed celebrating Armistice Day, saddened for the soldiers who lost their lives fighting wars.

After hearing in my home of a Southern, undoubtedly racist woman, say in an Armistice Day crowd, "Many a mother's heart is broken today and many a mammy's, too," filled me with great displeasure.

All babies are conceived and birthed the same way regardless of race, creed or color of the parents.

I will never forget that bigoted slur.

Mammy was a dehumanizing, derisive, slavery-time moniker originated by the brazen Southern whites through self-empowerment, forcing uneducated blacks into involuntary servitude, denoting their superiority.

Every Armistice Day, the band paraded. Sometimes I beat the cymbals, others I carried the bass drum and was jarred and thoroughly shaken by the loud boom, boom, booms bouncing in my head.

I had a uniform, white pants, purple coat and cap with the band symbol above the bill. I really enjoyed marching with them but not nearly as much as I would have, had I been able to toot the licorice stick, a clarinet.

I really had myself to blame for not owning one, as a friend had an Abbott System, never mastered it and wanted to sell it to my father for $4. When I saw it, I immediately said I didn't want it because the one at school was a Boehm system. I had no idea what difference it would have made, probably none. Outsmarting myself, an adolescent who knew nothing, but thought he knew it all, at maturity I wished I had asked Father to buy it for me, missing my chance to get a horn and maybe becoming a band member and musician.

I missed another chance when Mother bought a new self-playing piano with three dozen rolls of music. One song that I recall was very, very pretty, *Am I Blue*, and went like this: "Am I blue, am I blue, ain't these tears in these eyes telling you?" It was the ticket to awakening feelings of love and romance, even to a preteen. A neighbor friend of my parents and her paramour came to our home, bought several shots of moonshine and danced in the front room as I pedaled. Mama and Daddy joined them occasionally.

Mother had great hopes for sister and me and offered us lessons. She knew an elementary school teacher who taught piano lessons for twenty-five cents per hour and wasted no time in contacting him. He was a short, dark, bespectacled, very quiet, polite man. He gave each of us our first lesson, playing the "C" scale over and over with one hand, then the other and in unison. Mother looked on proudly. After writing down the name of the music book, we left, mission accomplished.

Mother bought the book and everything was O.K. until my baseball buddies saw me with it under my arm on my way to his home. Audibly whispering "Sis-ay, sis-ay, sis-ay." That was just too much, very embarrassing and revolting to me. Reaching home, I begged Mother to please let me stop. To assuage my displeasure, she reluctantly agreed, but now I regret that she acceded to my immature feelings.

I really liked music and began composing songs when I was 15. I wrote the words which just seemed to pop into my head, then composed the tune while walking around singing to myself. Eventually, I haunted Professor Green and another friend, John Banks, to write the music for me. They delayed me with promises for years. My efforts were all in vain until, as a young adult, I met a professional composer, "Sweet" Lou Halmy, in Hollywood.

As time passed I really became interested in writing. *Don't Be A Holdout, I Saw You First,* and *Life Is So Sweet When Love Is Young* were three of my earliest and best numbers. I wrote many others.

Some were the fallout from my fantasies of love and romance that I observed in the movies and from the young lovelies at school and my community who were not yet allowed to date. I could only dream about them. At that time in my young life I thought of becoming a musician and a doctor later in life.

Later switching ambitions, becoming a postal railway mail clerk caught my fancy. I saw many mail cars on passing passenger trains with workers sorting mail as I sat on the front porch wondering where they were going. The tracks were less than a block away. I'd get a magazine once in a while with an inviting advertisement by the Franklin Institute in Philadelphia about the particulars of obtaining the job. After hearing from them, I didn't have the money to buy the instructions necessary for preparation to take the test. I was too young, anyway. I finally gave up on that impossible dream.

Approaching my third year of high school, I decided to quit and take a job as delivery boy for Burris' grocery store at $6 a week. I give Father credit for not letting me drop out, when with a resounding, "No," he said, "you are going to finish high school," and that settled it.

I began my third year with the desire for perseverance and settled down to the task of tackling the books and an ongoing interest in girls.

My horizons spread and the early teenage explosion of male hormones soared. Marie Fernandez caught my eye, a Smithfield cutie. The girls in my neighborhood whom I saw at church and school didn't impress me especially after the Louise McGee debacle.

I began talking to her at lunch time. Finally I got up the nerve to ask her if I could have the break, street smart for young teens to express their desire to become sweethearts. She said, "I'll let you know tomorrow." Her anticipated answer rattled around in my brain for several days, as everyday her original answer became standardized. Finally one day after I reminded her of her promised answer, she said, "Tomorrow never comes." I was crushed, walked away and never looked back.

Looking around Woodlawn, there was Mary Olivia Harris, very attractive, taller than I, an only child, whose lusciously appearing lips were as inviting to me as the nectar from the honeysuckle vines to butterflies and bees visiting them daily in droves.

Olivia was a tenth grader and I an eleventh. Riding the same bus and streetcar daily, I was fortunate to sit beside her on many occasions. As we talked about school, at the risk of receiving a nasty no or maybe, her dimpled smiles stimulated me enough to believe she'd be receptive to my asking if I could come see her. Smiling, she said, "I'll tell you tomorrow." Tomorrow did come in this case, as I'm sure she had to get her mother's permission, who along with her father knew my parents very well. Mrs. Harris passed our home twice daily as she went four blocks down the road to Dr. and Mrs. Kinkead's home where she worked for years. Sometimes I would be in the swing on our front porch or sitting on the bench in front of our watermelon stand. We always spoke politely to each other.

Olivia's father often bought a large watermelon from Father and shouldered it more than three miles to their home. He was sure it was a good one, as Father was almost perfect in judging the quality of his melons, which were fully guaranteed. He never returned one, which was a plus for me; the negative was Father's reputation as a bootlegger. However, it didn't hurt my chances of seeing Olivia. The next day she told me I could come over Sunday afternoon at three o'clock. Olivia and her parents were regular churchgoers, their church was across the street from First Baptist, where I attended. They were African Methodist Episcopalians, A.M.E.s.

Already dressed after having left church services at 1 p.m. and eating dinner at 2 p.m., I constantly watched my trusty $2.50 Ingersoll wrist watch, which ran slow most of the time. It kept good time this Sunday as I checked it against our striking clock in the bedroom, which was almost always correct.

The sun was very hot and the humidity high. My shoes sparkled, but I knew after walking across four railroad tracks, trudging through dusty Froggy Bottom, crossing another set of railroad tracks, up a rough, red clay road leading to the foot of Shades Mountain, much of the shine would be gone.

Olivia's home was a stone's throw from the mountain. Checking the time as I climbed the four steps leading to the porch of this very large beautiful home, it was exactly 3 p.m. I knocked lightly, not wanting to appear aggressive. The front door was open and I could see through the screen while standing at attention. Instead of Olivia answering, here came Mrs. Harris, all five-foot-eleven inches of her, looking straight at me not cracking the slightest smile, calling back to Olivia a few steps behind,"Edwin is here." I froze in my tracks, hoping she would be happy to see me as she had known me all of my life.

"Good evening, Mrs. Harris," I said nervously, as she opened the screen door and stepped onto the porch with Olivia following closely. I was speechless as she directed me to a seat in the large swing hanging from the ceiling. She sat in the middle, to my disdain, not wanting her with us on my first date and not knowing what I was supposed to do, especially since three people were always known to make a crowd. I had heard some of my teenaged friends, old timers, talk about dating, but with no explanation.

Olivia sat quietly on the far end. No one said anything until Mrs. Harris asked, "How are your parents?"

"Fine, Mrs. Harris." We sat looking straight ahead, not uttering a sound. I could read Mrs. Harris' mind and was sure she was thinking, *I'd like to wring your neck and don't want my only child to start thinking about boys.*

Finally I said to Olivia, "How's school?" I couldn't think of anything else to say.

"Fine, I have a science exam tomorrow."

"Are you studying hard?"

"Oh, yes."

Her mother chimed in, "You'd better get a good grade."

I read this as a hint for me to get my mind off of her daughter, as school was more important than I.

I said, "I have an exam Tuesday in English Lit."

"I'm sure you'll do well," Olivia replied.

That was the end of our conversation. Telling them it was time for me to go, I really didn't care what time it was, just freedom from that stranglehold. Mrs. Harris walked to the steps with me. "Good riddance" flashed across my mind. I left and never looked back. My Ingersoll said 3:30 p.m. when I hit the road for home. It had been thirty minutes of torture for the three of us and I knew I'd never be a part of that scene again. I didn't even wave goodbye. I saw Olivia on the way to and from school, but never asked her for another date.

We had a wonderful choir, one hundred voices

strong. Mr. P. W. Wilkerson was director and also taught carpentry. One day as I loitered in the boys building I met him."Young man, where do you belong?"

"Tailoring," I politely replied.

"Don't you have anything to do?" he asked.

"Yes, sir. I'm on my way there now."

"Let's go down to Professor Lindsay and see if he can find something for you."

He and I went to the tailoring shop where he told Professor Lindsay I was loitering in the hallway.

"Come in here, young man and let's see if we can find something for you to do."

Mr. Wilkerson promptly left. Professor Lindsay knew me very well, as he lived on Oak Ridge Hill next door to my Aunt Mary. We saw each other often. He had me open my coat and voila, the lining was loose.

He said, "Sit down and fell-stitch that lining."

I procured a needle and thread and repaired it. When I showed him the finished work, he was satisfied and emphatically told me not to loiter in the hall anymore. I never did again.

Dolly Brown, a nice looking mature appearing eighteen-year-old from Kingston, two stops before we reached Woodlawn, was an excellent soloist. We rode that same rowdy special streetcar to school every day. I loved to hear her sing *I Don't Mind A Skeeter Lighting*, wonderfully groovy!

Eddie Crowder, a local adolescent, was also an excellent vocalist and really sang *Chloe*, to my heart and soul's content.

The choir sang monthly during the forty-five minute assembly. It was great. Mr.Wilkerson died in 1934. Mr. Wayman McCoo succeeded him, a handsome, bespectacled, great director and very frisky as he moved to and fro, across the stage. When he left for Alabama State College in Montgomery, Mr. William Henry became director. He got the job done, but in a nonchalant way. They were great and I always enjoyed the choir's performances.

Chapter 15
That Unforgettable Sunday

A single cock-a-doodle-doo from the chicken house every morning at 4 a.m. made me ill at ease until the second and final alarm, rain or shine, from"Ole 99" a passenger train that blared four loud woo, woo, woo, woos, as it swooped downgrade from Irondale three miles away warning everyone to clear the tracks at the Sixty-fifth Street crossing and alerting me to rise and shine.

"Remember the Sabbath day and keep it Holy," was a part of the scripture Mother always insisted we observe, faithfully.

Bleary-eyed and trying to straighten my twisted body from the crumpled sheet, I finally hit the floor and began checking the stinging, itching bumps over my body, no surprise as I heard the zinging mosquitoes when the room darkened. They had quite a few blood meals at my expense despite my being covered from head to toe, even on hot humid nights.

To the kitchen I went to start the fire, getting the stove ready for Mother to begin preparing breakfast.

Peace of mind wasn't everyone's pleasure as

the devil's evil spirit found its way to our home on that beautiful Sunday afternoon, the fourteenth day of September, nineteen-thirty-four.

Uncle Sandy, one of Father's older brothers, was six feet-two, ruddy-complexioned, with high cheek bones resembling an Indian and quite stoop shouldered from years of working in the red ore mines. He ruined my day. He and his first wife, now deceased, had two daughters and one son. He lived in his beautiful white home on Oakridge Hill, across the railroad tracks two miles from us. He never owned a car and walked to our home or wherever he wanted to go around the neighborhood.

Without much schooling, he developed a keen insight into living through mother-wit and survival from adaptations to the hard knocks of life. When he came to our house he smoked his pipe, which he always filled with George Washington tobacco. The smoke was fairly strong, but not too offensive.

The tone of his voice sounded combative after a few drinks of moonshine, but he was harmless. Like most adults in those days, he believed children should be seen and not heard.

He was my favorite uncle. Listening to baseball broadcasts was his favorite hobby. We discussed baseball incessantly. I liked his lingo. For a strike-out he'd say, "The pitcher greased him by putting wrinkles on the ball. He bumped the wall if the batted ball rattled it for an extra base hit. The bases were drunk if occupied by three runners." I considered him a real buddy. He was my friend.

For some unknown reason, he nicknamed me Plunk and Annie Ruth Zoo. She and I were overjoyed on his payday, because he always brought

us a large Hershey candy bar from the commis-
sary. While visiting us he'd sit with his legs crossed
and sister would sit on his foot for long periods of
time, as he bounced her up and down.

I was always happy to see him but thought his
fifty-seventh birthday would be his last. After two
or three shot glasses of hooch he announced to
sister, Mother and me, this was his fifty-sixth birthday. "I was born January 12, 1885. I'm fifty-six."
That awoke my arithmetic mind. I was always
putting two and two together to see if they equaled
four and began checking to see if he were really
fifty-six. Sister was seven and could also count.
We came to the same conclusion, adding and adding until the total was fifty-seven. "I'm fifty-six,"
he continuously maintained.

"No, Uncle Sandy, you are fifty-seven." We
counted on our fingers, then got paper and pencil
to prove we were correct, but to no avail.

His voice became louder and higher, "I'm fifty-
six," his moonshine speaking loud and clear.

Since we couldn't convince him, Annie Ruth
decided to settle the matter her way, one I never
would have conceived. I imagine she was just tired
of his noise, went to the kitchen, took the box of
cayenne pepper from the shelf, returned to where
he was sitting with his legs crossed and eyes closed.
"Open your mouth, Uncle Sandy."

He obliged and she filled it with a copious quantity of red pepper. Instantly he began sneezing in
such rapid succession, he became short of breath,
his cheeks reddened and nostrils ran like a water
faucet. I thought he was going to die. Mother arose
from her rocking chair close by, "Sandy, are you
all right?" He couldn't answer as he was still sneezing. Mother turned to sister and said, threateningly, "Why did you do that?" Sister was silent for

fear of getting a thrashing. Her expectations were on target. Mama got the strap and gave her a good one, all the while observing Uncle Sandy who, at last, began settling down. The sneezing and whipping came to a halt. "Are you all right, Sandy?"

"I think I'll be all right, Ginny." Everything settled down and we never discussed his age again.

I was fascinated by his carbide lamp, which was fastened above the rim of his miner's hard hat. One day I asked, "How do you turn that light on?"

He smiled and said, "You just put some of that white powder, which we call carbide, into the lamp, wet it and snap the switch in this opening and a sharp blaze will come out." It was real neat. He gave me a little powder and advised me to be careful handling it because it would burn my fingers. I wet a small amount, lighted it with a match and a white cloud of steam penetrated my nostrils. It smelled like gun powder. I was careful to keep my fingers free of the spewing carbide and never experienced a burn.

The appearance of his heavy work shoes coated with red ore dust, always stuck in my mind.

He had no romantic interests until he met Katie Nelson, sister-in-law of Mr. James Hutcherson, an old friend, whom he visited quite often. She lived and worked as a presser on the south side of downtown Birmingham. She was a divorcee with a late teenaged daughter, Vester. He saw her occasionally when she visited her sister, who was married to Mr. Hutcherson and was attracted to her by her peaches and cream complexion. He went ga, ga, goo, goo over her and couldn't wait until Mrs. Hutcherson introduced him to her.

He had a half-dozen peach trees in his back yard, the largest, reddest and sweetest peaches any earthly being had ever tasted. To him, she was symbolic of those delectable qualities, hence his pet name for her—Sweet Peaches.

She was a tall, straight, very fair skinned lady with smooth, combed-back jet black hair wound into a neat, medium-sized ball on the back of her head. A staid but friendly smile complimented her always flushed appearing face. Vester was short, light brown, very quiet and also worked at the cleaners. I only talked with her a few times, but often waved at both of them as they passed our home on the bus going to and from work. They never visited our home.

It wasn't too long before Uncle Sandy announced to Father and Mother that he was going to marry Sweet Peaches.

After hearing of his wonderful find, Daddy asked him where she lived. "She lives at Twenty-Eighth Street on the south side." Father was very familiar with the area, as he peddled fruits and vegetables throughout the city.

Henry Eskett, a fat, gravel-voiced, slow talking, past middle aged man who Daddy knew well was a fellow bootlegger and when his usual supplier was out of whiskey he bought two or three gallons from him. One day, Father asked if he knew Katie Nelson. He said, "Yes I know her, she's a big, yellow kinda rough woman, works at Jones' Cleaners.

Daddy was a bit puzzled, "You know my brother Sandy met her at her sister's home in Woodlawn and plans to marry her."

"I wish him luck," Mr. Eskett said with a smirk.

Daddy didn't rush to tell Uncle Sandy what he heard about Sweet Peaches, but one day when he stopped by for a few drinks, told him what Henry Eskett said about her. He took a big gulp of moonshine, almost choking from what he had just heard, lowered his head for a moment, straightened up and blurted, "I won't marry her or try, I'll marry her or die."

Daddy smiled, shook his head and said, "San, if that's the way you feel about her, go ahead."

Their conversation was disturbing to me because I didn't want Uncle Sandy to die. Finally on my way outside, I picked up my tennis ball and bat, hitting and missing a few and soon forgot about their conversation.

The wedding took place in the mid-twenties at Uncle Sandy's home. Mother and I attended. Father and sister stayed home. Mother and Aunt Katie became instant friends and remained so over the years. They often ran into each other at Aunt Mary's and had a laughing good time.

Things seemed to be going along well between them until Uncle Sandy began telling Aunt Mary about their troubles. Aunt Mary visited us often and after a few shots of moonshine, told Mother about their problems. It was disturbing to me, when I heard her say she thought they both drank too much and wished they would stop and maybe their troubles would end.

I always looked forward to Mother making a batch of her famous rolls when Sunday rolled around. She made them four or five times a year, to my delight. Oh, what a welcome change it was from 360 days plus of biscuits, biscuits and more biscuits. Usually thoroughly disgusted with the results, she always made them late Saturday afternoon so they could rise overnight and be ready for baking Sunday morning. I can see the big black square pan covered with brown paper that she used to bake those delicacies. To smell them baking would make my taste buds go crazy. They had failed to rise more than a third of an inch so many times, I decided to take a peep to see how they were doing, knowing full well Mother didn't want them disturbed for any reason. I could see they weren't doing too well and carefully lowered the paper and went about my main job of building a fire. So many times, instead of a roaring fire I'd find none at all and had to start over. I would add kerosene, when we had some, to the bed of paper,wood and coal. When lighted it sometimes went, swoosh, as the sudden flame leaped upwards sending me scurrying across the kitchen to escape getting my eyebrows singed. Once the fire was burning well, I would go outside, around the house to the front porch to get the Sunday paper. I knew better than to go through the bedroom as Mother might have been in the process of dressing. With my chores completed, I could now enjoy reading the sports section of the paper while sitting on the back porch. When Mother finally came to the kitchen I could hear her remove the brown paper and disgustedly exclaim, "Aw shucks, those rolls didn't rise again. Guess the yeast from Tombrello's store was too old and flat."

Upon hearing this outburst, I knew she was upset so I'd put the paper down, go into the kitchen, smile, hug her and say, "Your rolls are always tops with me."

After trying to lift her spirits, I took the key to open the watermelon stand, as a customer had stopped out front. "Are these melons any good boy?"

"Yes, sir. If not, just bring half of it back and you can get another one." That was Father's motto. They were always ninety-nine per cent good and very few were returned. That was Father's other expertise besides selling good moonshine whiskey and beer.

At that juncture, Mother was battering the chicken, the rice was boiling, seeming to take hours to cook as she skimmed it many times before it was done. The chicken now done, gravy made, rice ready and the rolls smelling mouth-watering good, it was time to eat. When she removed the rolls from the oven, hot and less than a quarter inch high, her feathers fell again. She was always looking for that perfect batch. As we began to eat, I would boast about the delicious rolls and she would look at me and just smile. The pan emptied, so they couldn't have been too bad.

After my breakfast settled, I began thinking about taking a bath and getting ready for Sunday school and church. I would get the number 3 wash tub, bring it into the dining room, put it behind the heater and fill it with medium hot water. In the winter, Saturday night was bath night because I didn't want to go out in the morning after a hot bath and take a chance on catching a cold.

Classes began at 9:30 a.m. The one-hour lesson, held in a private room, was implanted in my mind and nurtured my Christian faith. Mr. Henry A. Pearson, my teacher, was an early role model. It wasn't hard for me to see the devil at work, for bootlegging and emotional abuse were daily occurrences in our home. I knew it wasn't right for Father not to have a legitimate job like his customers. Selling intoxicants to them to subsidize our livelihood was his way of making a living.

Church services began at 11 a.m. I always took a seat in the middle aisle because I wanted to escape the tremors from Brother Jackson's shudders when the pastor's message touched his religious soul very deeply. He sat on the left side. Scanning the congregation, I wondered who would shout first in the deaconess' amen corner—Sister Huff, Sister Willingham or Sister Lewis—and who would be the first deacon sitting across from them to close his eyes, maybe in deep thought about the sermon or just taking a nap?

After the choir had sung a soul-stirring song following a moving sermon by our pastor, Mrs. Mary Elliott, a bespectacled, light brown skinned, serious looking, less than five feet tall lady, stood up in the middle of our thirty-five member choir and set every soul on fire, including mine, when she sang *His Eye Is On The Sparrow And I Know He Watches Me*, or *Just A Closer Walk With Thee*. Divine bonding with thoughts of Jesus made me ever more conscious of my spirituality, the same feeling the shouting sisters of the church exhibited. My soul felt full and humble as tears came rolling down my cheeks in God's divine chapel. To me, that's what religion was about.

I also loved the songs sung by the congregation after a soul-stirring sermon. My favorites were *Dwelling In Beulah Land*,—especially the words, "I'm drinking from the fountain that never shall run dry."—*Rock of Ages* and the most often sung, *Amazing Grace*. My parents always gave me a few coins to drop in the collection plate. I proudly put them in and passed it to the next parishioner. When church services were over, I visited with my peers and a few adults for awhile, then headed for home.

Changing my Sunday clothes, I dashed to the stand for a cold five-cent quart bottle of strawberry Town Cola, diminishing the fifty cent profit from a case of twenty-four. Nehi and Try-Me were of superior taste and quality but only six ounces and just not enough to quench my thirst. I had to cool off for awhile as the church was very hot and the hand-fans from Echols-Strong and Welch

Brother's Undertakers didn't quite do the job. Leery of the thoughts of an undertaker and so afraid of dying, they always reminded me of the many funerals I had attended.

I was now ready to sell watermelons in or outside of the stand, delivering all curbside sales. I never received a tip, but a polite thank you was readily acknowledged and appreciated. Between customers was a delightful time to cool off, as the stand was covered by a huge elm tree which extended symmetrically over and around the stand almost to the back gate of our home. A huge canopy of very thick green leaves provided shade from that more than fifty year old tree for a welcome retreat.

Before the gang congregated at 2 p.m. to listen to the baseball broadcast, I had begun to think about Sunday dinner, as I knew it was the feast of the week. We would have baked chicken and dressing, candied yams, Jell-o salad, ice cream cranked by me in our two-quart tin freezer, and cake or perhaps roast beef or pork, string beans, collard greens and, of course, cornbread always. After enjoying one of Mother's Sunday specials and feeling stuffed and lazy, I rejoined Father at the stand where we waited for the neighborhood crowd to gather and hear the ball games broadcast over WAPI. Ours was the only radio on our block. They would refresh themselves with a soft drink of their choice for a nickel or a slice of cold melon at the same price.

My peers, Nay Felton, Pete Hardy and Freck Felton arrived. Freck had no freckles but because he was very fair complexioned, as was Wilson May who had many, many, I nicknamed him Freck. Father's friends, Mr. Moot Felton (Louis, Sr.), Mr. James Collier and Mr. Clarence White were there, but notably missing was Uncle Sandy, Father's brother, a devoted baseball fan and loyal booster of the Birmingham Barons and their manager, Clyde Milan. He hadn't arrived when the game began and I wondered why.

Little did I know the winds of doom were swirling through the disgruntled minds of him and Aunt Katie. They had been separated for several years and their home was divided into separate living quarters, she on one side and he the other.

She continued to work at the cleaners and invited her co-workers over. They all lived on the south side where she previously lived. Drinking, smoking, loud music and talking went on all day Sunday. He didn't enjoy their frequent get-togethers and let her know it, because he felt this was his house, having worked hard to pay for it before they married and no one was going to run over him. He worked for a criminal attorney, Reese Murray, part time and was off on Sundays.

Now that they were separated, confusion reigned supreme with accusations, cursing, threats and general denigration of each other's character. Uncle Sandy was a regular visitor to Aunt Mary's and talked of his domestic troubles. They often visited our home, that's where the tea was, good old exhilarating moonshine whiskey. They got into their tea quite heavily and spilled the beans about everything that bothered them. Aunt Katie's name came up often because they saw her as evil and a trouble-maker. I picked up on bits, pieces and chunks of negative feelings about their many troubles. My parents never took sides, just listened.

Unfortunately, their feelings had turned to hate and on that Sunday he became fed up with the boisterous frolicking next door, rapped on the wall with a cane and hollered, "Stop that damn noise." The loud talking continued. He rapped harder the next time and used the same language.

She hollered back, "Stop knocking on that damned wall disturbing me and my friends." There was no lessening of the noise and, for the third time, he rapped even louder. The breeze from the stick fanned the smoldering fire built from her hate, disgust and hostility towards him, and burst into a raging inferno as this very light-complexioned lady's cheeks turned a hot, flaming red. She went around the front to Uncle Sandy's door, cursing all the way, "I'm sick and tired of you bothering me and my friends, I'm gonna shoot the hell out of you."

He didn't reply, but really felt the heat of her wrath from the threat of being punctured with hot lead. He said he grabbed his hat and high-tailed it up the hill to his sister Mary's house. She was cooking dinner when he burst through the front door excitedly, "Ag" as he called her, "Kate is going to kill me."

"Aw, naw," flat southern talk for, oh no, "What's the matter San?"

"She and her cronies are down there drinking and keeping all kinds of noise. I rapped on the wall and she came around to my side of the house with a gun threatening to kill me."

"Go down to Tom and Ginny's and wait till she cools off. I don't think she'll go down there."

He took her advice and went out the back door on his way to our home, two miles down the hill. Shortly thereafter Aunt Katie burst through the front door at Aunt Mary's shouting, "Where is he? Where is he? I'm gonna kill that S.O.B. Come on outta there."

Poor Aunt Mary said she was scared to death, hardly knowing what to do, and was so stunned she couldn't even say he's not here. They had al-

ways been very cordial to each other. Aunt Katie
wasn't her usual self, face flushed and using ex-
plosive language when Aunt Mary said, "What's
the matter, Sis Kate, San's not here."

She was extremely agitated and kept repeating, "Where is he? Where is he? Tell him to come
on outta there, bet he's down to his brother Tom's.
I'm gonna kill that S.O.B."

Aunt Mary tried to cool her off, repeating,
"What's wrong, Sis Kate?" That was the end of their
conversation. She stormed out of the house, down
the steps leading to the yard and down the alley,
the same trail he had just taken on the way to our
house.

I was perched atop the large icebox filled with
ice cold melons and soft drinks so I could see the
curbside customers when they stopped to buy a
melon or a soft drink. Birmingham was playing
the New Orleans Pelicans and the usual gang had
gathered. Everyone was engrossed in the game
when I looked up and saw Uncle Sandy, at long
last, walking rapidly towards the stand. As he approached the side door, eyes bulging, sweating
profusely and almost out of breath, he quietly said
to Father, "Old Man," as he called him, even though
he was ten years older, "come here quick." Dad
got up, went to the door and I heard him whisper,
"Katie's got a gun and is going to kill me." The two
of them walked over to the side gate of our yard,
talking quietly. Suddenly, out of nowhere, she
appeared alongside Mrs. Jenny Fagan's fence,
ready to cross Georgia Road. She crossed the
street, bypassed Mother and Mrs. Bertha Petty who
were sitting in the swing on the front porch, not
uttering a word, headed towards the back gate,
red as a beet and obviously angry.

I plainly heard her say, "You can't come down

to your brother Tom's for protection, come on outta
there, I'm gonna kill you." Wearing an apron, I
didn't notice her hands, but two witnesses said
they were underneath and presumably clutching
something. With the commotion brewing, I leaped
from the icebox and ran to the door. By that time,
he had gone into the house as she reached the
gate and was talking to Father. I didn't hear anything she was saying except, "Come on outta there,
I'm gonna kill you."

Suddenly he appeared on the back porch bran-
dishing Father's sawed-off, single-barreled shotgun, which was kept behind my parents bed. I don't
know how he found it. As I was exiting the stand
door, I saw him raise the gun and aim at her, then
that horrendous blast, as I frighteningly turned
and ran towards Mr. Griffith's home a few yards
away. Mrs. Griffith screamed, "Oh, my God," as
she walked to the edge of her porch upon hearing
the commotion and had a clear view of the back of
our house. I was stunned momentarily because I
thought Father might have been shot as he was
standing at the gate talking with her. Slowly, I
looked around and saw Aunt Katie lying on the
ground and Father still standing there. She had
been killed instantly. I returned to the stand without going over to see her.

A crowd began to gather. Vester had been
alerted by Aunt Mary and arrived just after her
mother had been shot. Two witnesses said they
saw her pick up a gun. Father said he didn't see a
gun and was there when she fell.

The policemen came, handcuffed Uncle Sandy
and placed him in the back seat of their car. It was
sad seeing my favorite uncle arrested. An ambulance came and took her away.

Uncle Sandy was released on bail after a week

in jail. He had recently begun working part time for Mr. Reese Murray, a very prominent Birmingham criminal attorney, who defended him. When he visited our home he looked very sad, face drawn, deeply lined and not his usual talkative self. The baseball season was over and so was his favorite subject, the Birmingham Barons. The crux of his conversation with Mother and Father was, "I'm gonna come 'clair'," meaning clear, "cause Katie, no more Sweet Peaches, was gonna kill me. Ole man, did you see a gun?"

"No San, I didn't see one. She had one?" Daddy asked. Father told him, "Moot Felton was in the watermelon stand listening to the ball game and saw us walk toward the gate and heard her loud talk. He was exiting the stand when the shotgun blast sounded and after she fell, said he saw a gun by her side."

"Will he come to my trial and testify?"

"I'll ask him," Daddy replied.

"I'd be much obliged if he would."

Father asked Mr. Felton and he said he would.

Uncle Sandy was exonerated at trial. The next time I saw him he still looked depressed and went downhill, health-wise, from that day on.

I really liked Uncle Sandy and was sorry to see his life ruined. For me what began as a grand and glorious day of Sunday school, church and dinner, and later the baseball broadcast, became a disaster.

I smelled the odor of gun powder that permeated the air through the silver dollar sized hole in the screen every time I left by way of the back door, always reminding me of that fatal shotgun blast that killed Aunt Katie. I can still visualize Uncle Sandy as he raised and leveled that shotgun, and hearing a sound like a frightening clap of thunder, following a huge streak of lightning during a storm almost paralyzing me with fear. At age 15 upon witnessing the most dreadful event of my young life, an unexpected, cold-blooded murder, the tragedy shall forever remain embedded in my memory.

Chapter 16
The Scourge Of Early Adolescence

I became aware of the dreadful disease tuberculosis when I was in the second grade. Madeline Brown, a sandy haired, very thin, Indian red complexioned classmate with velvety skin who lived on the north side of Woodlawn was a victim. I really wasn't impressed with its contagiousness. She, Grover Price and I were very good friends. Grover was her sweety. Blessed with a beautiful voice, she sang at our annual second grade concert about a girl who was murdered by her mother for stealing a pear. Grass grew over her grave and when Johnny, her brother, attempted to pull it, a song echoed:

"Johnny, O' Johnny, don't pull my curly hair, 'cause mother has killed me, for only one little pear." It was very touching.

She died from tuberculosis during the next school year.

Consumption was the name given tuberculosis, for which there was no cure in those days. The only treatment was residence at a fresh air camp, way out in suburbia, cod liver oil and a raw egg whole milk cocktail three times daily, in addition to other high caloric food if the patient had an appetite. The wasting effect of the body increased as the appetite decreased.

I became frightened of the disease as I saw Emma Carrie Woods and Olivia Cornelius, two beautiful young neighborhood ladies, waste away and die. Community talk about them and the disease were distressing to me. I weighed myself every time I went downtown and saw a penny scale. I was stuck at 128 to 130 pounds, wanting desperately to advance to 150 or 160 and couldn't gain another ounce. I thought I might have consumption. Mother told me I was going to weigh myself away.

Developing a dry cough and pain in my chest during early adolescence scared me stiff. I had heard of indigestion resulting in chest discomfort and belching produced relief. I always sat up with Mother until 3 a.m. Sunday mornings while she prepared and sold barbecue. Father and sister had long since gone to bed. To get quick relief from the pain, I added a pinch of salt to a bottle of coca cola and quickly ingested the instant foam. That combination produced a big belch and temporary relief. The problem continued intermittently.

Mrs. Rosa Kidd, a neighbor, invited her fourteen-year-old niece from West Virginia to visit her every summer. She was very thinly built with keen features and large eyes. We became friends and after a while visitation began two doors away, sitting in the swing beside her and talking. The relationship became friendly enough for me to begin putting my arms around her. Guess she became attuned to my vibes and we became puppy lovers. One night we were out back and as she leaned against a telephone pole my advances were persistent enough to close in on her. She responded as I kissed her but several times, she raised the red flag when I tried to get more intimate and all action ceased.

I didn't know she was ill with tuberculosis until three summers later after she died in West Virginia. Her aunt told Mother the cause of death, maybe she didn't know about the contagiousness of tuberculosis to tell Mother I should be checked for that scourge of a disease.

Mother took me to Dr. Broughton for a checkup who did a tuberculin skin test. It was four plus, meaning the germ had entered my body. He referred us to Slossfield Health Clinic in North Birmingham, where Dr. Kelly Joseph diagnosed me as having primary tuberculosis, inactive, per chest x-rays. One tablespoon of cod liver oil in an ounce of tomato juice daily was prescribed. A public health nurse visited me weekly for six months. I never developed a fever. My body had placed calcium around the tuberculosis germ, walling it off to prevent spreading. I returned to school in September, feeling fine.

Chapter 17
Errant Childhood Sexuality

When innocent teenaged adolescent males hormones start rolling, associates can help channel them in the wrong direction. Experimentation was nothing new and stories of their escapades seemed exciting and intriguing.

I was introduced to my first and only house of prostitution by Johnny Hood, a year younger than I, who told me about his visits to one, which sounded exciting. The fifty cent fee for services was within my range so I asked him if I could go with him sometime. He laughed and said, "Yeh, man." This is a good way to get into a whole lot of trouble. Neither he nor I discussed condom use as protection against venereal disease and I had no real knowledge about them, except hearing they were called merry widows. I had seen a few abandoned ones on the streets.

He agreed to take me along one beautiful Sunday afternoon. We took the streetcar across town to the ghetto to a rather shabby looking house for the fling. A young woman let us in after a gentle knock. Johnny, the veteran, went into headquarters with her as I waited. When she was ready for me she collected the fifty cents I had been instructed to give her. That was a bit disconcerting, as I expected to pay after I had been serviced. She was too wise for that. When I couldn't ready myself for some action she attempted to unbutton my trousers. I resisted, as this was ego alien to me. Embarrassed at not being able to perform, I requested the return of my fifty cents. That was a no-no. Overhearing a loud argument in progress, Johnny came to ease the tension. "Ed, what's the matter?"

"I want my money back."

He didn't ask why. "Come on Ed, I'll give you your money back."

On the way home I told him I couldn't get ready. That brought a sniggle and, "Don't worry about it, that happens sometimes." We never discussed that episode again, nor did he return my fifty cents. We remained friends until he left for Chicago and never returned.

Call it what you may, boy talk, girl talk or facts of life, parents should have heart-to-heart talks beginning with their eight year old boys and girls about sex and its consequences. Their fear that introducing discussions about sex to preadolescents will awaken their desire to experiment is erroneous. It's hard for children to escape being indoctrinated by their school chums and neighborhood peers, who probably know more than you think. Your talking frankly with them might prevent venereal diseases and pregnancies later in childhood and adolescence.

Mrs. Rosa Ferguson, a big dark lady with a very pleasant personality, and her coal miner husband had three sons and a daughter. They lived just adjacent to us at the end of an alley. She was very religious and a member of the Holiness Church.

Robert, 18, the oldest, was very tall and weighed over 200 pounds. I was eight and my sister five-and-a-half years old. The six of us congregated on the grass of a large vacant lot adjacent to my home. We chatted, laughed and just hung out. Robert began carrying sister on his back. That was harmless enough until one day he propositioned me to let him have sex with her and I'd have sex with "Sang," as he called Lucille, age 12. That raised an immediate red flag and "No-o-o...." I didn't tell my parents but never let him carry her on his back again.

Just as fathers are protective of their daughters, it is in the genes of boys not to want any male to make a play for their sisters, even though he likes other boys' sisters.

I was angered many times when older boys called me "Brudd-un," meaning brother-in-law. I didn't appreciate that association.

"Sang" slipped through the back fence of our yard and we had several twisting sessions behind the outhouse. No excitement was ever experienced.

The "no-no" word around any home is sex. Everyone is aware of it, but afraid to touch it, as they would a rattlesnake. I wish my parents had told me the whys, wherefores and dangers of being premature in becoming a participant. My failure to become a parent was caused by six months of untreated gonorrhea that clogged the passageways of my reproductive system, sterilizing me for life.

I wasn't sexually precocious, but an experimenting participant. "Let's do it," was the expression used to ask for sex. The girl across the street, a very nice looking lassie, two years my senior, started me. Hide and seek or High Spy, as we called it, was a very popular game played after dark. We sat on our front porch in the swing, rocking chair or the bench in front of the watermelon stand, chatting in general until the game began. When the counting started the participants scattered in all directions, to the shrubbery behind the house and grape vines for places to hide. The theme song for the game was "Chicken, chicken with the web toes, when I got back my chickens was gone, what time it is for the witch, all hid?" When all was quiet, the caller ran to find the players. Upon finding one, a foot race to the calling place ensued. Everyone had to be found before the game was over. The last loser called the next game.

Louise and I had a designated hiding place. She would lower her underwear and I was ready for action. No particular thrill on my part came forward, just bumping and grinding, a strange act that I didn't understand.

The act was transferred to the back seat of Father's car when Mother went downtown and he was at work. At age eight I had heard the term joy riding in automobiles. Lovers sat in the back seat and enjoyed hugging and kissing. We imitated them. To prove our immaturity, we alighted from the car and did our thing standing up, her back against the wall. She staged a description of the depths of my penetration. As for me, I was just an obliging participant.

Louise's first cousin, Mary, was my second act every Wednesday after her grandmother went to work. She conversed with sister and me every day from across the street. When Mary told us she was going into the house to take a nap, that was my signal to cross the street two doors down between Mrs. Felton's and Aunt Edna's homes, across the back to her house and through the gate. We kissed, wrangled and twisted for a longtime, nothing exciting, just a premature mischievous act on our parts.

As I grew older, associations with my male peers brought enlightenment about neighborhood sexuality. Some girls were termed "easy" and others "hard to get." It really didn't matter to me because Mother would have skinned me if she thought I ever contemplated such behavior. Even though she never cautioned me about venereal diseases, she saw pregnant, unwed girls and warned that if I impregnated one she'd see that I married her.

My Aunt Mary warned me about venereal disease. One day while visiting us she was three shakes in the wind, i.e, mellowed out from several shots of 135-proof moonshine. She said "Edwin, don't go around here ravishing these fast gals, you get clean 'poozy'." I knew what she meant.

Well, I didn't take her advice very well, because butcher Pete, one of my best friends, was known for his reputation with girls, caused me to get my first and last case of gonorrhea.

"Hey, Egg," as he called me. "Why don't you get Big Alice? She's a pushover."

"Have you done it to her?"

"Yea, man, many times."

I planted this filthy seed in my mind and one Sunday night after church services, no less, I convinced her by saying, "Come on Alice, let's go around to the school house and have some fun."

"I can't go around there."

"Oh, yes you can, come on," as I grabbed her hand, pulling her in the direction of the school four blocks away.

"Naw, I can't go."

"Come on, yes you can," I kept saying. The tugging stopped when we reached the school. The business I had in mind was completed. She and I went to our respective homes.

I had become too wise and precocious and picked up a case of gonorrhea. I never told anyone of the burning, yellowish discharge oozing from my genitals and the frequency of urination a week after that encounter. Ultimately, a wet circle appeared on my underwear and trousers, which became whitish when dry. I felt ashamed and didn't want to face the anger and disgust of my parents because our lines of communication were disrupted by a dysfunctional environment and my ignorance about venereal diseases and their complications. I wish I had told them, maybe they would have taken me to a doctor sooner, before I reached the stage of being unable to urinate.

Father suspected something was wrong and, for some reason, didn't confront me, either out of anger towards me or to teach me a lesson. I learned a life-long one. He finally confronted Mother, "Virginia, something's wrong with that boy."

"What do you mean?"

"He's got the clap."

Mother looked astonished and asked, "What's that?"

He turned around disgustedly and said, "He's been messing around with some nasty gal."

She looked perplexed and asked, "Who?"

He angrily said, "I don't know," and left the room.

Mother looked me in the eye and said, "Edwin, who have you been messing around with?"

I dropped my head and said, "Nobody." That ended the conversation. She never got involved in quizzing me about what Daddy had brought to her attention, to my detriment.

In the meantime, the discharge became so copious I procured a Bull Durham tobacco sack to enclose my genitalia, hoping to keep the discharge from wetting the front of my trousers. Mother noticed my soiled underwear and took me to Dr. T. Y. Young, a white general practitioner. He prescribed a small bottle of Sweet Spirits of Nitre and a dropper, with directions to instill a dropper full three times daily into my urethra. That did no good, so Mother took me to Dr. K. J. Kinkead, who had treated me for a gunshot wound. Dr. Perrin Long of Tulane University discovered sulfanilamide in 1948. I took a course of forty-eight tablets. The discharge ceased, but I wasn't home free.

One night, six months later, I couldn't urinate. My bladder became more and more distended and my abdomen very painful. Father and Mother took me to Hillman Hospital where I was placed in a large bathtub of hot water to see if my urethral sphincter would relax, allowing my bladder to empty. No such luck. I began to hurt more and more. The doctor had to pass several small catheters, called filiforms, until he could get one past the stricture of my urinary passage into the bladder. That wasn't painful compared to the pain in my abdomen from a greatly distended bladder. He finally succeeded in getting one into my bladder, a larger catheter was connected to the filiform and urine flowed freely. Oh, what a welcome relief that was. He referred me to the Urology clinic, but when we were social-serviced, the worker said we were ineligible because of home ownership, horrors.

Afterwards, my urine flowed moderately but the stream over the few years slowed to a trickle. The urinary canal has to remain open so the urine won't back up and affect the kidneys. I have had to have my canal stretched (dilated), from weekly to monthly for many years and will forever. The cold steel instrumentation is no picnic.

I succeeded in getting what I thought I wanted, but not wanting what I got.

That was a case of child abuse, pure and simple, by both parents for not talking to me about sexuality or taking me to a doctor when the overt signs showed something was wrong.

Parents should try to know the whereabouts of their children at all times.

I heard a real fallacy from older youths that if you didn't have sex, your nature would go to your head and run you crazy, you had to "get some" in order not to lose your mind. I never discussed anything like that with my parents, just played it by ear as life went on.

A few of my peers found out in many wrong ways about venereal diseases and pregnancy. Those maladies would surely disturb the mind of any male or female, child or adolescent.

A real boner was, if one had gonorrhea, a way to cure it was to have sex with someone who didn't. Nothing could have been further from the truth. It only spreads the infection to an innocent person and results in all kinds of complications if untreated.

Chapter 18
The New Arrival

I was really bewildered and puzzled when Father had sister and me arise from our nice warm beds early one very cold morning in January and told us he had to go get Dr.Broughton. "Your mother is ill." It was January 6th and extremely frigid. He had built a roaring fire in the heater in the dining room. We huddled close to it, a little frightened, wondering what was wrong with Mother. The bedroom door was closed, that was a little unusual, too. We sat quietly after Daddy left and suddenly I heard a strange sound coming from the bedroom.

"Is that a baby crying?" I asked sister.

"I think so."

"Where did it come from?"

She was as stunned as I. I hadn't heard my parents say a stork was going to bring us a baby. I had always heard the old folks say that's where babies came from.

Dr. Broughton's wife told Daddy he was out on a labor case. He continued on to Dr. T. M. Young's home, a white doctor, who lived about a mile and a half away. Mother never sought any prenatal care. It was about 1 a.m. when Father knocked on his door. He answered and Daddy asked if he would come to see his wife who was about to have a baby. He agreed, dressed hurriedly and followed Father to our home. The baby was born when they arrived. Dr. Young took care of Mother and the baby. Mother never saw him again.

The first look at my little brother, whom I didn't know was on the horizon, was cute. He was light-skinned and kinda gleeful. Despite being three days short of my fifteenth birthday and a sophomore in high school, I wanted to stay home and play with him, but Mother quickly put an end to that. She told me to prepare my breakfast and go to school. I fried some bacon and eggs, ate them with a couple of slices of white bread and hustled out the door to catch the bus. I rode the bus part way and transferred to the streetcar.

I enjoyed science classes tremendously. The eleventh grade was my introduction to chemistry to study components of units which built substances and compound mixtures. Water, H_2O, hydrogen plus oxygen, carbon dioxide, CO_2, filtered dioxide, which we exhale, carbon plus oxygen, entered my memory bank. Wearing a white lab coat for the first time gave me an air of importance. Picking up an expression from James Williams, a classmate, "I'm scientific," after successfully completing my first experiment was sensational.

Mr. George Hudson, the teacher, was a stern man. He made sure we followed his very strict rules of being careful. His strictness paid off in the long run, no accidents.

English Literature was highlighted by Geoffrey Chaucer's *Canterbury Tales*. They were written in "Olde English" and interpreting them was equivalent to learning a foreign language. Miss Myrtle Clark, the teacher, a bespectacled, small lady, was very tough. Other author's poems and works were thoroughly analyzed.

Geometry proved to be my nemesis. We were taught to never memorize the propositions but use the theorem, which would guide us step by step to the end to prove the triangle was congruent or similar. Due to my ability to remember speeches and poems verbatim, why not memorize them? I remembered every statement in solving the propositions and the reasons. Well, I said the propositions with honors but the day of reckoning came when we had to solve geometrical exercises at exam time. To my puzzlement, I came up empty. Richard Macon, a lifetime acquaintance, was a math whiz, stating the propositions excellently and easily solving the exercises at the end of the lesson. At exam time, a little reckless eyeballing could have solved my dilemma, as he sat alone in front of Grover Price and me. He was too slick for that, covering his paper blocking my view. Needless to say, I blew the tests. Lucky for me the grades for stating the propositions and the written test scores were averaged. "E" plus "D" averaged an "S" for satisfactory. That was quite ego dystonic, going from "E" for excellent in mathematics and algebra to "S" in geometry.

That taught me to follow the rules throughout life. There are no shortcuts.

Chapter 19
My Senior Year In High School

Summer vacation was drawing to a close and I had begun to put the happenings of the past three months behind me and started thinking about my last year of high school. My friends and I had talked at length about our future plans after Industrial. Grover, Richard and I often talked about college. I didn't know from whence the money for tuition was coming, but always said I wanted to go to Tuskegee Institute, Tuskegee,Alabama, 98 miles south of Birmingham. Grover and Richard said they would probably go to Miles College in Vinesville about 22 miles from Woodlawn. That was well and good, but I still had to finish my senior year, so my thoughts were again focused on good old Industrial High.

I could now shed those khaki trousers all boys were required to wear the first three years, for black or dark blue. I never wore khakis again. Being an upperclassman put a special spring in my steps as I strolled the hallways to and from various classes.

Of the five or six teachers I had my senior year, Miss Dessie Harris stands out in my mind. She taught American History. I did fairly well in answering daily questions and thought I had it made after reciting Lincoln's Gettysburg Address to her satisfaction. The day of reckoning came when she gave the first written test. Forty-five minutes were allotted for completion. It consisted of five long, involved questions. I wasn't racing with time but answered the questions in about twenty minutes and promptly took my paper to her. She looked up, her large brown eyes flashing in disbelief, "Are you through already?"

"Yes ma'am, Miss Harris."

"You couldn't be. Go back and start thinking again."

Returning to my seat in wonderment, I reviewed the questions, answered each one in much more detail and after about fifteen minutes, returned my paper to her. A soft smile lighted her face as she took it and said nothing. I slowly walked away thinking, next time I will write, write and write throughout the period. I received a "B" on that test and earned an "A" on future ones. American History was one of my favorite subjects.

Advanced science came along with physics, very different from general science, biology and chemistry, dealing with natural laws and processes and the states and properties of matter and energy. It slowed my academic prowess substantially. I only made a "C" from the chairman of the department, Mr. Noah Wills, a very good teacher.

Thanatopsis, by William Cullen Bryant was the big memory deal in American Literature. I fortunately remembered it well. Miss E. O. Wyatt, Chairperson of the English Department, was my teacher. I made an "A", a "B" and a "C" for each six weeks grade.

The twelfth grade was our only elective subject year. We could take either Business or Spanish. I outsmarted myself, coming to the conclusion I was never going to Spain, so why take Spanish? I could have used it to great advantage in later years when I moved to California where many Spanish speaking people live, and were among my numerous patients.

Things were really getting exciting now, graduation time was near and we were busy preparing for the ceremonies. There were several rehearsals, marching into the auditorium and taking our seats on the stage. Next going downtown for our cap and gown fitting. They were sent to the school just prior to graduation. The rental fee was $2.50.

Being a commencement speaker, I had to rehearse daily and of all people, Miss E. O. Wyatt was in charge. The theme was, "Some contributions of our race to American Literature." There were sixteen speakers.

She gave me a proverbial fit as I tried to present a poem by Phyllis Wheatley. I heard, "Stop singing that poem!" so many times I wished I weren't on the program. Finally getting it right, I was the first speaker introduced by a classmate, Daisy Winston.

Phyllis Wheatley was born in 1753, perhaps along the Gambia River, Africa. She arrived in Boston Harbor on July 11, 1761, aboard the schooner Phillis and was bought shortly thereafter by John and Susanna Wheatley for a trifle, apparently named for the vessel which had transported her.

A vocal solo by Eddie L. Crowder was beautiful. Selected spirituals were rendered by the class.

A total of 283 received diplomasJune 11, 1937, an increase of 46 over the January class. It was a glorious occasion for Mother and me. Father and sister did not attend.

The senior prom was the final celebration. No formal gowns or tuxedos, just a simple dance in the school cafeteria from 3 p.m. to 6 p.m. Fess Watley's band played. I couldn't dance worth a nickel, had never been to a dance and only attempted a few times at church socials. Alma Beavers, an attractive classmate lived on the north side of Woodlawn. I was sort of sweet on her even though she had a regular flame. I wrote her notes in class, asking if she were going to be sweet to me at the dance, as we had decided to go together. She told her boyfriend Bernard Morgan, my whist partner in our Casanova Social Club, and he nullified that arrangement so I took Julia Cobb. She was quiet and very attractive. After the school dance she asked me to go the Owl's Club, a very popular night spot downtown, to an after-party. I couldn't go per orders of Mother, who had told me to come straight home after the prom. That was one of the few times I told her she must have thought I was her oldest daughter rather than her oldest son. Julia never forgave me and I never saw her again.

As strict as the teachers were for academic excellence, college was never a topic of discussion. We had many excellent educators speak to us at Assembly two or three times weekly, depending upon whether you were in your junior or senior year.

We had home room, with class officers and a teacher sponsor. I do not remember any discussions or encouragement as to whether or which college we planned to attend.

Only once did I hear Father mention Miles College, where I finally matriculated, as he heard me say I wanted to attend Tuskegee Institute. Maybe Mother was silent, though she had heard me express my desire to become a doctor because she knew they could ill afford to send me to college.

Several of my lifelong school mates went to Miles in Birmingham, one to Knoxville College in Tennessee, a few to Talledega College at Talledega, Alabama, 52 miles north of Birmingham, some to Alabama A & M in Huntsville, Alabama, 115 miles north and a few to Alabama State College in Montgomery, Alabama. All of their parents were able to send them.

Despite the Great Depression, being a high school graduate I thought I had the world in a jug and the stopper in my hand, believing all I had to do was go into the workplace and a job would be waiting for me. I walked eight miles with Hartz Jordan, an adult neighbor, to Stockman Pipe & Fittings Company many mornings waiting at the employment office for the manager to emerge— never any luck.

There were a few pitty-pat jobs, such as drug and grocery store delivery boys, custodial jobs in stores and curb boys at laundry and dry cleaning establishments. The maximum pay was five dollars per week. News of vacancies spread quickly throughout the community and were filled promptly. I was lucky once when Marshall Canada quit his curb service job for another one five blocks away. It was too tough for me, scrubbing a cement floor more than necessary, and I was fired after two weeks.

I watched the newspaper help wanted column daily and told my parents of a job downtown for an office boy. They weren't enthusiastic, stating those jobs were for whites only. I found out how right they were. I scratched up fourteen cents car fare and away I went. There were about forty white youths waiting outside the office. Being the only black, the word "nigger" was blurted out several times with no retaliatory rebuttal from me. Finally, I was told by the employer the job was not for coloreds and I sadly returned home.

Two years following high school I decided I still wanted to go to Tuskegee Institute but was constantly being encouraged by friends to attend Miles, a local institution. That was music to Father's ears because he and I knew the family resources were not favorable for me to attend such an institution of higher learning. He filibustered about my going to Miles, but offered no encouragement. Deciding not to go to college if I couldn't go to Tuskegee, I proceeded to hang around with fifty or sixty other unemployed neighbors and friends playing rise and fly whist, some for free, the type I played. Others played for a quart of nickel Town Hall soda, all flavors, orange, cola and strawberry. We played at the home of Mr. and Mrs. Lima Canada, who had a very large back porch and yard. They were super people. She and her husband Jelly Belly, who had a large protuberant abdomen, tolerated no cursing, fighting or misbehaving of any kind. I visited their home so often Mother jokingly told me she was going to pack my clothes and send me around there to live with them.

Times got no better. Everyone was resigned to let the time pass in a jocular vein, playing cards and checkers all day, every day, except Sunday. Friendships were genuine. Mrs. Canada barbecued and sold it by the sandwich on Saturdays. Her husband was a barber. They meant so much to me, guess I should say their home was my home away from home.

My best paying job came out of the blue one day when James Oliver voluntarily asked me if I wanted his paper route. He threw *The Birmingham Post*, one of two evening newspapers. I immediately said yes. He gave me his hard-back-covered route book with 36 customers' names and addresses neatly recorded and said, "Come with me and I'll teach you the route." I gladly went with him over the fifteen mile route throughout the neighborhood, beginning in The Bottom where I lived, across four railroad tracks, up steep Oakridge Hill, downhill about a mile into Cracker Town, so named for the poor white people who lived there, onward across the Seaboard railroad tracks to the foot of Shades Mountain. The circle was completed when I walked a mile in the opposite direction northward across Oakridge Hill to the bottom where I began, and three blocks further to the office. I was young, full of vim and vigor, and that route over hill and dale didn't deter my enthusiasm.

The newspaper sold for twelve cents per week, no Sunday edition. I knew all of the customers well, made a little profit and started a small savings.

It rained very often and extreme care had to be taken to keep the papers dry. On those days I covered the bag carefully with the flap and placed each customer's paper behind their screen door.

There was plenty of thunder and lightning during the many rain storms I encountered trudging along between customer's homes on that long route, taking shelter under the nearest large tree I could find in the middle of no-man's land, not cognizant of the extreme danger of the affinity of lightning for trees. The good Lord spared me many times from injury or sudden death.

The crowning point of my paper route was a contest sponsored by the branch office manager,

Mr. James Fletcher, a raw-boned, thin, white gentleman. There were forty carriers and only one of color. For each new customer who took the paper for one week at twelve cents, the entire amount was mine. I went to work in earnest. I knew ninety-nine per cent of the blacks in Woodlawn and at the end of the week I had 102 subscribers, 66 new ones continued taking the paper. I, as well as the branch manager, was very well pleased. Most customers were well meaning and paid on time, but I had lots of trouble collecting from others. Mr. Walker, who worked for the Public Works Administration, was paid every two weeks and caused me many nights to walk four miles in absolute darkness to collect. He liked to read but was slow to pay.

His wife, Mrs. Rosie, was pleasant and felt sad for me. He would finally pay, when I could catch him. Rayford Jones, an ice man with six children, a stutterer and awful liar, owes me a goodly sum until this day.

Fortunately for me, the paper increased to sixteen cents a week and increased my earnings substantially. For the first time in life I accumulated a small bankroll. I really wanted to attend Tuskegee, but it wasn't nearly enough. I didn't have the insight or courage to find out the particulars for matriculation. I had been told by two of my life-long play and school mates now attending Miles that the initial registration and quarterly fee thereafter was thirty-five dollars. Their encouragement for me to follow suit brought forth a reevaluation of Booker T. Washington's dictum, from his book, *Up From Slavery*, "Cast down your bucket where you are."

I now began thinking seriously about Miles to prepare myself for a professional education of becoming a physician.

Chapter 20
Teenaged Numbers Runner

How do parents teach honesty and morality? By words or deeds, and at what age?

I could have been any type crook I chose to be if I had acquired the devious methods so prevalent in my home of scheming a livelihood without gainful employment during personality development in my preteen years. My younger years were spent trying to live down the shame from the constant stream of daily visitors in and out of our home buying whiskey and playing numbers.

I wondered what our neighbors were thinking, was I going to be a bootlegging, good-for-nothing individual when I became an adult, like my father? Or would I make something of myself?

I was taught to respect all adults, not sassing or being flip towards them, always greeting them with "good morning" or "good afternoon." All responded in kind, returning the greeting. I heard quite a few say, "He's such a mannerable boy, he's gonna make something out of himself." That could have been a rebuttal to the example engendered by my environment. It made me feel good to think someone thought there was something good in me.

It's hard to unlearn something you have lived, but I knew there was a better way to make a living than bootlegging and writing numbers. I knew what breaking the law meant and wanted no part of the criminal justice system to ruin my character.

Our neighbors knew Father was a sinister character. Summertime, during watermelon season when he was at the stand, his cursing and indifference told the whole story. His unstable gait and the sagging seat of his trousers accentuated his unstable emotional tirades. Pete Hardy, a playmate, called him "Loaded." I couldn't take it any longer so one day I told him Pete called him "Loaded." He ran Pete away with his customary bombastic cursing barrage. As is said in psychiatry, abused children always try to gain acceptance from an abusive parent, anything to calm that devil was worth a try.

What kinds of references did my peers hear from their parents about my home life? I wondered for sure. In the classroom I tried to excel to let my peers know there was some good in me so they wouldn't smear my mind with possible smut emanating from their parents. Their parents weren't living the type life prevalent in my home. Mother was also a victim.

As an example of dishonesty, I bought a package of cinnamon rolls, six for a dime. Upon opening them, a very large green fly was readily seen embedded in the icing. "Daddy, Daddy, there's a fly on this cinnamon roll.

Inspecting the contamination, his wheels started turning, blurting out his usual, "I be damned," fetched the slop jar, broke two slices of bread, threw them in, added some water to make it look like vomitus. I was told to get in bed and he would call the doctor. I hadn't eaten any of the rolls, mind you, but was ill in his thinking, seeing greenbacks, something for nothing. The doctor came, saw the fake vomitus, examined me and said I'd be all right. Father consulted his attorney the following Monday and told him our troubles. The attorney wrote the bakery and later Daddy received a settlement. I don't know how much, but it was something for nothing.

I saw a more severe act of dishonesty and chance taken by him. There was electricity in our home, the monthly light bill was cheap. A copper penny or a straightened hairpin placed in front of the fuse properly placed into the meter, slowed the registration of power. He removed the illegal gadget the morning the meter reader was to come. The meter was on the back porch. One morning he was almost caught red handed when the reader arrived just a he was hurriedly removing the hairpin. "What are you doing?" Father didn't reply and got away with that illegal act.

People often did those dangerous tricks at the risk of setting their homes on fire and destroying them.

Gambling and bootlegging were a way of life for many people in the community, even though they were illegal. Craps on a street corner, in a convenient alley or a home among friends was fairly widespread. Coon-Can, a popular card game, was also played in homes for money.

In addition to bootlegging, Father became involved in two gambling games, The Clearing House and Policy.

Just like an epidemic spreading through a community bringing on spells of sneezing, coughing, sore throat and aching muscles, causing much pain and suffering, the big question was, what kinda bug is going around? Our community had its own epidemic, the gambling bug, that struck daily. It was the 3rd, 4th and 5th numbers of the total thousands of bonds sold that day on the New York Stock Exchange, published in the pink sheet of the late edition of *The Birmingham News*. The numbers ranged from 000 to 999.

"What's the Bug today?" players wanted to know if they had caught one of their numbers. Those who were lucky enough to catch it were jubilant. Dream books were very important, as specific numbers were assigned to objects, people and happenings from a previous night's dream. An example, if one dreamed about clear water, the number was 123, 612 for spareribs and 527 for whiskey. A penny on a winning combination paid five dollars and a nickel paid twenty five dollars. Boxing meant turning the number around giving one six ways to win; it cost thirty cents. Boxed double numbers, like 330, only went three ways and cost fifteen cents. Either one could be boxed for a penny.

What a great Christmas present when Daddy heard 077 had hit the evening of December 24, 1937. It was Mr. Clarence White's number on which he had played fifteen cents daily for many months. Father couldn't wait for him to come by about 6:30 p.m. to give him the good news, imbibe a few shots of moonshine and play his numbers for the next day. Roosevelt McClendon was the pickup man. Mr. White and Daddy chatted jubilantly, awaiting Roosevelt, who worked for the Pullman Company and came by our home every night with the payouts. About 7:30 p.m. the welcome rap, rap, rap on the back door was music to their ears. Father jumped up and quickly opened the door, knowing it was Roosevelt with the $75.

"How are you, Mr. Witt?"

"Come on in."

He walked past Daddy and joined Mr. White eagerly awaiting his windfall. Roosevelt just sat down, showing no emotion. Daddy and Mr. White were observing him closely, awaiting the loot which didn't seem forthcoming. Finally Daddy volunteered, snapping, "Clarence hit 077 for $75, where's the money?"

"Sure 'nough, well, they didn't give me any money."

"You'd better go back and get it."

"I can't get it until Monday, Mr. Witt."

Daddy looked at Mr. White, then turned to Roosevelt, "Take off your overcoat, we'll hold it till Monday."

"It's freezing cold outside, Mr. Witt, please don't take my overcoat, it musta been overlooked. I'll get it Monday for sure."

In the meantime, Mr. White went home, got his silver barreled 38 Special and returned. "I want my money, Roosevelt."

"I know you do, but I just don't have it, Mr. White. I'll get it for you Monday."

I was observing the action from my seat behind the heater in the dining room, a little nervous, wondering what was going to happen. Mr. White didn't threaten Roosevelt with his gun and finally said, "Mr. Witt, give him his overcoat. I'll wait till Monday." I was relieved when he put his gun on the dining room table because I knew he was a mean man and could become very rambunctious.

Daddy gave Roosevelt his overcoat, who in his high-pitched tenor voice said, "Thank you, Mr. Witt, I'll get the money to you Monday."

That was undoubtedly the first time in history an overcoat was held hostage for an unpaid numbers hit. I heard the back door close and knew Roosevelt had left and was greatly relieved.

The payoff was consummated Monday. Daddy got his five per cent and Mr.White the remainder. Everybody was happy. He continued to play 077 to no avail until the vice officers closed down the numbers racket in Birmingham in the late thirties.

Roosevelt possessed a beautiful tenor voice and sang with the Pullman Jubilee singers, a magnificent group I heard quite a few times at my church.

In the summer of 1939, lady luck smiled on me once again. Eddie Osberry and L.T. Robinson, two lifelong friends who worked at the Merita Bakery, asked me if I'd like a job. I happily said yes and was hired at forty cents an hour, eight hours a day, unloading one hundred pound sacks of flour from a railroad box car. The temperature outside was over one hundred degrees and the humidity equally high. By noon, there wasn't a dry spot on my body. Fortunately, there was a cafe across the street where a large bowl of lima beans or black-eyed peas cost a nickel. I bought a bowl of each, needing the nutritional reinforcement to sustain the strength of a 130 pound late-adolescent.

After throwing off about twenty sacks, I jumped down and helped a veteran employee stack them to the ceiling. It was less hard but rugged enough.

Luckily, I received a promotion to go upstairs to sweep the floor where the ovens were going full speed. That was a snap. I ate dozens of vanilla wafers, salted crackers, cheese, cheese checks, marshmallow pies and a fruit mixture used to make fruit cakes. I didn't gain an ounce that summer, but increased my bankroll towards my college tuition.

A memorable incident happened one day when

I was asked to relieve a worker on the line extracting large pans of vanilla wafers from the huge, red hot oven. Donning a baker's apron, placing a pad in my left hand suspended from my wrist, I took a long, hooked rod by the handle and attempted to remove one. It flipped and struck the back of my left forearm, Mr. Earl, the boss, applied baking soda which slightly relieved the pain. A faint scar resembling the state of Alabama still remains. I enjoyed the sweet goodies of those old bakery days, but haven't eaten a vanilla wafer or a marshmallow pie for many, many years.

The great desire to become a doctor was still foremost in my mind. I had told my lifelong friend, Thelma Lyas, who graduated from the Meharry Medical College School of Nursing, that I wanted to become a doctor. She told me the requirements. First, I would have to complete my premed education, then apply to medical school. I took her advice and began to make plans to enroll in the premed program at Miles beginning in September 1939, reaching for my goal of becoming a doctor.

Things had not changed around our home, the bootlegging business was still in full swing and gambling was rampant throughout the community. The hub of both activities centered around 6218 Georgia Road.

The numbers games were most embarrassing for me. Father became the station man, that is, all of the writers brought their books to our home to be taken to the downtown headquarters. At the outset Daddy took them,. That was all right, but he became hot with the police suspecting him, so I was chosen for the job, an innocent and unsuspected teenager.

I also received the dubious duty of going to Father's players' homes, night and day, to write their numbers in a book the size of a store clerk's receipt book with a carbon to give the player a duplicate. We kept the original, taking it to headquarters for the day's action. I had to walk through our neighborhood where my school chums saw me daily, going to the same house feeling guilty and very ashamed, wondering what they thought. They knew something wrong was happening, passing within fifty yards of Grover C. Price's home, my school seat mate and Sunday school classmate, every day.

None of them ever asked me what I was doing and Lord knows, I never brought up that conversation.

One house I visited was in death alley, a section where dice games, card games, prostitution, bootlegging and quite a few fatal stabbings and shootings took place. I wrote numbers for the lady of the house and her husband. I wished to become invisible each time I entered the alley from First Avenue South, but had no fear of the alley cats who hung around there day and night. Neither she nor her husband took any mess from any of them. I knew they wouldn't let any of them bother me. The psychological trauma from my peers seeing me visiting those places was worrisome. In addition to the physical abuse to Mother and me by Father, that awful burden was added. Mother didn't like the way we were living, often telling him he should get a job and stop the rackets selling whiskey and writing numbers. It never fazed him.

I walked eight miles to Groveland every day, five days a week, to pick up the books from two women writers. I was unknown to the police but still was afraid of being arrested. It was such a long walk and I believed someone along the route was sure to draw dead aim on me and become suspicious that I was doing something too repetitiously and that it must be wrong. They were so right.

One morning two vice detectives knocked on our door. Father answered and, to his dreadful disdain, admitted them. Mother detected something was wrong and began clearing the dining room table of the gambling slips. Opening the door of the heater as the officers entered raised their ire because she was trying to destroy the evidence. Well, she didn't get all of them. Detective Goldstein gathered the remainder and announced, "Both of you are under arrest." I notified the operator of the numbers game just as soon as they left and he bailed them out.

When they went to trial, Mother was exonerated after the operator's attorney went to bat for her and said she had nothing to do with writing numbers. Father was fined $103, which was not paid by the numbers boss because so many writers had been arrested, the boss' money was depleted. Daddy was remanded to the city jail and worked on the street gang for one week until I gave Mother the money to free him.

Being abused verbally and physically many times apparently made me try to be accepted by Father, paying my hard-earned money from my paper route to get him released. To get revenge would have been to let him complete his sentence. Mother and his sister, Mary, went to the jail on the far south side, about 12 miles away, to get him. The three of them returned home a little past noon. He immediately started drinking and was soon loaded for bear. He began cursing, shouting and swearing, saying I shouldn't have given Mother the money to get him out. I was crushed because

I had worked so very hard to save that money to finally get into college after being out of high school for two years.

In more cases than not, children are taught honest work ethics at home, or by examples in the community. They learn early in life that work is an integral part of survival. From parental example, choices are mentally assimilated.

The vice squad officers were very, active and feared by me as I had seen Abe Goldstein and H. L. Darnell, two very tough detectives, arrest my parents for possession of illegal gambling materials and didn't want them to arrest me for any reason.

My character was almost blemished by Willie Jones, an elementary school classmate. Call him a pimp, stool pigeon or informant, he deserves it. He oiled the jaws of law enforcement to clamp down on me for something I didn't originate, but for which I was almost victimized.

One morning Father and Mother were in court to ascertain their fate after an arrest for possession of gambling paraphernalia. Willie came by as usual, played his numbers and left. I was in charge, in Daddy's absence, totaled the slips, minus the five per cent commission, resulting in a paltry but respectable sum of $3 during the depression, placed the slips in a coin envelope and prepared to leave. The three one dollar bills were new and crisp. I placed them and the rubber bound envelope in my right coat pocket. Leaving the house, I walked towards 62nd Street when a familiar sight, Car No. 5, which patrolled our area, appeared. When I saw it something told me to prepare to rid myself of that hot contraband. As the shiny black Birmingham Police Department car came abreast of me, I became very paranoid and made ready to seize the envelope and discard it. Officer V. W. Gore, the driver, began yelling, "Boy, don't throw that stuff away, don't you throw that stuff away." They knew who they were looking for, as Willie had given them a complete description of me. My first attempt to grasp the envelope failed as the three crisp dollar bills were loose and in the way. His admonition, "Boy, don't you throw that stuff away," kept ringing in my ears. The second attempt failed but divine intervention by my Lord and Savior, Jesus Christ, gave me the power and strength to grab the envelope on the third attempt, extend my right forearm and with quick reflex wrist action tossed it underneath the car. The Lord blacked out the officers' fixation on arresting me and relaxed the jaws of the law which were about to clamp down on me. They plainly saw me reaching into my pocket. The other officer, A. C. Sowell, alighted from the car, came around and instead of looking underneath, opened the back door and ordered me in. The package was plainly visible if he had looked.

As the Lord would have it, my fourteen-year-old sister and little brother were seated across Georgia Road on the steps of Mrs. Talley's home. She saw me throw something towards the police car from fifty feet away, dashed across the street, picked up the contraband, put it in her pocket and casually returned to the steps and sat down to wait for Mother and Father to exit the bus.

Instead of driving the car forward to see if anything had been thrown underneath, Officer Sowell got in and away we went to the house where he searched me and seized the three crisp dollar bills from my right coat pocket. "Where's that stuff, boy?"

"What stuff?"

"Them numbers, boy, you know what I mean."

"I don't have any numbers, sir. He looked at me for a few seconds and finally said, "We didn't catch you this time, but we will."

Chills ran all over me anticipating their leaving and returning to the spot where they stopped me, and finding the package that I threw under the car. They drove away in the opposite direction to Georgia Road and I heaved a huge sigh of relief. The month was July, very hot, humid and my anxiety level reached its peak from the heat. My nerves would have been much less flayed if I had known of the heady job done by sister. The package was secured in her pocket, but my nerves were shattered.

I escaped the embarrassment of having my wrists placed behind my back, bound by a pair of shiny steel handcuffs inscribed with B.P.D. (Birmingham Police Department), taken to the city jail, mugged and fingerprinted. My hopes of becoming a doctor would have vanished.

About thirty minutes after the near catastrophe of getting caught and arrested for racketeering, Mother and Father arrived. I nervously told them what had happened. Mother was livid and almost speechless but managed to softly utter, "How did you keep from getting caught?"

Father only had a deceitful grin on his face, all the time plotting the route I should take downtown with those near calamitous bets. He said, "Catch the bus, get off in Woodlawn, transfer to the downtown streetcar and, if you see any officers, raise the seat and dump it." As fate would have it, no one was on the streetcar. I felt free until I saw Abe Goldstein and Henry Darnell, two tough vice officers who had arrested my parents twice. I raised the seat in anticipation of dropping the package but they didn't see me, thank heaven. Going out 5th instead of 1st Avenue North, I made it safely downtown to the gambling connection.

The real threat to the ruination of my prospects for a career in medicine were the hideouts
and maneuvers designated to place the bets. There
were two fine pickup men with whom I became
acquainted; Slim, a six-foot-four young man in his
early thirties and an older man of forty-five, known
as Smitty, both all-business. Smitty, a little more
caustic, seemed hardened from trying to stay free
of being arrested for handling the numbers and
the vicissitudes of the depression years in general. Our rendezvous was in the vicinity of 17th
Street and Fourth Avenue North. Approaching either one, accepting the bets on the street in a very
swift manner and pocketing them was routine. If
the vice squad officers were in the vicinity they
signaled me with a twist of the head to keep walking. I'd go uptown, wasting thirty minutes to an
hour, or to Brock's Drug Store and have a malted
milk shake. At age 17, being "hot," that is, having
a pocketful of unlawful gambling material, was
threatening to me. I figured, as did Father and the
pickup men, that the officers were not suspicious
of me and maybe I would not be stopped and
searched. I always altered my route as a safety
measure. One day before reaching the corner of
17th Street and 4th Avenue, my blood curdled
when I noticed two plain-clothed detectives sitting
with the door on the passenger side open. I just
looked straight ahead and kept walking but
couldn't help wondering if they had suspected me
and would suddenly get out and say, "Hey, boy,
come here." All Negro males were "boys" in the
eyes of the law. Arriving at the corner, the light
fortunately was green and I kept on trucking. This
time the stash for the bets was a garbage can outside the back door of Nancy's Cafe in 3rd Alley off

of 17th Street. I walked to 18th Street and 4th Avenue, down 3rd Alley to the stash and deposited the cargo. Relieved of another clandestine mission, I walked to 17th Street and 1st Avenue and boarded the streetcar home. Another triumph, to the satisfaction of Father, as well as myself because I knew the danger associated with getting caught by the police and the consequences.

Another extremely dangerous spot to stash the bets was a garage, little used, located between 16th and 17th Streets and 4th Avenue. There was a very small, dark room just inside the main entrance. Inside the door was a shelf for the package to be placed. I could visualize a vice officer mugging me as I raised my arm to deposit the contraband, a handcuffing ceremony and jailing to follow. My squeaky clean record as a law-abiding citizen would be blighted forever. That was a scary, scary mission.

Mother never knew of the danger and couldn't have done anything about it anyway. I had been taking the stuff to town regularly and the possibility of becoming "hot," a suspect of the vice squad or their informants whom I didn't know, was very real.

Father asked Clara Johnson, a devoted numbers player, if she would take over carrying the numbers to town. She would receive five per cent of the weekly totals of the books. She was unemployed and accepted the offer. She was unknown to the police and the money would be a financial boost. She accompanied me downtown, chatting all the way about some of everything as we walked from the streetcar line to the stash. "Here it is," as I opened the door to that small pitch dark room, resembling a hole in the wall. Her mouth popped open, she couldn't speak. I thought she had had a stroke or heart attack. She was a dark-complexioned woman and her face seemed to have been splashed with a peck of white talcum powder, she was so pale. I showed her the shelf to place the books. She never uttered a sound until we were safely on the street.

She was still horrified when she said to me, "Everett," which she always called me, "I ain't coming down here no more. It's too dangerous, going into that dark place." She, like I, knew it was an ideal hideout for the cops. I was right back to square one, carrying out the shameful and extremely hazardous mission forced on me by my deceitful, scheming father.

Recurrent thoughts of the terror I felt of possibly being grabbed by a vice squad detective as I opened the door still haunt me.

Another numbers game called Policy was Father's newest venture. It was a spin-off from the old Japanese game, Keno, played in Las Vegas Casinos. The core and mainstay of Policy was the Gig, played by putting eighty numbered balls into a sack, from which twelve were drawn twice daily. Anyone having three of the twelve numbers drawn caught a Gig worth $11.50, for ten cents. If two of the three numbers played were pulled, it was called a saddle and paid fifty cents for the dime. Catching three numbers for a nickel paid $10, but no saddle. If you played two numbers for a nickel it was called a flat and paid $2.50 if drawn. ⁻

A stove pipe horse was a combination of five numbers costing a dollar and a half and paid $50 if you caught all of them. If you caught three you were paid $11.50, and two paid fifty cents as for a gig.

S. J. Burton was the policy writer and tickled me by pronouncing policy as "Polish-ey." I remember seeing him one very hot, humid July afternoon hobbling on his two wooden legs, cane and all, sweating profusely as he approached our home. When Father stepped out the back door, S.J. was grinning from ear to ear and smacking on a big wad of chewing gum while exclaiming, "Tom, did you have black man today? It fell out." Black man was 14-41-70, the number in the dream book players always consulted after dreaming of one.

Father answered snappily, "Hell no, I forgot it, did you have it?"

"Yes, I did."

"Did anybody else have it?"

"Annie Kate and Frank Erskine had it. You shoulda had it, Tom."

"Well, I slept it today."

S. J. picked up the evening numbers and happily waddled away.

Big Doc, the pickup man for the policy game, arranged for this particular nights' drawing to be held at the home of Mrs. Elsie River in our neighborhood. They were held all over town. The middle bedroom was the site of the purported fix. I was the tool. Standing outside of a raised window, I was to record the first three numbers into "The Book", tear out the slip, place it in an envelope and seal it. The date and amount of the tickets were prerecorded.

I was to rush into the house just before the drawing was over, out of breath, with the sealed manila envelope in hand, exclaiming excitedly to Big Doc, "I'm sorry I'm late."

The operator smelled the rat and refused to take "The Book." Big Doc's and Father's underhanded scheme, with me in the middle, went down the drain.

Although I knew it was wrong, at my young age, I had to go along with Father's orders and was relieved when that scheme fell through and there were no further attempts.

Chapter 21
Out In The Cold—Homeless And Jobless

A feeling of uneasiness always prevailed at home due to verbal outbursts from my drunken father. Family values were nil and not part of his relationship displayed towards mother and me. Often, for no apparent reason, false accusations would come forth. You'd be darned if you sat without uttering a sound and be darned if you just looked at him. His distorted mind reacted when he perceived you were condemning his drinking. *Why are you looking at me?* must have been his innermost thought.

Anyone could gather discarded, old creosoted cross ties for the price of removing them from alongside the railroad tracks. There were always a few by the fence outside our yard for firewood. If I were sitting in the house, he would order me out to chop them with our old dull axe. They were almost impossible to cut and the job was doubly hard under the broiling hot sun and extremely high humidity. I would whack away, hoping he would finally sober up, come out and say that's enough.

Mother suffered an even crueler fate, having to endure the cursing and emotional torment of being called useless. She was a tireless worker. I never dreamed, after many threats from him in the presence of Mother, he would put me out.

One night in early fall, his always present anger with me exploded. "Get out," placing me in a complete state of shock. What did he mean, where was I to go? There was no explanation from him nor any questions from me. Mother looked on in disbelief as I left slowly by way of the back door. My mind's eye turned immediately to the watermelon stand about fifty feet away. It was empty, as the season was just over, and the door wasn't locked. I had been in and out of it hundreds of times but never thought it would become my home. It was almost completely enclosed except for the upper part which was screened to the ceiling. After having slept on the davenport for the past eight years, stretching out on a bed of rough concrete covered with sawdust was hard to fathom. I tried to decide what course to take the next day as I had no money and no place in mind to go. It was a very scary situation for an inexperienced teenager to be homeless.

Flashbacks of the hoboes who came to our door during the depression for a handout invaded my thoughts. I lay there thinking, who would help me, a homeless, inexperienced teenager? I became very restless and decided to get up. I stumbled over a chair in the dark, striking the lower lid of my left eye on a sharp corner of the icebox receiving a one inch laceration, just missing my eyeball. I had a handkerchief in my pocket and applied pressure. Fortunately, it wasn't too deep and the bleeding stopped.

Around 10 p.m., I looked out and saw my cousin James Washington, whom we called Bunch. I called out to him, he came and I told him my troubles. We talked late into the night and he came up with the idea that we could hobo to Chicago. Despite his experience at hoboing, having been as far as Chattanooga, Tennessee, and several other cities in between, I wasn't impressed. "You remember Emmett Matthews got half of his foot cut off up there on Sixty-fifth Street catching a train. He was a good boxer like Joe Louis and coulda made lots of money."

Bunch listened and finally said, "Yeah, but he wasn't careful enough. Let's go, nothing's gonna happen."

"Who do you know when we get there?"

"Some first cousins. We'll find our way around."

"I have never hoboed and am too afraid to try," was my final reply.

We agreed that anything would be better than bunking on sawdust in the watermelon stand. He said, "O.K., you can stay at my house."

"All right, maybe I can stay with you all for a while until Daddy lets me come home." We talked ourselves to sleep. The next morning after Bunch went home, I decided to go into the house to see what kind of thinking was going on in Father's mind.

Both parents were up as I entered with my long, sad face, not saying a word and was greeted with the same silence until Mother saw the cut underneath my eye.

"What happened to your eye?" I told her and she said, "That's too bad," applied some Vaseline, then asked, "Are you hungry?"

"Yes, ma'am." She prepared some bacon, eggs and biscuits as Father sat silently in the big overstuffed barbers chair, where he always slept off his drunkenness. I finished eating, thanked her and prepared to leave. She asked where I was going. I quietly told her I was going to Aunt Mary's, but after walking out the door decided to go by Mrs. Clara Johnson's, who lived alone, and ask if I could stay with her because Daddy had put me out. I had known her since early childhood and went to her home daily to write her clearing house numbers for Father's gambling book. I tapped lightly on the door, she appeared surprised to see me so early in the morning. I told her Daddy had put me out. She looked a bit puzzled, "What did you do Everett?"

"Nothing, Miss Clara."

"He should be ashamed of his self, with this kinda carrying on. He's just that way with his dirty self, with this kind of carrying on. Go down and ask him if you can stay with me and if he says yes, it's O.K. with me."

"Yes ma'am," knowing good and well I wasn't going to confront him with any kind of request, especially that strange and unusual one. Turning towards the door, I said "Thanks, Miss Clara. I'll see you later."

I left and walked up the pathway, across the railroad tracks to Aunt Mary's. She greeted me at the door, "Good morning, come on in, Edwin."

I immediately said, "Aunt Mary, Daddy put me out and I have no place to stay."

Without hesitation she said, "You can stay here as long as you want to. Bunch told me that he spent the night with you last night in your daddy's stand."

"Yes, ma'am."

Aunt Mary, a wisp of a woman, not five feet tall but stern and fair, was a widow with five children, her youngest five and the oldest 18. She took in washing and ironing from rich whites and used smoothing irons heated by a charcoal fire in a bucket. There were pine needles on the end of the ironing board to cool the iron and smooth its surface before ironing white shirts and other very special clothing. Both daughters did day work for rich whites.

Aunt Mary visited us often and was fond of Mother, nicknaming her Cook. She ate dinner with us once in a while. She liked a little toddy, as she called moonshine, to relax her troubled, hard-working soul. Mother was good to her teenaged high school daughters, giving them dresses and jewelry and often took sister and me to visit them.

Food was very scarce in their household. They could hardly feed themselves during those depressed times, let alone a growing adolescent like me. The older daughter was slightly resentful, but the younger one, Cora, was happy for me to be sheltered and fed at their home. I slept with Bunch and his brother, Bo Diddly, whose given name was William.

That was the first time I'd had food placed on my plate, it was rationed so everyone could get a little bite. I got along very well at Aunt Mary's but the guilty feeling kept gnawing away to get a job and find another place to live to relieve the over-crowding.

One day a friend of mine told me I could get a job washing dishes for $5 a week at Drewry's Inn. I went over there and was hired, working 6 p.m. to 6 a.m. seven days a week. Drewry's Inn was a large green, hut-like building located on the corner of 60th Street and First Avenue North, the main thoroughfare from East Lake to downtown. Vehicular traffic was always heavy. The big Drewry's Ale and Beer sign was a natural magnet for travelers in need of a thirst quencher and food.

Surrounding the inn were numerous old, well-kept homes. Many large trees lined the streets. The neighborhood was lily-white.

The inn had an expansive kitchen, an 8' x 4' icebox full of cold beer and soft drinks, a huge brick pit for barbecuing large beef and pork shoulders. A rear storage room was stacked to the ceiling with hundreds of cases of Drewry's Ale and Beer.

A large circular serving center was out front with stools for seating and a dozen booths, each accommodating four to six customers.

That all white Inn was open 24 hours daily, specializing in barbecued beef and pork sandwiches. Milk, soft drinks, Planter's Peanuts, Hostess Cakes, candy, Drewry's Ale and Beer, from which the establishment got its name, were the main beverages. Mr.Sam Wood, a short, stocky, aging, grey-haired gentleman, was the owner. He was kind to me and said only a few words beyond, "Good morning," or "Good afternoon."

Mr. Payne was the sandwich man, Howard and William Mullins, Mrs. Mary Lewis, my acid-mouthed boss, and Miss Prather served the customers. There were three curb boys, young white adults, Lawrence Cason, Junior Bridges and Mayo Rickman. During my three months there I got to know them quite well as they were headquartered in the kitchen where they placed their orders, picked up and delivered them. We got along very well, laughing and joking quite a bit. I had had no close contact with whites my age, except Jo Jo Tombrello, whose father owned the neighborhood grocery store. Jo Jo played center field on the 62nd Street baseball team, I played right field. He was good.

I was the dishwasher and floor scrubber. There were hundreds of glasses and dishes to be washed, resulting with my developing a severe case of dishpan hands. The back of my hands were as thick as an elephant's hide and always sore. Vaseline at Aunt Mary's relieved the pain, but not the unsightly roughness.

The curb boys picked up the customer's debris, made good tips, but never shared them with me, despite the rule that I had to share in the glass losses, which were substantial as the customers on many occasions drove away with them. A large tip quelled the curb boys' displeasure. I complained about having to help pay for the missing and broken glasses, but management said the boys were accountable for any glasses I might inadvertently break by dropping a tray.

I got along well with all of the adults except Mrs. Mary, who couldn't help showing her racist colors and Alabama upbringing. One day in my presence she asked the laundry man who delivered the white uniforms if a"nigger" had ever worn any of them.

He said, "I don't know," the tone of his voice implying, what difference does it make?

She looked me in the eye and said, "Ed, you know I don't like niggers, don't ya?" I just walked away without uttering a word, feeling very hurt.

No racial slurs were ever expressed by any other employees; however, the first time I was blatantly called a nigger was early one morning when I went to the front counter to get the morning paper. Sitting there was a heavy set, beer-drinking, middle-aged white man. As I reached underneath the counter he angrily scowled, "Get back to that kitchen, nigger, you don't belong out here." I picked up the paper and returned, sat down and began reading, ignoring his remarks. No other employees were there to hear him, so no further problem arose. I didn't tell anyone about it until this day.

At age 17 life had put a double whammy on me. I had been kicked out of my birth home and working 6 p.m. to 6 a.m. Besides my racist female boss, I had to contend with orders from a creaky, peg-legged, rocking horse-gaited customer who arrived five mornings a week at 2:30 a.m. and decided upon entering if the floor needed scrubbing. From the kitchen I could hear that thunderous voiced employee of *The Birmingham News* hollering, "Where's Ed?"

When I heard that familiar voice I just automatically walked to the front, "How are you, Mr. Tunderberg?"

"I think the floor needs scrubbing."

"Yes, sir," I'd fetch the bucket and mop, prepare some hot sudsy water and go to work, while he sat at the counter smoking a cigarette and drinking hot coffee. I could feel his eyes critiquing every slosh across the floor and every squeeze of that boring old mop.

Three meals daily and a five dollar per week salary compensated me for that displeasure, because I needed a job. I was still living at Aunt Mary's.

I had heard a song in my church, an old slavery-time hymn, *I'm So Glad Troubles Don't Last Always*, and looked forward to becoming free of my troubles some day.

That racist waitress really got stung early one evening when Grover C. Price, Jr., a friend of mine, came in the front door as all whites did and gave her his order. The few blacks entered the back door. He was light-complexioned, with freckles, wearing a Lindbergh cap which covered his sandy, coarse hair. The flaps fastened underneath his chin covered most of his face. He looked white to her until she saw him wave at me. On closer observation, she decided he was a "yellow nigger." Her face really turned red as I observed the interaction between the two of them. I was standing slightly behind her as she seemed to swallow her tongue before being able to blurt out, "Next time you come in here, you'd better come to the back door."

Grover was a college junior and very bright. He retorted, "There will be no next time," as he turned and exited the front door.

I was laughing inwardly all the way to the kitchen as she turned to me. "Ed, tell that smart-alecky nigger the next time he comes in here he'd better come to that back door."

"Yes ma'am, Mrs. Mary."

I saw Grover a few days later and told him what she said. We laughed heartily, we knew the score.

My biggest triumph was the morning I helped the bakery goods delivery man, who was white, figure the bill for a large quantity of goods. I didn't think of myself as a high school graduate hot shot or smart aleck, but felt compassion and sympathy for him as he was having great difficulty trying to figure the bill. He and I were alone and I corrected the bill for him. After heartily thanking me, he collected his money and left. I never saw him again but felt gratified for doing a good deed for that day, despite my own plight of having been kicked out of my home.

Drewry's Inn was a popular stopping off place for the hordes of people on their way downtown to work or shop. Livening up cafes, ballrooms, bars and speak-easy homes with music was the introduction of the juke box. The Inn sounded like a real honky tonk joint every night. There was no dancing but country and cowboy western music lighted up many a lonesome, beer drinking soul. I was into the big band sounds of Count Basie, Duke Ellington, Benny Goodman and Fletcher Henderson, with their tender, sweet ballads and country music wasn't my bag.

I distinctly remember one hillbilly tune, "I Saw Your Face In The Moon," until this day it was played so often. It's a nice tune and goes like this:

I saw your face in the moon honey.
You chunked a smile at me.
You looked as if you were happy,
But in your eyes I could see
You were hiding from old bygones,
Places you and I once knew.
I could see your smile fading with the gloom.
When I saw your face in the moo-oo-oon,
When I saw your face in the moon, da, da, da, da.

I ate my meals at the Inn so Aunt Mary's family didn't have to share their food with me at that point. After three months on that job, someone told Father they saw me at the Inn. Out of guilt, I guess, he came over and pronto, ordered me to come with him. We walked home together and all he said along the way was, "I'm gonna give you a good whipping," and he did, soon as we reached the house. Just more abuse as far as I was concerned.

I was back in the same old dysfunctional home again.

Two blocks from the Inn was Wadley's Drug Store, where a tragic interracial murder occurred early one Sunday evening. The victim was James Kemp, a seventeen-year-old youth, who Father said was a distant cousin. They lived on the north side of Woodlawn and we on the south side. We never communicated, even though we were the same age.

The drug store was moderate in size, with a

beautiful soda fountain and stools for whites only. It was very professional in appearance with sliding glass-door-enclosed shelves of medicinals and a back room for dispensing prescriptions. Dr. Wadley was a slightly balding, past middle age, medium height, man with spectacles hanging from the tip of his nose. There was always a cigar dangling from his mouth, even when talking, making his speech garbled and grumbly. He paced the floor constantly. My family, as well as many other blacks, had their prescriptions filled there. Once I worked one-half day as a delivery boy before being fired for being too slow.

Trouble began to brew for the pharmacist when an elderly, shabbily dressed black man known as Brer Rabbit, who lived on the north side, ambled in appearing frightened. He was a wanderer, who always carried a stick in his right hand and a bag full of who-knows-what in his left. I saw him numerous times in our neighborhood but never said anything to him. Somehow, that evening he ran into James Kemp, who followed and irritated him. He rushed into Wadley's Drug Store and asked the pharmacist to stop James from bothering him. Dr. Wadley went to the back of the store, picked up his .45 automatic and came to the front door where James was standing. James saw the gun, turned and ran down the sidewalk towards the back door of the store. One shot was fired, striking him at the base of his skull. He dropped dead instantly by the back door.

Word spread quickly of the shooting. I ran immediately towards the store. Upon approaching the neighborhood mortuary, I was told the victim was there. I knew the mortician and asked to see the victim, as he was a distant cousin. He took me into the embalming room, removed the sheet covering James' face revealing nostrils filled with blood, indicating he had suffocated. It was a pitiful sight, another life snuffed out needlessly.

Dr. Wadley was acquitted of any wrong doing. Community blacks boycotted his store. We went to Shifflett's Pharmacy a mile away for our pharmaceutical needs thereafter.

Chapter 22
That Special Leather Belt

I'll bet my bottom dollar if I asked a dozen people if they had ever seen a "Jelly Belly", they would say yes, from observing protruding abdomens hanging below the belt many times. Some heard a funny tune of yesteryear, "It must be jelly, cause jam don't shake like that."

If I asked if they had ever seen a Lead Belly, they would say, no.

During early childhood, I heard of black belt champions, but didn't attach any great significance to the meaning. I became the owner of a very important new black belt given to me by Mr. Benny Hayes for Christmas. Mr. Hayes was a small man, an excellent tailor with stooped shoulders from years of bending over a sewing machine, slew-footed, very fair, with straight hair and could have passed for white. He worked for an exclusive white tailoring shop downtown.

He became fond of me during his nightly visits to our home for a couple of shots of 135-proof moonshine to relax himself. When out of his favorite Chesterfields, he bought cigarettes from me at a penny each, which I made from good old Ripple tobacco and rolled on my cigarette machine.

Sammy Lee Simmons was the only boy of four children in his family and a high school student when they moved to Woodlawn from Avondale, six miles away.

I saw him daily. He played first base on our baseball team and lived next door to Tombrello's grocery store where we traded. The Knight's of Pythias Lodge Hall was just across the street and was a favorite hangout for the unemployed teens of the neighborhood every day, except Sunday when most of us went to Sabbath school and eleven o'clock church services. We sat on the steps and kibitzed about everything from girls to sporting events and school.

Though it wasn't a topic for ridicule or praise, Douglas Truss, a round-shouldered, late teen, nicknamed Old Fess, did his spider act, sucking on a reefer cigarette butt held by a straight pin to keep from burning his lips. Marijuana cigarettes were referred to as reefers in those days and sold for thirty-five cents each. He sucked on that thing until it became invisible. I had no idea of its effects, just knew it was against the law to be caught with one.

I quit trying to smoke corn silk in a make-believe pipe which I made from an acorn shell with a long hollow pod inserted to make the pipe stem. Sam, Floyd and Harvey Holly smoked Camels, Lucky Strikes, Old Golds or Chesterfield cigarettes which sold for a penny each, unable to buy a pack for fifteen cents. Mother would have fanned me real good if she had smelled cigarette smoke in my clothes.

For many months Sammy Lee exhibited his lethal weapon. He undoubtedly had evil intentions, as it was common knowledge he would cut a piece of lead from a pipe, shave it to fit the barrel and place it into the end of a blank cartridge. The cartridge contained a wad of paper and gun powder. When fired, the gun projected a potentially lethal missile. He often drew it on whomever he came in contact, always exclaiming, "I'm gonna kill you, nigger!" Everyone tried to evade him but when face to face would say,"You better put that gun away before you shoot somebody." I was afraid of him as he was physically larger, older and stronger than I and the sight of that loaded gun terrified me. Knowing I couldn't wrest it from him for acting so stupid, I avoided him as much as possible. He always kept the hammer cocked, securing it with his thumb.

On several occasions when he pointed that ready-to-fire gun at me, I said, "Sam, take that gun offa me, it might go off."

He would just say, "I ain't never shot nobody yet, it ain't goin' off." All the while I was watching the precariousness of his thumb holding the hammer. Little did I know I'd be his first victim.

Just a few days later on a hot July afternoon, my deepest fears came to pass. While standing in front of me, gun in hand, suddenly like a clap of thunder, a loud "bam" rang from that gun. A cloud of black smoke emanated from the barrel. I cried out, "You shot me!" clutching my right side and bending forward. He stood there, stunned, not saying a word as I looked up at him. Immediately a contingent of our peers who heard the blast a few feet away from where they were perched on the lodge hall steps came rushing to me.

"What happened?" I heard one of them ask.

Another who saw me holding my right side, exclaimed, "Egg's been shot."

James "Spitty" Morgan, so named because he spat all the time (didn't chew gum or tobacco, just an acquired idiosyncrasy), accompanied me as I slowly ambled towards home, a block away. When we entered the back door, Mother was in the kitchen. She saw me holding my side and quickly asked, "What's the matter?"

"Sammy Lee shot me."

"I've told you about hanging around with those bad boys."

Father was in the dining room snoozing as usual to get rid of his ever-present hangover. He jumped to his feet after hearing me tell Mother I had been shot. "What happened?" he asked when he saw me bent over gripping my right side.

"Sammy Lee shot me."

"For what?" he retorted angrily.

"I don't know," as I unbuckled my belt and lowered my trousers, revealing where blood had stained my shirt a dark red, an area the size of a fifty cent piece. When I lowered my shorts oozing, dark red bubbly blood was visible at the point of entry of the missile.

Daddy said, "Let's go to Dr. Broughton," who lived about two blocks away. The four of us left on foot, Spitty disappeared en route. Soon we were joined by Sam's father, who had been told by his wife when he returned from work that Sammy Lee had shot the Witt boy.

Mr. Simmons caught up with us about half way to Dr. Broughton's asking: "Is he hurt bad?"

"We don't know," Father replied.

"I'm so sorry," he said, walking alongside Mother, Daddy and me. Neither of my parents expressed any anger towards him for what his son had done.

Mr. Simmons said, "I'll pay the doctor's bill."

When we arrived at the doctor's office, he wasn't in. There was a round, plastic clock on the door indicating that he would return at 7 p.m. It was 6 p.m. Father decided to take me to Dr. Kinkead, an excellent white physician who lived about five blocks across the line dividing the white and black neighborhoods. We had used him on a few occasions. He made house calls on many of our neighbors who spoke highly of him and Father liked him too. On our way home to get the car for the drive to Dr. Kinkead's home, I began to feel faint and very weak, almost collapsing from the shock of the gunshot wound. Mr. Simmons and Father assisted me while Mother looked on excitedly. We climbed into the car and drove to the doctor's home.

Father knocked, Mrs. Kinkead answered and said, "How are you, Thomas ?" She knew us well as she was a regular patron of our watermelon business.

"Edwin's been shot."

"Oh, that's too bad. Come on in."

She unlatched the door and crumpled-up me, assisted by Father and Mr. Simmons, entered the living room. By that time I was sweating, my mouth was dry and I felt like I was going to faint as I eased down on their beautiful couch. Dr. Kinkead came in, greeted us and asked Father what happened. "Mr. Simmons' son shot Edwin."

At that point I vomited all over the floor and really excited Mother who jumped to her feet, exclaiming, "Mrs. Kinkead, I'll clean the floor for you."

"Oh, no, that's all right. I'll take care of it."

Dr. Kinkead looked at the small oozing hole filled with frothy, dark red blood, felt my tender abdomen and decided the bullet didn't enter the abdominal cavity and injure any internal organs. He bandaged the wound and said he would come by our house the next day. Mr. Simmons told him he'd pay the bill and for all other care I might need.

We returned home, I eased into bed with assistance, where I remained for seven days. I got up and around slowly. On the tenth day when my parents took me to Dr. Kinkead's office, we entered and registered at the receptionist's desk, however, she promptly told us to go outside, have a seat in the hallway and wait until she called us. His white patients sat in the waiting room. Just another reminder of the deep-rooted policy of racial segregation.

Dr. Kinkead was a kind, gentle and caring person. At examination he said the wound was healing well and I could resume my normal activities.

Nine years later, I was taught in medical school that penetration of the abdomen by a bullet, knife or any penetrant below the seventh rib required an exploratory surgical procedure, that is, the abdomen should be opened to see if the intestines or the aorta, the largest artery of the body, had been ruptured. The outpouring of the intestinal bacteria, into the virginal peritoneal cavity, which houses the abdominal organs, causes peritonitis and death. There were no antibiotics in those days to combat such a virulent infection.

An X-ray of the abdomen was in order to locate the bullet and determine if any organs or blood vessels were damaged. I could be called Lead Belly because of that lead missile fired into it by a short, dark, burly, bluffing neighborhood bully named Sammy Lee Simmons.

To this day, when I get a study of my large intestines, X-rays reveal that missile encased in scar tissue in the right lower quadrant of my abdomen. Fortunately, I haven't had any complications from that foreign body.

Chapter 23
The Sign On The Wall: College Entrance

It is now June 1939, the end of my second year out of high school. My former classmates, Grover Price and Ducky Wilson are juniors at Miles College majoring in English and mathematics, respectively. There I was, in the same old rut, with no way in sight of going to Tuskegee Institute. My aspirations of becoming a doctor were on a tight hold.

Ducky and Grover had been proselytizing me regularly about going to Miles. It cost $35 to register and quarterly thereafter.

My dilemma was about to come to an end as I was trying to work it through. If I wanted to become a doctor, I'd better lower my far-reaching ambition of getting an education at some far away institution, follow the advice and patterns taken by my progressive schoolmates and attend Miles.

My paper route had provided me a sense of frugality, as I saved my little money and the nest egg was now large enough for a college beginning.

Late adolescence, I was 19, didn't afford me enough wisdom to exercise restraints in helping a friend when I entered Miles. Little did I know that an elementary and high school classmate, Ducky Wilson, would get me involved in a conspiracy to help a friend cheat on the math entrance exam, a requirement for all freshmen. An exam was also given in English. It could have ruined my chance of getting an education in pursuit of my dream to become a physician.

Ducky Wilson's father ran a grocery store on neighboring Oakridge Hill. Roosevelt (Pops) Davis, a life-long friend of ours, lived around the corner from the store and was a regular customer. Pops, fifteen years our senior, finished high school in 1927, had a job at Tennessee Coal, Iron and Railroad Company and lived with an older sister in their deceased parent's neat, small, shotgun house. He bought a new Buick every other year and waved at me when be passed our house on many occasions. I spoke to him quite a few times when I visited Uncle Sandy, who lived across the street, but never had any conversations with him. Pops knew Ducky was at Miles and told him he would like to begin attending, even though it had been a long time since he finished high school and might be a little rusty handling the books.

"Great, I'm sure you'll get in the groove once you start."

"How much does it cost?" Pops inquired.

"Thirty-five dollars to register and each quarter thereafter."

"That's not bad. When do classes begin?"

"September First."

That rang a bell in Ducky's head. He knew I was at last planning to enroll at Miles, as was Walter Jones, another friend. Since Pops had a new car, a ride with him would obviate our having to take the streetcar 30 miles to and from school.

Pops developed a fantasy that if he went to

college, a halo would glow around him and his beautiful car, then he could crash the "Circle," so-called members of the elite society, school teachers and other professionals.

Later Pops told Ducky he was going to enroll and Ducky said, "Walter and E. T., the Witt boy, are going to enroll, too, and we can ride together." Ducky knew Pops wasn't a good student from news circulated in the community by his former school chums and asked Walter and me to help him with the math entrance exam. The strategy was for Walter to sit in front of Pops and me behind him. Preliminary to the test Mr. Shepard, the monitor, gave each individual the list of questions and a yellow sheet of scratch paper for calculations, with the stipulation it had to be turned in with the completed exam, no exceptions. I didn't find the exam too difficult and casually glanced over Pops' right shoulder. His wheels weren't turning well, his paper clear as the palm of my hands. I tried, stealthily, to show him my paper, but he ignored my generosity. Walter sneaked a look backwards and saw what I had seen, no progress. Ducky, Walter and I had come to the conclusion before the exam that Walter and I would try to help him in any way we could. Since he wouldn't copy and Walter was in clear view of the monitor, I decided the best way to help was to switch papers and write his exam. Since the monitor didn't know us, when time was up we didn't exchange papers so as not to arouse any suspicion of collusion. I wrote Pops' exam with his name on it, of course.

Mr. Shepard finally announced time was up.

All was well and good except for Pops' feeling of guilt, as he arose slowly and let me precede him. I handed Mr. Shepard Pops' paper and the yellow sheet full of calculations. Suddenly, it seemed like lightning had struck a pine when Pops handed Mr. Shepard my exam paper and no scratch sheet, which he held crumpled in his left hand, void of any calculations. The professor said, "Mr. Witt, where's the scratch sheet?"

Pops spoke softly, "My name is Roosevelt Davis."

"What are you doing with Mr. Witt's paper?"

Mr. Shepard couldn't believe what he was seeing or hearing, beginning to look bewildered as Pops volunteered, "I'm a little rusty in this sort of thing."

I listened nervously to the exchange as my feathers fell. Mr. Shepard was speechless as Pops and I left the room, realizing I was in serious trouble for using poor judgment in my first affair of this kind. Pops, Walter and I met Ducky at the door, the instigator of this hookup, for a convenient ride to Miles.

"How did everything go?" Ducky asked. I told him what happened.

"That's too bad, but I believe everything will be all right, E.T." I was too shaken to respond. Upon arriving home I didn't tell Mother or Father what happened.

The Director of Instruction and the Professors of Mathematics and Biology had an urgent meeting. Nothing like that had happened in any of their experiences, therefore, their decision would set a precedent. The monitor explained to the committee members what happened and immediately a unanimous decision was made to deny my admission to the college, until fortunately for me, one member reconsidered. "That Witt fellow seems to be very bright, maybe we should modify our decision; he might help humanity someday."

After further discussion, another one suggested, "Let's have him take sub-freshman math with the five he caused to fail by raising Mr. Davis' score." The members agreed.

Well, the next morning the four of us returned and went to the auditorium. The first order of business was the monitor's request to see Mr. Davis and Mr. Witt. We arose and went to the Director of Instruction's office to face the committee.

"Mr. Witt, what happened?" the chairman asked. I told them I wrote Mr. Davis' paper and was sorry. "That's very unfortunate. We were supposed to refuse you admission to the college, but decided after reviewing your exam to have you take sub-freshman math for one quarter, for which you will not receive any credit. You caused five other participants, who would have passed, to fail by raising Mr. Davis' score." Thanking the members of the committee, we left for home, I felt very depressed. I told my "friends" I wasn't going to enroll. I didn't discuss my plight with my parents, they wouldn't have understood as I wasn't encouraged to go to college by them anyway. My companions encouraged me to go along with the decision. I listened, however, the only thing that really caused me to accept the committee's decision was that huge sign on the wall in college colors, purple and gold, "FEES PAID TO THE COLLEGE WILL NOT BE REFUNDED." I had worked too hard for that thirty-five dollars to forfeit it. I began taking 12 units plus sub-freshman math with 20 others and after two weeks became the teacher. After fulfilling my penalty, I began taking 15 units, a standard load, increased it to 18 and ended up taking 20.

My rusty academic friend, Pops, registered and continued to work at the steel mill from 3 p.m. to 11 p.m. five days a week. His college days soon ended, not lasting a month.

Miles Memorial College, named for its first president, Bishop James A. Miles, began its efforts dating back to 1898 by the Colored Methodist Episcopal (C.M.E.) Church, located in Vinesville, Alabama, six miles west of downtown Birmingham, as a two year non-denominational teacher's training college.

In 1939 when I entered, it was a four year Liberal Arts College with just over a hundred students, offering Bachelor of Arts degrees in Mathematics, English, Chemistry, Biology, History, Education and General Science.

Dr. William A. Bell, President, was a native of Atlanta, Georgia. He was a little past middle age, mulatto complexioned, slightly stout, an eloquent speaker and administrator, who loved the institution. Our accreditation ranged from A to B and B to A. He was one hundred per cent anti-smoking and didn't allow it anywhere on campus.

Leaving the quiet, ordinary but neat, Vinesville residential area and focusing beyond Avenue H, acres of tall pine trees nestling two moderately large red brick buildings, home of Miles College, came into view.

The Administration Building, largest of three red brick structures on campus, housed his office, the Director of Instruction's office—there was no dean—and classrooms for History, Sociology and English. In the basement were classrooms for Music, Education and the laboratories for Physics, Chemistry and Biology.

The red brick, two story, girl's dormitory and Home Economics department were west of the administration building. The single story, old Welch's mortuary science building, on the east side down a hundred yard paved walkway, served as the Physical Education lecture hall and dressing room for the football teams.

There was no dormitory for boys. The few who were from out of town roomed with families in the neighborhood.

A wide sidewalk with lush green grass on either side led to the steps at the entrance of the Administration Building and was flanked at the top by two large pillars on the porch leading into the foyer. A half circle driveway of red clay covered with crushed rocks, bordered by green grass and very tall pine trees, made an impressive approach to the campus.

Behind the buildings was a huge grove of pine trees and a large athletic field where the Golden Bears, our football team, played their home games. There was no gym. Softball was the only activity in which the physical education class engaged.

The ride from Woodlawn with Pops didn't last long and many were the days I exited streetcar No. 30, at the end of the line in Vinesville, Alabama, six miles from downtown Birmingham, then began a foot job, three blocks to 55th Street, left up a gradual one mile incline, passing many nice neighborhood homes, Stephen's Cleaners and Montgomery's Grocery Store, one block off the route, finally reaching Avenue H and the entrance to the college.

Fairfield, Alabama, contiguous to Vinesville, with a population of 14,000, one third black, and seat of the city and county government, began at 60th Street. Tennessee Coal and Iron Company (T.C.L to the community) was the main industry, hiring many blacks who lived in both locales. Acres and acres of tall pine trees surrounded the vicinities.

The faculty was excellent. Mr. Marion E. Zealey,

Director of Instruction, and my premed major professor, was a very nice energetic gentleman. He was an alumnus of the University of Minnesota with a Master of Science degree. There was no official designation of Dean at the college, so when we attempted to call him Dean Zealey, as he was acting in that capacity, he thwarted our efforts defiantly by retorting in a somewhat sour tone, "I'm not the Dean, just the Director of Instruction." He didn't resent our calling him Prof, which we did always.

He depended on me for the smooth running of the class; chemicals on the tables, beakers and test tubes out of the cabinets was my daily assignment. When things were in disarray he would say, "Mr. Witt." I'd look around and get things in order, pronto.

I was made very unhappy one day when he asked, "Where are the tongs used to hold the test tubes?"

"I think," and before I could finish my reply, he snappily and slightly belligerently spurted, "With what?" Fortunately I forgot about that insult and never encountered that type remark again.

I declared my major to be premed. Mr. Zealey was an excellent teacher and very interested in the 10 premed students, himself having been a premed major.

We sashayed around the chemistry lab proudly in our long white coats, addressing each other as doctor. There were four young ladies taking chemistry to satisfy their science major requirements.

Among us was Robert (Bay Bay) Coar, a veteran health coordinator for the Jefferson County Health Department and a former mortician until his uncle went out of business. He decided he wanted to study at Meharry Medical College in

Nashville, Tennessee, and become a doctor. He worked with many black physicians at Slossfield Health Center, a county facility, who were graduates of Howard University in Washington, D. C.and Meharry. They were the only medical schools blacks could attend after Leonard Medical School, an affiliate of Shaw University of Raleigh, North Carolina, closed in 1910. The University is still operative.

Bay Bay was impressed by them and their work and engaged in conversations about becoming a doctor. He often spoke of how they said, "Them niggers at Meharry study in groups of six to eight to master that medical curriculum." College to this point had not been too difficult for me; my eyebrows raised, as that was where I planned to matriculate. Little did I know in the ensuing years I, too, would study in groups.

In premed I took three years of chemistry, inorganic, organic, qualitative and quantitative analysis. Qualitative analysis was interesting when we weighed substances to be analyzed. The scale was gold plated, the weighing pan the size of a silver dollar.

To see Professor Zealey dust the pan with a small brush, despite the fact it was kept in an enclosed cabinet under lock and key, was interesting to me.

When producing oxygen, rubber tubing was connected to the flask which contained the chemicals and placed outside a large, open window because of its explosiveness. Prof Zealey did that experiment himself.

Exams in college were a new experience for me. The professor passed each student a blue book where the answers to the exam were to be written. It cost fifteen cents. I guess the color blue was chosen because of the symbolism with the way you'd feel if your input between its binds was less than satisfactory.

The most shocking question of our initial chemistry exam was, "Who is the author of the textbook used in this course?" I, along with everyone else, was baffled, looking around the room at each other as if the answer were floating about somewhere in space. No one answered that question, but were ready for the others.

Mr. Shepard, my biology teacher, an alumnus of the University of Kansas in Lawrence was a fine gentleman, a few years this side of middle age. He told me he taught his course just like Histology and Embryology, were taught at Meharry. That was music to my ears, as I was trying to prepare myself to attend that institution when I graduated from Miles.

I worked very hard in the laboratory, dissecting a fetal pig and a frog, outlining all systems. I began to think I was on my way preparing to study medicine.

The Department of Religion was chaired by Reverend James McKenzie. He was short, stocky, very fair with straight hair, past middle age with heavy, slightly garbled speech. He was a divine Christian gentleman of the cloth and pastored a Colored Methodist Episcopal Church in the surrounding community of Fairfield. The devils in my class always prefaced their prayers with, "Dear Lord, bless Rev. McKenzie," that meant an "A" in the course. The course lasted one quarter. Religions of the world, Shintoism, Buddhism, Hinduism, Catholicism and Christianity were studied.

Physical education was taught by Dr. T. J. Knox, all-American linesman from prestigious Talledega College, a four year Liberal Arts school

52 miles north of Birmingham. He was coach of the Golden Bears and a registered pharmacist, working nights at Temple Pharmacy on 17th Street and 4th Avenue. Yesteryear's pharmacy graduates received PhC degrees, Doctor of Pharmaceutical Chemistry, and were called doctor, but not so today.

Classroom work consisted of lectures about the fundamentals of tennis, golf, basketball and football.

The library was on the second floor of the Administration Building. There were many periodicals, reference books, novels and encyclopedias. Periodically I had to use the reference books for a report. I never had time to go sit, study or just do some extra reading.

Mrs. Mae Shepard was librarian, a very sweet, fair complexioned, middle aged, average height woman. She received her Master of Science degree in Library Science from the University of Kansas.

The English Department was strong with Miss Carrie C. Robinson from Langston University, Marshall, Texas, as chairman and Miss Eugenia Perkins from Stowe Teachers College, Washington, D. C., and Miss Mary Mollette as assistant professors. Grammar, composition, English and American Literature were the courses taught.

Miss Robinson, a beautiful, light brown skinned lady, had a magnificent soprano voice. She and Dr. Long, our Sociology teacher, harmonized melodiously. I thought they were second to no one, including Jeanette McDonald and Nelson Eddy. I was deeply moved when they sang, *Make Believe* by Jerome Kern.

The Department of History was chaired by Mr. James Regan, who taught Ancient, American and

European History in a very interesting manner.

Mr. Russell Ragland of Iowa University taught math, commercial algebra, trigonometry, calculus and the theory of equations for math majors. He organized a group of students in the commercial algebra class to form a bank. We loaned money to students at 10 per cent interest per week. A few of the students borrowed up to a dollar and never paid their loans. It was fun.

Sociology was taught by one of our two PhD's, Dr. William Long, a graduate of Miles and Indiana University. He was a local poor lad, living with his grandmother two blocks from the college, working his way. Students got a bang out of him, his being Southern, returning to Miles calling text books, "tech" books. We laughed behind his back. He was an excellent teacher, and had a magnificent deep baritone voice, appearing on stage occasionally. He sang *Old Man River* and *Go Down Moses* to perfection. They were my favorites.

Our other PhD was Dr. Gordon West from Kansas University. He headed the Education Department. My most memorable concept of education was his love for the theory, "Education is Life," by John Dewey.

He sponsored the Education Club, which met monthly and bought and sold candy at Saturday football games. I was one of the super salespersons.

Mrs. Jane West, his wife, was the teacher training professor. She was short, stout and a very strict lady, according to her students.

French was the only foreign language offered. All students were required to take one year. Miss Jean Chandler from South Carolina State College was an excellent teacher. I haven't forgotten all I learned in her class and on a few occasions find friends to check my competence.

Our choir was well trained by Mrs. Gregory Durr White, a stout, moderately tall, brown skinned lady who could really play the piano. There were thirty to fifty members in the choir. I was never a member but enjoyed hearing them practice as they rehearsed in the basement of the Administration Building next to the room where my class in Education was held. They presented programs for the student body during the school year.

Mrs. Edith Tate Jones, a fair skinned, heavy set lady, taught typing and home economics and was all business. The expression, "rough on rats" fit her well, according to her students. There were no vocational trades for males.

During the depression days of 1939, the Federal Government passed legislation initiating an aid program for needy students, called the N. Y. A. (National Youth Administration). It paid $30 a month for a job assigned by the college. I couldn't have gotten a worse job as a prisoner. I was given the job of sweeping the biology classroom concrete floor. The cloud of dust was so thick I couldn't see across the room, in a basement with four large windows which only opened at the bottom. The dust settled on desks, walls, blackboards and onto the floor from which it ascended. The most important concern should have been for my respiratory tract which I am sure suffered immensely. It could have been laden with every pathogen known to man. My respiratory tract had to work overtime, for sure. Fortunately, I survived that serious threat to my physical well-being.

Things began to beam brightly for me when I became a member of the freshman debating team. There was an annual competition between the freshmen and sophomore teams. In twenty years of competition, the freshmen had never won. Teaming with classmate Cora Wimbush, we won, to the surprise of the student body. I really enlivened the audience during my speech when I attempted to rhyme Naziism with Fascism and said, "Naziism" and "Fatzi-ism." The roaring laughter was deafening.

I appeared in many plays, recited poems and appeared on stage for programs throughout my college years.

Students assembled in the moderately sized auditorium with a small balcony three times weekly for convocation, plays, educational and musical programs and information regarding the status of the college by President Bell.

Speakers from out-of-state black colleges and universities graced our stage with inspiring messages. The most notable quotation that I had ever heard was given during a speech by Dr. Benjamin E. Mayes, President of Morehouse College, Atlanta, Georgia. "Squeeze all the juice from the intellectual orange." There is plenty of far-reaching thought and application from that sage advice for anyone trying to educate oneself in order to succeed in life.

In the summer I delivered the papers myself, but during the school year I had to have help some days when I remained to practice for a play or chapel program. I paid Jack Whitlow, a ten year old, $2 a week to throw them for me. He was very undependable. His single, sickly mother tried to jack him up, but to no avail. I returned home on a few occasions during the winter months and had 102 papers to deliver. It was exasperating. I guess my customers forgave me as I didn't receive any flack or cancellations for lateness. I knew a change had to be made. Edward Patterson, about 12 years of age, was dependable and a valuable replacement. I never had any worries after hiring him, paying him $3 per week.

I was in my sophomore year when the United States declared war against Japan, December 7th, 1941, and was 20 years of age. The first draft for military service in 1940 was for young men 21-45. The second draft was for those who became 21 after December 7th. I became 21 one month later and registered. The draft board's ruling was for deferments of college students in premed programs, math and science majors, if their grades were satisfactory. The dean of the college, in my case, the Director of Instruction, forwarded my grades to the draft board quarterly, as Miles was on the quarter system. Fortunately, my grades were good.

I was half way into my sophomore year when another form of emotional abuse from Father came forth. He instructed Mother to tell me I had to pay $2 a week for room and board. That shocked her for she knew what a struggle I was having paying tuition, transportation, books and school supplies and now this. Being hurt deeply once again, she had no alternative. The paper route was my main source of income plus the small stipend I received from the college for cleaning a classroom. I began paying the $2 weekly and gave the first payment to him. Because of his extreme guilt, when I attempted to pay him next time he said, "Give it to your mama." Some weeks I'd come up short with so many customers not paying on time, she would give me the $2 from barbecue and whiskey sales to keep down his rage. I'd make sure he saw me give it to her, because on several occasions he asked her if I had paid. I survived this emotional trauma only because of the help I received from her.

My romantic feelings were now more mature, the territory looked more robust and inviting; however, the first quarter was spent with my mind primarily set on getting out of the sub-freshman math class.

The 35-minute trip from downtown Birmingham to Miles offered me an opportunity to sit next to the coeds, talk and attempt to make an impression on them. We talked about our aspirations and desires, filling time pleasantly and meaningfully.

The 20-minute walk uphill from the car line gave us an opportunity to sound each other down, a courtship cliche.

I finally decided to make a play for Friendly Mae Oliver, her given name, with beautiful big brown eyes, short, shapely and an interesting conversationalist. We became an "item." Many a courtship was begun on the steps of the Administration Building where big pillars adorned each side of the dozen steps leading to the foyer. We made this one of our courting places.

The campus was surrounded by very tall beautiful pine trees and strolling among the shady whispering pines down the rolling, lush green hills was a favorite pastime for young lovers like us.

I didn't have a car, but streetcars were cheap and convenient. I could go from my house to hers and return for eighteen cents. We attended school affairs and football games that way, also.

Things went well for us and we were inseparable for about a year when along came a matronly but very glamorous married woman, who, after a few weeks, latched onto me as we had several classes together. She entered Miles to take some science courses required to enter a school of Pharmacy.

Sally Newton and I became very friendly and

going home after school we'd walk to the streetcar line and sit together. Our adopted theme song featured by Glenn Miller's band, *At Last My Love Has Come Along*, made her fantasize, truthfully or untruthfully, that we would get married when I graduated from medical school. That was false because she was already married. I was single and didn't really have my mind on marrying anyone and surely didn't want to ruin my reputation forming a triangle.

Occasionally on Saturday night she took the streetcar from downtown to Woodlawn where I'd meet her. She held a newspaper in front of her face to keep from being recognized. I introduced her to my parents, not telling them she was married. We sat on the davenport, talked, hugged and kissed. One Saturday night I suggested we get physical, she exploded, "You old heel, I'm through with you." It was near graduation and I wasn't needed anymore to assist with her heavy academic load.

I walked with her to the streetcar line, that was all for us.

A short while before our breakup, she and I were walking to the streetcar line from school side by side and Friendly Mae suddenly appeared out of nowhere, grabbed my left arm and swung me around. I froze, not knowing what to do. Friendly screamed loudly, "Come on and leave the married woman alone." I didn't say a word. Sally turned red as a beet. The three of us walked on, boarded the streetcar, sat together all uptight and uttered not a single word. I was relieved when Sally exited and a few blocks later Friendly Mae left, but not without rolling those big eyes at me.

Afterwards at school I failed to convince her that I wasn't in love with Sally and we slowly drifted apart. I decided to pick up the pieces and get on with my life.

Later I became friendly with Ernestine Moseley, a real charmer who lived in Kingston not far from Woodlawn. We rode the same streetcar. One day I asked her for a date. She accepted and we went steady until I graduated from Miles and left Birmingham for medical school in Nashville. Afterward our romance dimmed as time went by and slowly sank like the setting sun into the deep fading western horizon.

Miles is a sister Methodist school to all-white Birmingham Southern College, located in Wylam, Alabama, about fifteen miles away. One day the Dean of Religion was our assembly speaker and spoke very eloquently. To top off his visit he invited the student body to come over to his school for a picnic. We were startled, living in separatist Birmingham, but accepted, readily believing we could soften racial tensions somewhat and help make Birmingham a better place for all people to live in harmony. The Dean returned to his school and informed his student body at an assembly of our accepting his invitation to visit their campus for an all day get acquainted picnic. I don't know how the student body as a whole took it, but a young lady who wrote for the campus newspaper published it. Guess the name of the newspaper— it was *The Tattler*, how ironic.

Unfortunately, one of the students took the paper home and her mother read it. Well, as things go, *The Tattler* really did its job, blowing that mother right out of her prejudiced mind. She immediately called the President and asked him what he meant, inviting those "niggers" from Miles college to Birmingham Southern to socialize with her daughter. She was so adamant the President asked the dean the nature of the complaint. The dean told him and he was non-committal.

Dumbfounded and not knowing what to do, the Dean lingered with his dilemma as long as he could before calling Dr. William A. Bell, apprising him of the woman's anger. Aware of the racial climate in Birmingham, our president thanked him and called off the visit to prevent any further repercussions. He thanked President Bell and asked for a return visit to express his sorrow for the incident. He gave a very conciliatory, compassionate speech on "Why we love and why we hate," a beautiful message, indeed, graciously accepted by our president and the student body and the avoidance of further embarrassment was averted.

One night a friend of mine and I took two coeds to a school dance at the Owl's Night Club downtown. We were frolicking around, not drinking, when a fellow Milean, Mark Smith, solicited by a dining car waiter, dropped by about 12:30 a.m. looking for an additional person to replace two waiters missing from an L & N Railroad dining car. The train was leaving at 1.30 a.m. Even though the job was to be for only one trip, I accepted and asked a friend to escort my girlfriend home. She understood my plight as I hurriedly left the dance hall with Mark and the waiter. I didn't have any way of informing my parents, as we had no telephone. We went to the station, boarded the train where I bedded down on six dining room chairs, as did the regular waiters, and shortly was on my way to Mobile, Alabama, 265 miles away. After breakfast the next morning I was to be given a return ticket.

Upon arriving in Mobile, I immediately sent Mother a telegram, telling her I had gotten a job as a dining car waiter. By that time I'm sure she had grayed considerably and was almost out of her mind, knowing I had gone to a dance, and was about to call the police notifying them of my disappearance. After receiving the telegram, all was well.

I had no experience waiting tables, but bussed dishes at the Britling Cafeteria downtown for two weeks one summer. All the waiters tried to help me, telling me how and what to do, and especially not to go flying through the window holding a tray as the train swung around one of the many deep curves en route to Mobile. I tried to be careful and do my very best, as I needed the job.

There were eight stations. I was given station one, it was closest to the kitchen. In talking to one of the waiters who had been on the job for 25 years, I told him I was a senior in college. That really rang a bell with him as he had always wanted to go to college, but his family was too poor to afford him such an education. He told me he would ask the steward to keep me all summer to earn much-needed extra money for school. He did, and the steward said he would give me a chance. I was thrilled, but had much anxiety as to how I could adapt to becoming an efficient waiter.

Like a shepherd watching his sheep, seven veteran waiters watched my every move carefully, but no critical comments of the many mistakes a greenhorn waiter, like me, was sure to make. They saved their laughter until old flat-footed, loud mouthed chef, Melvin Jenkins from Louisville, announced, "Come get your rails." Everyone was sitting and relaxing after serving dinner. I looked perplexed when the veterans began to sniggle, as one by one, they made their way to the kitchen. I wondered what a rail was, not the ones on which the train was traveling. The chef laughed, looking at me, "Hey, school boy, come get your rail." To clear my head about what he meant, Fred Saffold from Montgomery, Alabama, smiled and said, "Fool, go get your dinner." All the waiters were now breaking up with laughter. I went to the kitchen, got my "rail," carried it to my station, sat down and enjoyed a delightful meal. I never suffered from missed meal colic the entire summer on the diner.

The dining car lingo tickled me. The chef is the big man in the kitchen and greeted by the waiters with "Hello, chef." He answers, "Hello." The order number is given and how it is to be prepared. Old chef repeats it and goes to work. I finally got the hang of it.

I almost met my Waterloo early one morning when the engineer almost failed to see the open draw bridge over Biloxi Bay in Mississippi as we headed for New Orleans, 75 miles away. I was in a deep sleep when the six chairs on which I was sleeping suddenly scattered in complete disarray, slamming me against the wall. The screeching of the wheels and the violent sound of hundreds of dishes and glasses crashing, pots and pans banging loudly, found me sitting on the floor wondering what was happening. I didn't learn about the near catastrophe until later, being informed by the conductor as he passed through the diner. I picked myself up, dressed and went to the kitchen to help clean up the mess.

That was a narrow escape, indeed. Biloxi Bay is very deep and wide.

Everyone on the dining car had a job to do. There was the pantry man, linen man, salad man and silver man. I was the pantry "mule," scrubbing the kitchen floor and racks three times daily. It was quite lonely every day after the meal had been served, to be alone in the kitchen sloshing the mop through a sea of soapy water, scrubbing the racks and floor until they were spotless. I did that job until I was promoted to pantry man. I had never made a salad in my life, nor had I seen one made until I observed the pantry man, shredding cabbage, adding pickle relish, salt and pepper, so that's what I did. After each bowl was returned, I carefully checked to see if it had been eaten. The news was good, ninety-nine per cent of it disappeared and I was happy. Guess hungry people will eat anything.

I soon began to order ice cream and other supplies and gave the crew all the leftover ice cream they could eat and threw many gallons into Biloxi Bay to keep it from melting. I plastered my coronary arteries with fat from gorging it also.

My first misfortune on the job occurred one night after we arrived in New Orleans and quartered at the Page Hotel. After settling in my room I prepared to take a shower, placed my new Bulova wrist watch on the dressing table, undressed and stepped into the shower stall. A fellow waiter named Wheeler, whom I had just met, was in a connecting room with the door open. Upon returning, the table caught my eye; the watch was missing. Luckily, I didn't place any money there. The disappearance of my watch really shook me up frantically calling out to him, "Wheeler, did you see a watch on the dressing table."

"No, I didn't."

I was so shaken my lips were quivering, face flushed and I was in a state of almost total shock. I had no further conversation with him, being a 21-year-old greenhorn. We worked together all summer, my watch gone forever. I knew not where, but harbored a strong suspicion.

My much needed job almost ended before I got

started. A veteran yard man in New Orleans always came onto the diner visiting the crew. We became friendly and one day he asked if I'd give him some butter. Just as I handed him the package, up popped the steward, Mr. Jackson, a growling, fat, mean man, who was notorious for firing waiters on the spot for any infraction. "Hit the ground," was his motto. He and the yard man looked bewildered, and I was perplexed. He was in a good mood that morning and didn't fire me. I never did anything like that again and finished the summer financially enriched and wiser from the experience.

I was paid $1.46 an hour and time and a half for overtime. The train was always several hours late but I didn't mind as I needed the extra cash.

Chapter 24
The Darkest Day Of My Life

I was happy to get that railroad job. They kept me all summer, thus insuring at least, my railroad fare to Meharry Medical College in Nashville, Tennessee. However, just six months prior to leaving tragedy struck, Mother died. The numbers rackets brought the end to her life, I'm sure.

During Christmas week, mail at the terminal annex of the Southern Railway was very heavy and extras were hired. I was a senior at Miles and became friendly with B. T. King, a student and fraternity brother. He was a regular employee as a mail handler and procured a job for me and several fellow Mileans. The joy turned to sorrow because Mother was killed during the first week. If I had been home at midnight when she returned from a birthday party for a lady who lived across the street, perhaps I could have prevented the tragedy. Mother regularly wrote the numbers of the clearing house players as well as a multitude of numbers played by Father. His writing wasn't too cool, to say the least, and he'd want her especially, or me, to write them. After church on Sundays she always prepared my dinner. That Sunday, December 21, 1942, I was due to start work at 6 p.m. and expected her to have dinner ready at 4 p.m., totally unaware of the birthday party she was getting ready to attend. I became more and more incensed because she had not dished up my plate. With my mouth resembling that of a platypus, I helped myself and sat down to eat just as she sashayed into the kitchen, preparing to leave.

"How do I look?" she asked.

After a long pause, I said, "You look O.K."

"You wished you looked as good as me."

I said nothing when she left for the party at 4:30 p.m. with my seven-year-old brother. I was surprised she would go to that lady's home because of a falling out they had several years previously over Father. He was as handsome as he was crooked. Mother thought the woman was paying too much attention to him and told her in no uncertain terms. They made up somewhat over the next several years but not enough for Mother to go to her birthday party. That was the last time I saw her alive. She was in excellent health and good spirits when she left. I left for work by streetcar about 5 p.m. and was busy loading and stacking filthy, dirty, dusty mail sacks about 12:30 a.m. when my first cousin, Robert McCain, Chief Petty Officer on leave from the U. S. Navy and my future brother-in-law, Eddie Brown, came onto the scene. My first thought upon seeing Eddie, a playboy, was that he was putting one of his many women friends on the train, but seeing them together I figured something terrible had happened—and it had.

As they approached my cousin exclaimed, "They want you to come home, Edwin, your mother is very low-sick," an old Negro expression for a gravely ill person. I asked if a doctor had been called and Eddie said, "I think so."

I found B. T. and told him my mother was low-sick and I would like to go home.

"Okay, I'll tell the foreman." The three of us went to Eddie's car and hurried home.

Upon nearing the house I could see it was completely light from back to front.

I didn't know what to think, if the doctor had been there or was on his way. Upon arriving, I rushed into the front room, meeting Mrs. Jenny Fagan, a lifelong elderly lady-friend who had lived directly across the street from us since the day I was born. She said, "Your mother just passed." I was speechless. Mother was lying in bed in the next room, completely covered with a white sheet. I knew the meaning of that scene, death. Mrs.Fagan followed me into the bedroom.

"What happened" I asked. Father hadn't appeared; he was in the dining room.

She answered, "I don't know, your father said she just came from the party, went to bed and died." That's the fib he told her. Initially I thought maybe the lady across the street had poisoned her. The party could have been the proper setting to settle a long-time grudge.

I met Father in the dining room and he told me the same tale he'd told Mrs.Fagan.

"Are we going to have an autopsy?" I asked.

"You should be ashamed of yourself for thinking someone did something to your mother."

Dr. Young was summoned, pronounced her dead of natural causes and said the coroner would accept his diagnosis.

What could I do? Twenty-one years old and powerless to begin a fight with him, he was in control. My mind buzzed as to what really happened. Did I want to go after the woman who invited her to the party and finally got her revenge? I mulled the situation over and over in my mind. If an autopsy weren't done, there would be no legal grounds to accuse anyone. I was feeling too distraught to discuss my thinking with Father because he wasn't of the same mind. At least, he didn't express such. He seemed only interested in the undertaker taking her away and off of his hands, thus absolving him of any association with her death, showing no outward emotion. When he refused the suggestion of an autopsy, my thoughts turned to his implication in her death knowing he was very angry because she had stayed until midnight at the party. If she had been home by 8 p.m. and written the numbers she could very well be alive today, or at least lived longer.

Mother apparently had a premonition of her impending death while at the party. I was told by a friend of the family who lived three doors from us, Mrs. Pecola Cornelius, that she asked her several times at the party to pray for me to become a doctor. I had been accepted by Meharry Medical College six weeks previously and she and I were jubilant even though we didn't know how I would be able to enter such a highly financial situation without "eye water to cry with," an old Southern saying, hence, her turning to the good Lord for guidance and help for me. She would have done everything in her power to scratch my train fare to Nashville and more if she could.

Well, the murder narrowed to one person when several months after her burial the lady who lived next door for many years told me she heard noises and loud voices around midnight, as from a big altercation. She heard Mother say, "Stop choking me; you are going to kill me." That was the silent end. My seven-year-old brother was in bed and didn't witness the fight or was fast asleep at midnight, which I find very hard to believe as she was killed in the bedroom where the three of them slept. He never talked about the incident and I never questioned him. I should have become fearful of my own safety for insisting on an autopsy and I am sure father became more and more paranoid towards me.

As time went on I asked the undertaker's wife about the condition of mother's body and she said her throat appeared swollen when she dressed her.

During my childhood many so-called wakes for the dead were held the night before a funeral, most on Saturday and the funeral on Sunday, at the church. Coffee and home made cake were the menu. I tasted my first cup of coffee with evaporated milk and sugar at Mr. Hutchinson's wake when I was nine years old. I liked the taste. Mother only let sister and me drink coffee when we had a dry breakfast consisting of fried salt pork with the drippings poured over rice and hot biscuits.

The saddest wake I attended was Mother's in December, 1942. The undertaker brought the body home early Saturday evening. My seven-year-old brother played underneath the casket as it sat atop a catafalque, a strange sight to see. Father and his sister, Katie, sat on the davenport behind it talking about what, I don't know. My suspicions around her death never diminished and haven't until this day. She was strangled to death.

The burial was over and I had no know-how or finances to further pursue the cause of her death.

Returning to college to complete my last year was very difficult. My grief was very deep following her death because I knew she wanted to see me graduate. I was more determined now than ever to fulfill her faith in me.

Just before graduation the first fraternity was

established. Dr. G. E. C. Porter, a local physician and member of Tau Sigma Chapter of Phi Beta Sigma Fraternity, Incorporated, asked for and received permission from Dr. Bell to establish a chapter. I had never heard of fraternities and decided to join to see what they were all about.

There were eight inductees. The initiation was something else. Learning the history, fraternity hymn and names of all the chapters in the U.S. was part of our indoctrination. We were blindfolded, paddled, taken to an undertaking parlor, hugged a corpse, crawled across so-called burning sands of the desert and embarrassed in many other ways. The full-fledged members of the local chapter called us dogs until our initiation when we became full-fledged Sigma men. We were all glad when the initiation was over.

Phi Beta Sigma Fraternity was established at Howard University in Washington, D. C. in December 1895, by Dr. Samuel F. Morse, a clergyman. There are chapters all over the United States. Our annual conclave is held in various cities during Christmas week every year.

There are three other well known black fraternities, Alpha Phi Alpha, Omega Psi Phi and Kappa Alpha Psi. Miles had no sororities during my matriculation there.

I was elected chapter president and our fledging group had monthly meetings at the college and fraternized with our brothers of Tau Sigma during charity events held throughout the year and participated in their annual dance, a huge affair.

Our campus activities were limited in the beginning. Finding new members was our primary goal. Soon we had enough, 25, to apply for a charter from the national organization. Our goal was reached in record time as news of the fraternity spread. We became the talk of the campus, full-fledged Phi Beta Sigma Fraternity men.

Midway through my senior year I wrote to Meharry Medical College for an application to enter the freshman class of September, 1943. Their reply contained a request for a fee of $50 which was forwarded to the medical aptitude test preparers, who would send it to the Dean of the college to administer.

The test arrived at the Director of Instruction's office, as we had no official dean. He advised me of the date and time. He returned the test to the company which sent the results to Meharry.

A special honor was bestowed upon me before graduation when my major professor, Mr. Zealey, conducted a poll among the student body of 150 during an assembly asking who was the senior most likely to succeed. I was the winner. That was thrilling, after having been out of high school for two years before beginning college, no job or prospects of getting one until I accidentally got a paper route and saved enough money to enter Miles. The encouragement of two lifelong friends who were now juniors was extremely important, especially after a serious error in judgment, my innocently writing the math entrance exam for a friend and the vote of two out of three admission's members not to enroll me as a penalty. I had to take sub-freshman math one quarter after scoring high on the entrance exam. I was able to take a full load of twenty hours per quarter and became vice president of the honor society.

Many college students and their teachers between ages 21 and 45 were eligible for the military draft at the outset of World War II. Some were thwarted for years due to lack of finances. Thoughts of being deferred and entering medical school flourished in their minds when the Department of the Army announced it was taking over all medical schools, expenses paid. The news spread to all colleges and universities. The six hundred applications for admission to the freshman class at Meharry were the largest in its 67 year existence.

I was a senior premed student at Miles and hadn't heard of that huge bonanza. I was poor but hopeful of going to medical school some day, prepared myself and fortunately, had applied. It was an opportune time for me, even though I didn't find out about the Army Specialized Training Program (A.S.T.P.), a government paid education, until I received my acceptance in June, 1942. Classes were to begin June 23, 1943.

Even better news stated that the Federal Government would pay the expenses of students who qualified for the Army Medical Corps, as they needed doctors because World War II was in progress.

I graduated from Miles on May 23, 1943, Cum Laude, in a class of 37, with a B.A. degree. The speaker was Dr. William Bell, our President. A reception was held in the home economics building for graduates, parents and friends.

Throughout the past four years I had looked forward to that day.

Due to Mother's demise just six months prior to graduation, my emotions were a mixture of joy and sadness knowing she would not be there. My sister was living and working in New York and Father chose not to come and bring my seven-year-old brother.

After graduation, I did not tarry in Birmingham because in 17 days I was to enter Meharry Medical College. World War II was in progress, the

Army had taken over all medical schools and for the first time in its history, Meharry began a year round program. I was immediately inducted into the Army Specialized Training Program and promptly began the study of medicine and military science.

Chapter 25
Medical School And A.S.T.P.

Meharry Medical College, located in North Nashville, Tennessee, on 18th Avenue North and 21st Street, was established in 1876 as a Class "A" medical school by five Meharry brothers, white gentlemen, who were passing through Nashville on their way to another destination in Tennessee. A devastating storm had swept the city causing many deaths, injuries and much destruction in the Negro section. There was no hospital for them, so the brothers decided to remain and establish a medical facility where Negroes could receive much needed medical care in the future. The facility, appropriately named Meharry Medical College, is one of four predominantly black medical schools in the United States.

The original building, standing proudly amidst the several acre campus, is a two story, red brick structure in the heart of the black community. Fisk University, a prominent old, four-year liberal arts black institution, is directly across the street. The Meharry School of Nursing is adjacent to the medical school.

There are four black medical schools in the

United States: Howard University in Washington, D.C., established in 1869, was federally funded and always admitted three non-blacks but is now totally integrated; Morehouse Medical College, affiliated with Morehouse College in Atlanta, Georgia, was established in the early 1980s; Charles R. Drew Medical School, affiliated with U.C.L.A. and U.S.C. Medical Schools, established in Watts, California, also in the 1980s; all-black Leonard Medical School, affiliated with Shaw University in Raleigh, North Carolina, established in 1882 and closed in 1910.

There are presently 137 white medical schools. The Meharry School of Nursing, a four year school, had 125 students and granted B. S. N. degrees, Bachelor of Science in Nursing.

There was also a four-year school of Dentistry. Students at graduation receive D.D. S degrees, Doctor of Dental Surgery.

The four-year School of Medical Technology offered intensive training in the differential components of urine, blood, sputum, stools and body fluids to find the causative factors in diseases of organ systems. An M. T. degree, Medical Technologist, was awarded at graduation.

The School of Pharmacy was discontinued in the late 1930s.

George W. Hubbard Hospital, named for the first president, was a 50 bed teaching hospital. Private patients were excluded from student examinations. Adjoining the Administration Building was a multi-volumed, thoroughly utilized, library.

Dr. Edward Turner, a middle aged, soft spoken, white gentleman, an internal medicine specialist, was president when I enrolled. He resigned my sophomore year, going to the University of

Chicago as a Professor of Medicine. Old time students called him Uncle Ed, the great white father. I never had any interaction with him.

Dr. M. Don Clawson, a white dentist who succeeded Dr. Turner, was president of American University in Beirut, Lebanon, before coming to Meharry and remained throughout my stay. He was the First dentist in the United States to head a medical school. Dr. Michael E. Bent, a Panamanian, was Dean and an old timer at Meharry. He also taught Bacteriology, enjoyed telling funny jokes and was a fine teacher.

After registering, I was referred to the basement of the Administration Building, serving as Army Headquarters. I met my commanding officer, Lieutenant Colonel Jules Sims, a white haired, real military man, straight forward but fair. Captain Chatman, Administrative Officer, was tough as nails and no-nonsense, one hundred per cent military. Lt. Brownlee was very quiet and all Army. Master Sgt. Simpson was a happy-go-lucky drill sergeant and also all business.

All medical and dental students who joined the Army were called to order and told about being inducted as privates. Some were ineligible. A date was arranged for us to go by train to Ft. Benning, Georgia, just across the Alabama state line from Phoenix City, Alabama. I was returning to Alabama whence I had just left and knew the area very well. We arrived Monday at 1.30 a.m. and were escorted to the day room for processing. A six-foot-eight sergeant entered the room and told us to follow him after a clerk had given us an identification card with a string attached which was to be worn around the neck at all times. He warned us that if we lost that tag we'd lose our "asses." It contained birth date, home address, parents' names and whom to notify in case of emergency.

It was about 3 a.m. when we completed our official entry into the Army. I thought it was time to go beddy-bye, in as much as we hadn't had any sleep. Well, that huge hunk of a sergeant had news for us and in a very rough voice barked, "Follow me, men." We went to the quartermaster section, were given two sheets, two blankets and a pillow. After that task we marched to our barracks and were told to make our beds while he stood and watched. I presumed he wanted to see how well we could make bunk beds.When finished, instead of being allowed to disrobe and fall into the sack for some much needed sleep, I heard for the first time, "Fall out." That meant go out to the company street, an area in front of the barracks and line up. After lining up at about 5 a.m., he informed us that we were in the Army now and subject to Army rules and regulations. Believe me, they were rough, policing the grounds, clearing all debris until 6 a.m. then proceed to the mess hall for chow. Mind you, I had had no sleep the entire night and was really wondering what was happening, but soon realized the regimentation was worth the room and board, tuition, $100 a month, commissary privileges, cigarettes, candy, toothpaste and other necessities offered by the army.

We returned to the quartermaster's building for uniform fittings and permanent metal "dog" tags to be worn for identification at all times except when sleeping.

We were given the standardized Army intelligence test. Funny thing about it, I met John Mabry, a fraternity brother I didn't know was there who was in charge of administering the test. He offered me a copy of the answers, which I refused. I heard by the grapevine if you didn't make between 90

and 120, you could not participate in the Army
Specialized Training Program. That was frightening, but I had confidence it would be no problem
for me. Fortunately, I passed without the help.

A funny thing happened during the physical
exam. Six were detained for protein in their urine.
They didn't feel the urge to pass a specimen, so a
gracious friend had a large quantity and shared it
with them. All were eventually cleared during subsequent screenings but what an embarrassment.

We returned to Nashville, arriving at 6 a.m. at
Union Station downtown. The Lt. Colonel and First
Sergeant were there to greet us, as were four big
Army trucks. A truck ride wouldn't be bad after an
all-night coach ride. We were given our two big duf-
fel bags containing our Army gear and told to load
them. Sergeant Simpson snapped, "Fall in, men,"
meaning line up. We marched six miles from Union
Station to the gruff commands of "hup two, three,
four, hup two, three, four," on tired feet pounding
the route to our quarters at the dormitory of Fisk
University across the street from Meharry. That was
a tiring introduction to Army life.

After suffering through that tough march, I said
to myself, "Gee, I'm in the Army now." It was summer vacation, so there were no coeds or anyone
around Fisk. We were given room assignments,
two to a room. By this time it was noon and the
Sergeant ordered us to fall out and line up to go to
the mess hall.

The food was lousy and a strike was attempted
after about two months, to no avail. Colonel Sims
ruled us out of order. It certainly wasn't home cooking, but we survived.

The Army Specialized Training Program was
arbitrary. There were 238 medical and 140 dental
student soldiers and 22 civilians, twelve male and

ten female.

Two companies of soldiers, A and B, medical and dental respectively, composed the Army Cadet Corps. Each had its own commanders: a Major, the squad leader, a Lieutenant, a Platoon Leader and a Sergeant who conducted roll call for reveille at 6 a.m. and retreat at 5 p.m. We were transferred to a new platoon each quarter in order not to get too well acquainted with the leader, to prevent collusion among classmates, friends or fraternity brothers for unexcused absences from formations.

I attained the rank of Platoon Sergeant during my senior year and felt quite proud. Captain Chatman and Lieutenant Brownlee were always present at formations. After one year we were promoted to Private First Class, one chevron worn on the upper arms of our uniforms.

Student soldiers who failed in the classroom were sent to Camp Barkley, Texas. Unfortunately, there were two in my freshman class, only one returned. Another failed the sophomore year, both later returned and graduated.

Medicine was the toughest academic setting I had ever faced. Absorption of so much material in a specific amount of time was gut-wrenching and mind-boggling. After two weeks, I found myself miles behind, what with anatomy, histology and embryology every day from 8 a.m. to 5 p.m. A tall box with 208 bones, each of which the student was expected to give a classical description, as described in Gray's Textbook of Anatomy, was astounding.

During my years at Miles I was usually in bed by 8 p.m. but Meharry was an entirely different experience, 2 a.m. and 3 a.m. found me up many nights after beginning at 6 p.m.

Being in that freshman class of strangers composed of 65 males and one female, meant much hard work ahead. Some had master's degrees in biology, chemistry, physics, anatomy, embryology and math from such prestigious universities as Cincinnati, Chicago, Wisconsin, Atlanta, Lincoln in Pennsylvania and Missouri. I was from Miles College, a small church school in Birmingham, Alabama, unheard of by any of them. A classmate, who died in April 1944, during our freshman year, predicted I would be "punched." Punched was a popular term applied to those who failed that awful freshman year, a bit upsetting, to say the least.

One of my classmates from the University of Chicago was so proud to be in medical school he boasted, "We are in professional school now." That classification was new to me and I pondered its meaning without comment.

Meharry ended many a young man's or woman's dream of becoming a doctor. The hallways and walls were haunted by ghosts of their shattered dreams. The malignant attitudes of the professors were widely known. Feeling intimidated from the start, the initial impression of the dangers of being punched were imprinted in the mind of every medical and dental student.

The faculty was 99.9 per cent black and home spun, from the old school of hard knocks, "I've got mine, now you get yours." All were excellent teachers for the most part and highly charged. A few of the real old timers were rather dull. Dr. "Pops" Talbert in the Department of Anatomy, I'm told, was the possessor of a photographic memory. He graduated from the University of Pennsylvania Medical School with a straight "A" average and never let anyone forget his academic prowess, flunking many first-year students. He was a fancy dresser, womanizer and a "Spirits of fermenti" enthusiast.

Dr. James Lee, a tall, thin, outgoing gentleman from Richmond, Virginia, was the most classical lecturer and taught physiology.

Dr. John Hale, the pioneer black surgeon of Nashville and head of the Department of Surgery, was a tall uninhibited man. He often told of numerous wreaths which hung from the doors of Nashvilleans, upon whom he had operated unsuccessfully. In those days, wakes were held at the deceased's home, hence the wreath.

Miss Jane Dandridge, nurse anesthetist, was in charge of anesthesiology. She was a middle aged, very fair complexioned, slightly tall, stately built, all-business lady. She trained quite a few nurse anesthetists. There were no men in her program. Nowadays, only a few nurses administer anesthetics. Anesthesiology is a very sophisticated specialty, requiring five years of training for physicians who desire to enter that specialty.

Dr. H. D. West, Chairman of Biochemistry, was an alumnus of the University of Illinois and an excellent teacher.

Vanderbilt University Medical School, all white, was across town. Several of their faculty members taught gratis at Meharry. Dr. Charles McMurray, a fine gentleman, taught Gynecology; Dr. Daugh Smith, a tall, red headed, slow talking southern gentleman taught Gastrointestinal diseases; Dr. Charles Warner, a fast talking, very wealthy gentleman taught Diseases of the Eye. He was the descendant of a very wealthy family that owned the Warner Building, a large complex downtown.

Dr. Hamilton, a six foot eight, large, gruff talking man, lectured in the Department of Radiology. Dr. Matthew Walker, a prince of a gentleman, Chairman of the Department of Surgery, a protege of Dr. Hale, was an excellent teacher. His famous saying, "Make the correct diagnosis and treatment can be found in the Lady's Home Journal," was fascinating.

Dr. Edward Scott of Chicago, Illinois, taught Radiology. He was a very fine, fair-complexioned gentleman. Dr. Maddox, who was in charge of Pediatrics, was kind of mush mouthed in his lectures, but good.

The "Black Prince," Dr. W. F. B. James, Chief of Obstetrics, was an elegant dresser and lecturer.

Dr. E. T. Odom from Mobile, Alabama, headed the Department of Medicine, a very charged academician and well liked by all of his students.

Dr. Quinland, a superb lecturer was Chief of Pathology. He was getting along in years and was all business. He loved to ride his favorite boys, I was one, getting busted out daily.

Dr. S. H. Freeman, a handsome Sigma man, was Chief of Orthopedics and a super teacher. These are just a few of the mainstays in teaching at Meharry.

A dentist in Birmingham whose nephew owned a drug store where I worked as a soda jerk for a short time while in college, heard I was attending Meharry. One day he saw me and his question, "Haven't they punched you out yet?" made me angry.

"No," ignoring his snide remark. He knew how rough it was and that I didn't come from the upper crust of society like those living in Smithfield, his neighborhood, or Enon Ridge where other wealthy blacks lived. I was from Woodlawn, way out in east Birmingham. Fortunately, that had nothing to do with my academic ability.

Very soon in my freshman year, I found what Bay Bay Coar, a classmate of mine in premed at

Miles, said was true. It was necessary to study in groups of twos, threes and fours. The medical course of study was almost too voluminous for any one person to absorb. Students with photographic memories were rare, there were none in my class. My study group consisted of one student in Histology and two in Anatomy. We read for two to three hours and asked each other questions afterwards, a "bust out session."

Histology, an initial freshman course, was that branch of Biology which dealt with the minute structure of tissues. Our class became aware of an expression used by upperclassmen, past and present, called "peeping," because of having to look into the eyepiece of a microscope focused on a color slide to identify a cell or tissue.

Each student was given a box of fifty color slides for study the entire quarter. A microscope was also assigned, both could be taken home. The microscope and case weighed about 15 pounds. I shared it with Carson Parks, a sophomore who used it in Pathology. That was my introduction to using a microscope.

Gray's Textbook of Anatomy weighed about seven pounds and I lugged it along with the Histology and Embryology text books. I was weighted down physically and mentally with only a three-and-a-half block walk which seemed like three and a half miles.

All textbooks were furnished by the government. If, at the end of the quarter's courses I wanted them as my own, I could buy them from the supply sergeant at Army costs. I bought all of them to start my medical library.

There was a standing joke if you looked into the microscope and didn't see anything, that was a fibroblast, which is a spindle-shaped cell found in scar tissue and popular on practical exams.

Grades for all 66 students were posted weekly, the written Histology and Embryology grades were combined. One student took the Histology and the ones to his right and left the Embryology test, to prevent collusion.

The scuttlebutt from upper classmen was keep ten students below your name and you were safe. When grades were posted, it was gut-wrenching time.

My experience using a microscope almost caused me to get punched. Every week a practical exam identifying cells and tissues under a microscope was given, ten in number. I made a score of 20 out of 100 one week, which really had me down in the dumps. Clemmie Jo Eubanks and Otis McCree were monitors, both with masters degrees in Histology and liked me. Clemmie and Otis followed me the next week and made sure I made the correct identifications. I was right on the money and had no further trouble.

"Punched" was a new and very strange expression to me, now I was well aware of the meaning and tried at all times to avoid being "punched."

Meharry was notorious for flunking freshmen, so much so, the upper classmen had this expression, "If you see the Chiffon shimmering next spring," referring to the coeds of Fisk University across the street from Meharry, "you'll become a doctor."

Reading, reading and more reading was the name of the game. Classmates would make each other paranoid by saying, "Gal, don't read me out." If they saw you at Price's Drug Store or walking the streets, they would always say they were going home to get some sleep, but you knew they were going home to read three or four hours. We were soldiers as well as medical students and Camp Barkley, Texas, was your next station if you failed.

I can hear John Gaffney, a stuttering, excitable classmate saying to me, "ga, ga, gal, the canal is hot," referring to Guadalcanal in the Asiatic Pacific theater of war where the U.S. was fighting the Japanese in 1944. That would stimulate me to go home and read, read and read some more.

Anatomy is the science or branch of morphology which treats the structure of organs and the relations of their parts. I heard my classmates speak of a cadaver and didn't know to which animal species they were referring. I received a surprise awakening with my introduction to the study of human anatomy. Going into that refrigerated room and seeing greased human bodies hanging from hooks applied to the sides of their heads, wrapped in gauze, was a gruesome sight for a novice like me to encounter.

Four of us were assigned to a table and an elderly, very wasted lady's body was our companion for the next six months. My fingernails were quite long and upon handling her, became clogged with grease. I thought to myself, "Lord, I'll never eat again." She was unwrapped and put on the table for a topographical description, guided by a small manual. Eventually 5 p.m. rolled around and happily the 1 p.m. to 5 p.m. session of the first day of real anatomical study was history. Being hungry as a bear coming from a long hibernating winter's sleep, I went to Fisk where we were billeted, washed my hands and went to chow, after lining up with my platoon. I ate like I'd never ever eaten. I didn't have any trouble eating from that day on, gaining 65 pounds in three years.

I studied anatomy with Danny Thompson and

John Gladney many a night. We questioned each other after having read for at least a couple of hours to be sure we were well prepared.

One's survival instincts came into play early if he or she were going to deal successfully with the onslaught of material in a medical course of study.

Dr. E. P. Crump, anatomy instructor, was project-minded and assigned to groups of four a topic to be worked through as we chose and presented to the class. Three classmates and I were assigned the twelve cranial nerves, which exit from the brain. Our report was less than satisfactory, causing Dr. Crump to specify the nerves he wanted each one to present next time around. That was indeed threatening to me, a heavy hammer hanging over my head. What will happen with the next presentation?

Being assigned the ninth and eleventh nerves, the glossopharyngeal and spinal accessory which supply the motor activity to the tongue, voice box and throat, I studied like crazy, reading and memorizing the descriptions, just as in Gray, making sure there would be no flies in this presentation. It sounded so classical my classmates opened their textbooks and followed, word for word. I was right on target. Dr. Crump was pleased and gave me his O.K. The others also satisfied him. We were very happy.

Before my time at Meharry in anatomy, I was told, when the practical exam was given, the professor, who was as crusty and rough as the barnacles on a whale and mean as a junkyard dog, took a probe, threw it into the cavity of the cadaver and wherever it landed, the student began discussing it, be it a vein, artery, nerve, muscle or an organ. Quite a few didn't make it.

Dr. A. A. Williams, another professor, was

amusing as he strolled through the lab in his long, white coat, pockets full of bones, eyes roving in all directions and everyone digging deeper into the cavity of the cadavers, not wanting to make eye contact which might attract him to them. He was famous for visiting a table and pulling out a bone of the skull, wrist or extremity. He cracked me up, inwardly, when he handed one to a student saying, "Talk to de bone." His Jamaican accent sounded very strange to me. I dug deeper into the lady hoping he wouldn't call on me, then it wouldn't have been funny at all. He expected us to put muscles on the bone, give the nerve and blood supply and its function.

One day I was describing the frontal bone, or forehead. Within it is a bony projection which divides the frontal lobes of the brain and has the appearance of a cocks-comb, called the Crista Galli, which I didn't remember after having read the description thoroughly. There I stood, frozen and speechless. A few classmates tried to send me a message via "the radio," but I was too proud to look among them to pick up the signal. The rest of my performance was O.K., ignoring the signal didn't do too much damage to my final grade.

Some students sat in the back where their educated fingers could clandestinely manipulate the pages of their textbook and get some needed help. I sat in the front, not because that would keep me from cheating, but I knew the consequences of being caught. One classmate was guilty during a biochemistry exam. The professor took him to his office, prayed with him and advised him to never do that again. He graduated with me.

An advance copy of an exam was sometimes given to a student by his lover, who was secretary to the professor. It was called the "Eagle," which he shared with his friends. Some fellows spent more time calling around to their friends to see if the Eagle was out than actually studying. Access to it almost messed up six borderline students in the final biochemistry exam. They scored 99, wanting to be sure they passed. Their scores all quarter didn't come close to that lofty height and they were called in by the professor and questioned. He let them go.

I found the "Eagle" was out when a friend of mine tried to give me a small roll of paper which contained the answers as he left the room. I refused to take it for any reason.

"Charged," "heavy," and "light" were terms applied to students and professors. Every one of us was in that uphill fight to become doctors. Some times were better than others for each of us. It was not hard to get the feeling that the professors were out to get you as evidenced by the head-cracking sessions during lectures, in the lab or on the wards. They wanted to know if you were reading and taking good notes.

"Heavy" did not refer to the weight of the body, but to the amount of knowledge stored in the cranium. "Charged" meant sparkling brain cells with immediate responses.

When a student was asked questions from time to time and answers were slow to flow, he or she was referred to as "light." It was an indication that more and more reading was in order.

There was a large-legged, dark brown skinned, good looking freshman nursing student, Catherine Jones, from St. Louis, Missouri, whom I met and was interested in seeing, but found no time. Bet she wondered if I were straight. I only dated my medical studies, there was no time to make a play for the "shimmering chiffon." One had to have total dedication to his/her school work to make it.

It was eight months before my first date with a cutie from Pulaski, Tennessee, who attended Tennessee State College, eight miles away. Dates were not too regular after that until my junior and senior years when I thought I would become a doctor. Catherine, by this time, had lost interest in me and we never got together.

Fraternities were very active on campus and played an integral part in establishing good interpersonal relationships with classmates and members of other fraternities. There were chapters of Phi Beta Sigma, Omega Psi Phi, Alpha Phi Alpha and Kappa Alpha Si. The first quarter at Meharry, as members of the Armed Forces, all student soldiers lived at Jubilee Hall of Fisk University. When the coeds returned, the Army gave us $100 per month for quarters of our choosing. Phi Beta Sigma Fraternity had a house two blocks from school where I spent the rest of my school days with seven brothers. I was shocked when I heard them calling each other "gal" and "ole lady." They began those references at colleges and universities they previously attended. I had no problem with "Brother," as that's what all members of fraternities called each other, but "gal" or "ole lady" boggled my mind. It soon became a part of my lingo. Fraternities came into prominence not only for brotherhood but academic aid as well. Old exams left at the frat house by former occupants were handed down from years past and were very helpful. The same questions were not necessarily asked from year to year, but sometimes questions on an old exam that was given many years previously showed up on a current one, to the surprise and delight of those who had reviewed them. The satisfaction after a successful exam from knowledge gained from old exams or any source made one boast "I got him," meaning the professor didn't stump him or her that day. The feeling of getting a good grade on exams made a young adult student like me feel happy as a child getting a shiny new toy at Christmas.

Each frat brother had a roommate who paid his share of the rent and utilities. I began to call my roommate "ole lady" and vice versa. It was a common greeting around the campus, frat house or wherever we might meet. We were all one hundred per cent males.

Our sorority sisters were Zeta Phi Betas at Tennessee State College, Fisk University and in the City of Nashville. We fraternized in a brotherly and sisterly manner, having many good times and often laid our secret handshakes proudly upon each other.

The frat house was my home away from home. There were three bedrooms, a large dining room, living room, small kitchen and bath. Upper classmen were chosen to be President, Secretary and Treasurer. A division of our teams of two each swept and scrubbed the floors; there was no vacuum cleaner. We all did our share and there were never any problems.

We got up each morning on time, bathed and made it to reveille and breakfast. I had no time to do my laundry and engaged the lady next door to do it, except for shirts and uniforms which I took to a dry cleaner.

Medicine was our main topic of concern. Upper classmen busted out each other and under classmen in order to make sure everyone was reading. A lot of reading went on late into the night by all. Loud arguments ensued on many occasions when the sophomores thought they were correct.

Books were brought out to prove their points and the seniors were always right.

The sophomores were always on my case, making sure I was reading. Moose Moorehead kept us in stitches, sounding his alarm often, "Have you taken your bath? We don't want this house to become the house of Armstrong."

We relaxed on Saturdays, playing bridge and whist until all hours of the night. I had never attempted to play bridge before moving into the fraternity house. Doxie Green, a freshman, was my partner and a good player. I don't think he ever forgave me for a boo-boo I pulled one Saturday afternoon. The bidding started, went round and round until our good hands kept climbing into game territory, little slam and then grand slam, using the Blackwood convention, asking for kings and aces. I told him how many aces I had and passed when he asked for kings. He played the hand and made a grand slam, the only one I saw bid and made at the house. He was fit to be tied. I felt awful, it was all over, but not forgotten. I haven't seen or heard from him since 1946, when I graduated.

One Wednesday afternoon, a soror from "all white" Vanderbilt University across town called and invited us to a dance on Saturday night. That was a shocking surprise and a great big joke, despite the cosmopolitan culture of Nashville influenced by Vanderbilt and all-white Austin Peay, we knew better. We cracked up at the invitation and boastfully vowed we were going. When the time came, we backed out and went on our regular dates. We were for integration, but presumptuous, we were not. I loved living in Nashville, no racial tension when blacks and whites were in close proximity on busses, however, we had to sit in the balcony in the large theaters downtown. There was an all-black theater on Jefferson Street in the heart of the colored neighborhood and very nice, with first run pictures.

Fraternity life was for me. Parties and fraternization were great. We only initiated five brothers during my time there. Most of the students had committed themselves to various fraternities at black colleges before arriving at Meharry. A few who graduated from white colleges and universities were available, as they couldn't join the ones at white universities.

Not all were interested in joining fraternities. Overtures were made to them.

The new and old brothers are going to many different locations in the United States and it's always pleasant to know you can call on them when in their towns and receive a warm fraternal welcome, and vice versa.

We were friendly with other fraternity members, being invited to their annual dances, as they were to ours.

The sophomore year had a bugaboo, physiology, which is the study of the functions of living organisms or their parts. It was known to get the weak ones punched. A perpetrator of that malady was Dr. D. T. Rolfe, a massive man over 300 pounds called Moby Dick behind his back. He was at Cornell University doing some special work when I arrived. Everyone was happy. An oral and written quiz were given every week. With the tough one away we breathed easier. After six weeks, he returned and took over my group. He had a good sense of humor but was very tough. When I took my final oral exam at the end of the quarter, his first question was a simple one, "Mr. Witt, what is Proteinuria?"

"Protein in the urine."

His next question was, "Describe the meridia of the eye," meaning the description of the curvature of the eyeball. I fumbled for a piece of paper and pencil from my coat pocket. He said, "Here's paper and pencil."

I scribbled a picture of the meridia as he moved on to the rest of the group, finally returning to me. He collected my prized drawing, tore it up immediately and threw it in the trash can. Oh, horrors, I visualized Camp Barkley in my future, I passed the course so my drawing must have been satisfactory.

Once during a physiology written exam, Frank Avery, sitting across the table from me, grabbed my paper after I refused to answer a question he asked. Dr. Rolfe was at the front table three feet from us. I was shaking all over with fear because he had eyes everywhere and I just knew he would think I was part of a conspiracy to cheat. To my great relief, he didn't say a word, nor did he forget Frank at the end of the quarter—he punched him. Frank enrolled at the Pittsburgh School of Pharmacy and later died in a car accident before graduating.

Another classmate, Maxie Scott, was five minutes late with his notebook, came to the physiology department barefooted, collar open and wide eyed, having been up all night. Dr. Rolfe wouldn't accept his notebook and he ended up at Camp Barkley, but returned later and graduated.

Dr. Rolfe wasn't all mean. He could be comical at times. One day Robert Thornton was answering a question during an oral quiz. He wasn't sure of his answer. Dr. Rolfe looked him up and down quizzically and continued to file his fingernails, which he regularly did whenever he had one of us on the hot seat. Bob continued to talk on and on, finally asking Dr. Rolfe, "Am I on the right track?"

"Ha, you must think this is a Kay Kayser program." Kay Kayser was an orchestra leader with an entertaining radio network musical quiz show.

In what should have been a loud roar of laughter to relieve some of the pressure felt in everyone's mind from their fear of being in the same predicament later, only a few sniggles were barely audible.

Bob's light complexion became rosy red as he meekly sat down. Dr. Rolfe continued questioning us in his usual business-like manner.

Another problem arose during my sophomore year. The professor of pathology, Dr. Quinland, possessed exquisite penmanship and took exception to any student who did not exhibit the same qualities. I always received excellent grades in writing throughout elementary, high school and college, but in medical school the professors lectured so rapidly it was hard to keep up. One found out early if he interrupted the professor because of something he missed, he would think, *here is a dummy* and I'm going to get even by busting him out daily, that is asking him questions he probably couldn't answer. No observations were more true. Writing fast, I developed my own brand of shorthand. I never took a course, with resultant poor writing. He began to call on me daily before lectures. The questions were simple, but as the old saying goes, when I stood up my thoughts sat down. He wrote on a test paper, "Decide now if you want to pass this course." I took him at his word. His favorite expression to those who couldn't answer questions during lectures was, "you cane in here naked, you'd better put on some clothes." That was threatening, knowing the "punch out" record was high, especially during the first and second years.

Dr. Bent in bacteriology, was something else. He wrote comments on test papers, "Bunk," "What are you talking about?" "Did you mean this?" and many others. I didn't worry as none of my grades were below the passing grade of 75

Dr. James Holloway, a parasitologist, Dr. Bent's assistant, was a very learned man and acted like a stooge. Dr. Bent, with his Jamaican accent, would be expounding with reference to sexual promiscuity and would emphatically say, "Isn't that right, Dr. Holloway?" Answering in his very high pitched voice, "Yes, sir, Dr. Bent," cracking up the class.

Biological chemistry (biochemistry) was known as "a real man" to medical students, meaning it was real tough. Quite a few student's dreams of becoming a doctor ended there.

It dealt with fats, proteins, sugars, enzymes and the chemical reactions of the body.

Dr. H. D. West, a mulatto, stoutly built, bespectacled, slightly bulging eyed, very strict gentleman with a loping gait and a sneaky half smile, was department chairman. He co-discovered one of the ten essential amino acids, threonine, while working on his doctorate at the University of Illinois. An essential amino acid is one of ten from protein not made by the body and necessary for formation of cell protoplasm. He never let us forget that he helped discover it.

Biochemistry didn't prove too difficult for me. I made my highest grade in it on the Tennessee State Licensing Board examination. My premed major professor at Miles College, Marion E. Zealey, had his dream of studying medicine come to fruition through two of his trusted students, Hessie Jones and me. She graduated two years prior.

My work in biochemistry at Meharry was of

the quality that Dr. West asked the name of my college chemistry instructor and how he could contact him. I gave him his address. Mr. Zealey : accepted the offer and came to Meharry as an associate professor. He was on the Admission's Committee which ruled on my admissibility to Miles for writing a friend's math exam and getting caught. I don't know how he voted. Things that go around can come around.

Eventually Professor Zealey applied and was accepted to the medical school, a life long dream. He was in his junior year when his failing eyesight reached the point his eye doctor recommended against continuing. What a tragic loss to the medical profession. He would have been an excellent doctor. He continued to teach at Meharry and across the street at Fisk University in the Department of Biochemistry.

He prepared me well.

He and I were reunited my junior year at Meharry and had quite a few delightful chats about old times. In the interim, he received his Doctorate in Biochemistry from the University of Minnesota. The whole scenario made me feel very good.

Just before I finished my second year, while taking biochemistry I was given a project with two classmates. We divided the work into three parts, each to do his third and when completed, come together and have someone type all parts to complete the whole. Naively, I went along with the plan. At the library one Saturday I spent three hours getting my part together. Dutifully, Monday morning I gave my material to Oliver Smith who took it politely and said he'd add it to his. I didn't know he had in mind to add my material to his which would complete his report. Somehow, Henry Adams, the third member and a very good friend, was shrewder than I and did the entire report himself and never had in mind to share his material. Well, due date for the report arrived. I thought all three parts had been combined, typed and were ready for Dr. West. Happily approaching Oliver, I said, "I'm ready to sign the report."

He looked at me in a very indifferent way, with the report tucked under his arm and said, "This is my report, you should have done your own."

Here it was, the last minute and I had no report. My mouth became so dry I could hardly speak, my mind blacked out. Finally I was able to say, "What happened to the material I gave you?"

"I used it, you should have prepared your own, I didn't get anything from Henry. He must have done his and so should you."

I was furious. Henry approached and heard the discussion. He saw me getting angrier by the second and finally said, "Witt, I'll put your name on my report." That was the first my knowing he had done his fully. I would have done mine if Oliver had not told me to do a certain part, give it to him and it would be ours. I didn't know he hadn't made the same request of Henry and all parts would be combined. Accepting Henry's unselfish offer relieved my extreme anxiety.

At the end of each quarter we were given a week's furlough.

I returned triumphantly from a week of socializing with my girlfriend and family in Birmingham, looking forward to beginning the clinical work of my junior year. My heart sank when the registrar told me I had to go to the Pathology office before registering. I turned quickly and went to see about the problem. The secretary was a matronly, middle-aged woman with a kind, friendly smile. Upon greeting her, I was surprised to hear her say, "You didn't turn in your box of slides." Heaving a sigh of relief, I dashed to my locker, almost forgetting the combination, opened the door and "viola," there was my medical education's life line. I gingerly picked it up and returned to her office. Upon handing her that precious box, we both smiled as she announced I was cleared. I now knew I'd be a junior medical student after freely overcoming that high hurdle.

Whereas the freshman and sophomore years are classified as basic science or pre-clinical, junior and senior are known as the clinical years. Histology, anatomy, biochemistry, physiology, neurology, embryology, bacteriology, pathology and physical diagnosis are replaced by medicine, obstetrics, gynecology, surgery, pediatrics, psychiatry, orthopedics, ear/nose/throat, ophthalmology and urology.

The long white laboratory coats were replaced by short ones. For the first time, contact with patients in a clinical setting became a reality. A stethoscope with long connecting rubber tubing was exhibited for the first time swinging from either side pocket, a pocket flashlight, tongue blades and a fountain pen in the upper coat pocket were standard equipment.

One becomes a laboratory technician, learning to do complete blood counts (CBCs), red and white, with their several different forms and meanings and urinalyses by the dozens.

Accompanying the intern, resident and staff doctor on teaching ward rounds was very interesting. The biggest mystery to solve was listening to heart beats and identifying the sounds. Abnormal sounds, such as murmurs, can be soft or loud, the louder the better. The twitch of a muscle of the chest wall sounds like a murmur, as do hairs on a man's chest. You think you've heard an abnormality until the intern or resident clarifies it.When they hear a murmur they will let you listen in order to fix it in your mind. They remember when they were in your shoes and someone helped them.

Taking blood pressure was practised on each other in the physical diagnosis class during our sophomore year. The systolic pressure, the one above the line, represents the pumping action of the heart; the diastolic, below the line, is the resistance the heart meets in pumping blood to all parts of the body.

To observe your first surgical operation from the viewing stand can be intimidating if the sight of blood causes you to become unglued. I was observing a classmate, decked out in his cap, gown, sterile gloves and boots, standing at the foot of the operating table when suddenly he sank, the strings of his gown caught on a sponge rack, suspending him. He looked like Christ on the cross. It was hilarious as his dazed body was removed from that pose and revived.

Hearing fetal heart tones in the obstetrical clinic was exciting, as was observing in the clinics and picking up a pearl or two here and there. We took histories, did physical examinations, diagnosis and treatment, recorded them on the patient's charts. The official history, physical and diagnosis were done by the intern on that service in the hospital.

Nervous time began for me on medicine ward rounds after I gave the history, physical findings, diagnosis and treatment of a patient assigned to me. There was always a large audience, a dozen student nurses, the charge nurse, intern, resident and fellow classmates.

I was a favorite student of Dr. William Grant,

Associate Professor of Medicine, who was in charge. Medicine, per se, as a single subject confused me because I thought the two pre-clinical and two clinical years, all inclusive, were medicine. Cecil's Textbook of Medicine contained over eighteen hundred pages of diseases and syndromes, a group of symptoms indicating the possibility of a certain disease entity.

One day, before the huge audience, he asked me to percuss the apex of the lung of a patient. Percussion is the art of placing the middle finger of the left hand over the top of the lung above the collar bone and solidly tapping it with the middle finger of the right hand. If a hollow sound results that means no masses or fluids are present. After starting my feeble effort, you would have thought I had dug a six foot deep hole under a scorching sun, as beads of perspiration covered my face. He laughed, the students and others smiled when he said, "Witt, if I were paying a dollar for what you just did, you wouldn't get a dime." Everyone became hilarious at that juncture, except me. Those things happen and, as a consequence, draw one's attention to more detailed instructions in the future when examining a patient.

Sometimes he discussed a case, asking questions about other conditions presenting the same symptoms, known as differential diagnosis. I'd be hidden among the crowd on purpose, but could feel the heat coming. Sure enough he'd say, "Wi-i-tt,what is your diagnosis?" It stimulated me to read just that much harder in order to hopefully become a good doctor just like him someday.

"Peanuts and pearls," would make a good title for a song. Those words were imprinted into the minds of all medical students. The former produced mind boggling cerebral indigestion which embarrassed him or her when a question was asked orally or on a written test by the professor, taken from the small printed footnote at the bottom of the page which had been ignored.

Pearls were precious facts implanted in one's mind for future use in diagnosing difficult cases. Utilizing them for a patient's well being produced cerebral jubilation. Those recalled flashes of wisdom picked up from professors, resident and intern physicians and sometimes fellow students in clinics and ward rounds can aid in solving many a diagnostic dilemma.

The most star studded and glamorous part of the life of a medical student is the senior year. I actually felt like a doctor, accentuating the attire and tools of the profession acquired when I became a junior. My worries of punching out had all but vanished, however, anyone could be punched at any time, but very unlikely as a senior.

As a relaxed feeling, proud and dignified, emanated from my perspective, I stood tall on campus and observed underclassmen, wondering how they were doing and wished for their success in reaching this status. I could now see myself at the pinnacle of success, receiving the M.D. degree and having the ability to help mankind.

Now I worked on the wards and outpatient clinics: medical, surgical, obstetrical, gynecological, pediatric, ear/nose/throat and the emergency room. I examined, diagnosed, treated patients and wrote prescriptions which had to be O.K.d by the clinical professor, intern or resident, but signing the line which ended with M.D. produced a great feeling of accomplishment.

A requirement for completing the senior year in Obstetrics was earning four points delivering the newborns of clinic patients who had had one or more children. A point was earned for doing delivery and a half point for assisting. Four students made a team. We made our contacts for the deliveries with women who attended the clinic.

We checked their blood pressure, urine, height, weight, blood work—the abdominal measurement for fundal height to determine the growth of the baby—and listened to the fetal heart sounds for abnormalities. We knew the expected date of delivery and stuck close to the phone at that time and earlier. When the patient's labor pains began, the Obstetrical Department was called and the patient gave the clerk the name of the student assigned for the delivery, who then alerted his assistants. We were referred to as "doctor" by the patients. The well-stocked obstetrical delivery bag of supplies was ready. Transportation was furnished by the hospital. When the delivery was completed and the umbilical cord stopped pulsating, it was tied, cut, an antiseptic applied to the stump and bandaged. Silver nitrate was instilled into both eyes for protection against infection, the infant cleansed, examined and, if no abnormalities found, a sigh of relief was breathed by all and the newborn handed to its mother who beamed when told the baby was fine. It was now time to return to the hospital.

The practice of home deliveries ended at Meharry in 1945 after a mother received a routine cleansing enema before delivery, which did not return and she died. A very sad misfortune.

My professors liked me very much, namely two by the name of Walker: Dr. H.H. and Dr. Matthew Walker.

Dr. H. H. Walker, a local physician and surgeon, an early alumnus of Meharry, was in charge of the Surgical Outpatient Clinic. He was about five feet tall, very frailly built and always had a big smile. Upon entering the clinic he always greeted me with a very cheerful, "Hi wa ya, doctor?" as he clasped my right hand, bestowing his lodge's shake. Maybe he was a Mason, I never knew. I appreciated whatever it meant because he was a fine example of humanity.

"I'm fine," was my reply. He was a Major in the Army Medical Corps during World War I and in preference to "doctor" wanted everyone to address him as Major Walker, exclusively. He had a huge practice as evidenced by the large roll of greenbacks he sometimes displayed, plus the huge diamond sparklers on the fingers of both hands, very expensive suits and shoes. As senior medical students, we rotated through his clinic. That was our first experience dealing directly with surgical patients. We saw many as juniors on ward rounds but only observed.

For some reason, I was his favorite student and called the roll. He explained how wounds heal, the solutions used to cleanse them, the technique of suturing, the salves applied for healing and how to bandage. How to incise and drain boils and abscesses was a good experience. Penicillin had not arrived on the scene, but the sulfa drugs discovered by Dr. Perrin Long of Tulane University in New Orleans had. "Scarlet Red" was his favorite ointment and was applied to all lacerations. I received my first suturing experience with his guidance. He was a very patient gentleman and such a favorite and fixture in Nashville, the fire truck at the 12th Avenue Fire Station was named the H. H. Walker Engine.

I was happy to attend the Surgical Clinic five days weekly and being called "doctor" in front of, and in the absence of, patients. A wonderful man and a neat experience from a super instructor. The prince of all physicians, a gentleman and scholar was the late Dr. Matthew Walker, Chairman of the Department of Surgery. He lectured three times weekly and was every medical student's favorite with a priceless expression such as, "Witt," or any student he was addressing, "How are you fixed?" That elicited a smile from both of us. "Fine, Dr. Walker." There wasn't an evil bone in his body. An excellent teacher, clinician and technician, he trained hundreds of surgeons who are practicing all over the United States.

Surprisingly, one day he asked me to head a group of five students to conduct an experiment in the physiology laboratory. After anesthetizing a dog and tying the base of the appendix producing acute inflammation, a dose of castor oil was given causing the appendix to rupture, with resultant acute peritonitis. It was treated with penicillin into the peritoneal cavity, which houses the appendix and into a large muscle. That is why it is ill-advised to give anyone a cathartic like castor oil or Epsom salts for a stomach ache, which could be a symptom of acute appendicitis. That was the first time Penicillin had been given into the peritoneal cavity and a muscle for that fatal affliction. Penicillin had recently been discovered in 1946 by Doctor Fleming at Tulane University, New Orleans, Louisiana. Through the genius of that wonderful teacher and gentleman, the dog recovered, a miracle and a first.

After the successful research and recovery of the dog, he gave the group a champagne party, a new experience for me. I'd never drunk champagne and after the second glass began laughing and couldn't stop, becoming hilarious. It was as if I'd been given laughing gas. I didn't drink any more and recovered quickly.

That successful experiment brought about the only "A plus" of my school career. I wonder why I didn't want to become a surgeon rather than a pediatrician. Maybe it was because one night a classmate and I volunteered our services in the Emergency Room as big-time budding doctors. The intern in charge gave us another type surgical experience. A nice lady came in with an inch long horizontal laceration at the junction of her lower neck and chest. The intern let us attempt closure. We put on sterile gloves, threaded a small curved needle and grasped it with a needle holder. I was first to try. The needle easily pierced the skin but I couldn't tie the knot using the needle holder. There, with the frightful sight of the top of the lady's left lung going up and down as she breathed, I quit and let my classmate try. He didn't have any better luck. We were both sweating profusely and alternating, trying to tie the suture and couldn't. Twenty minutes after we should have been through tying one suture and not more than two, the intern returned and saw us struggling. He relieved us, putting on a pair of sterile gloves and skillfully closing the wound. That was the end of my medical school suturing days.

Midway through my senior year when at last I thought I would become a doctor, I began to think about an internship.

Before equal rights legislation was passed in 1964 and integration began, black medical school graduates could only intern and receive specialty training at George W. Hubbard Hospital, affiliated with Meharry Medical College, Nashville, Tennessee; Harlem Hospital, New York City; Homer G. Phillips, St. Louis, Missouri; Freedmen's Hospital, affiliated with 99 per cent black Howard University, Washington, D. C.; Grady Hospital, Atlanta,

Georgia, affiliated with Emery University School of Medicine; Kate Bidding Reynolds Hospital, Wilmington, North Carolina; Sydenham Hospital, New York City; Coney Island Hospital, Brooklyn, N. Y.; L. A. County General Hospital, California, which admitted a select few from Howard and Meharry; Provident Hospital in Chicago, Illinois; Provident Hospital, Baltimore, Maryland and Kansas City General Hospital No. 2.

One could take a rotating internship, one month each in obstetrics-gynecology, internal medicine, gastro-enterology, cardiology, orthopedics, pediatrics, infectious diseases, emergency room, dermatology, surgery and pulmonary diseases for a year.

Kenneth Young, a New Yorker, sat next to me and boasted about his desire to intern at Harlem Hospital, saying it was large, all-Negro, with plenty of clinical material for excellent training. I wanted to go to a place like that to apply the diagnostic skills and treatments acquired from four years of classroom instructions and teaching on ward rounds at George W. Hubbard Hospital by the professors and staff member community practitioners. Further training at a teaching hospital like Harlem affiliated with Columbia School of Medicine could only enhance my readiness to apply for specialty training or go on my own into private practice at the completion of a rotating internship.

I applied for an internship in December 1945 to Hubbard Hospital, affiliated with my alma mater, Los Angeles County General Hospital, Los Angeles, California, and Harlem Hospital, New York City. I didn't receive an answer from Hubbard or L. A.County. Finally, in April 1946 I received an acceptance from Harlem.

A fun moment came about one day when Dr.

William Grant, my Medical Ward teacher, cracked my head always looking for "Wi-i-tt." He was my tropical medicine teacher when I was a senior. He asked "Wi-i-tt, where are you going to intern?"

I answered, "Harlem."

"Class, you see, there's another Southern boy who's going north." A big laugh from the class soon faded. I was his "Boy."

The war ended in April 1945. I was still in the Army Specialized Training Program. Freshmen, sophomore and junior students were released from the Army and had to assume their tuition. The Department of the Army decided to let my class complete our schooling, as we went year round and finished in three years instead of four. We remained in uniform, doing our regular Army duties, military science two hours on Wednesdays, drills for two hours, reveille and retreat daily. We received $138 per month for lodging and continued to eat three meals daily at Fisk University's Jubilee Hall, lining up and marching there at 6 a.m. reveille and 5:30 p.m. retreat.

I received an honorable Army discharge June 6, 1946, and was placed in the inactive Army Reserves for five years, with the rank of First Lieutenant, Medical Corps, subject to active duty call-up any time during that period. That's a small price to pay for a poor young man given an opportunity to fulfill his almost impossible dream. I am thankful to the A.S.T.P. but sorry it had to take a war for fulfillment of my dream.

The melding of 60 total strangers with a common goal of becoming medical doctors wasn't too difficult, as spirit of cooperation and respect developed to conquer a voluminous task. Times of sorrow and jubilation were inevitable as results of tests and experiences that didn't meet one's expectations. I had my ups and downs during my 36 months of medical education.

The medical curriculum was more difficult than I ever imagined. Hours of studying were vast. Adjusting to the professors' style of lecturing, their idiosyncrasies and giving exams, contributed to some uncertainty as to whether I could weather the storm.

My senior year was great and after passing final oral exams, I knew I'd attained my goal of graduating and becoming a medical doctor. Graduation was June 6, 1946. I ranked tenth in a class of 60. Dr. M. Don Clawson was commencement speaker.

Graduation would have been much sweeter if my dear mother had been there. I believe she was in heaven smiling down on me, her last wish that I'd become a doctor had come to fruition. My eleven-year-old brother, Thomas Jr., Lillian Beverly, my girlfriend, Mother's aunts, Lela Spurling, Angie Rush, Pearl Evans and Johnnie Mae Rush, Mother's cousin from Detroit, attended.

I reserved rooms for them at Brown's Motel and Restaurant, four blocks from the college. After graduation we had a wonderful dinner and chit-chat in the dining room. They left the next day.

A requirement to practice medicine in any state in the United States, except Louisiana and Georgia, is a 12 month rotating internship in medicine, surgery, obstetrics and gynecology, pediatrics, emergency medicine and orthopedics. Passing the licensure examination is a requisite in all states, especially the one in which one wants to practice. Tennessee, the state where I took my exam in March 1945, is reciprocated by every state except New York and Florida.

I passed the exam, applied for and received

reciprocity to practice in Alabama and California.

The National Board of Medical Examiners gives a licensure exam at the end of a student's sophomore year for the basic sciences. If successful, during the senior year the second half in clinical competence is given. When both parts are passed, the candidate is licensed to practice in all fifty states.

Licenses aren't necessary while interning or doing a residency.

Specialty training in obstetrics and gynecology takes five years; surgery, five years; internal medicine, three years; psychiatry, three years; ear/nose/throat, three years; orthopedics, five years; radiology, five years; neurology, three years; neurosurgery, five years; emergency medicine, three years; gastroenterology, three years; oncology, five years, ophthalmology, five years; pediatrics and urology, three years.

Usually the top medical students apply to the Chief of Services of a hospital for a straight internship of 12 months in a specific discipline, with anticipation of continuing into the residency training program for the number of years required to qualify as a specialist. His or her acceptance is usually granted.

Conversely, interns who do good work are given the opportunity to apply for residencies in their fields of choice. Many are accepted.

After completing the residency training program, the candidate applies for certification to the Secretary of the American Board of his or her specialty. The Chief of Service's recommendation to the Board is included with the application. A reply is forwarded to the candidate, notifying him or her of the costs, time and place. A written and an oral exam are to be passed to receive a Certificate of Certification. A second exam is given those who fail the written, at no cost. A third and final try plus a fee, has to be granted by the Board with stipulations of further preparation, that is, a refresher course.

Successful candidates may now go to places of choice to practice their specialities and apply to hospitals for staff membership and privileges.

Even though I was overjoyed to have been accepted at a 1,000-bed hospital where there was an abundance of clinical material for further training to add to the skills learned at Meharry, I felt some apprehension going to the largest city in the United States. I was concerned about the salary, $45 per month, but believed the experiences would more than make up for that. I was definitely beginning another chapter in my life.

When the train pulled into Grand Central Station in New York City, I was all eyes, anxious to get off and on my way. Hailing a cab, I found my trip to the hospital exciting, to say the least, zipping in and out through a maze of traffic, screeching brakes, very tall buildings and hordes of people rushing somewhere, I finally reached my destination—Harlem Hospital.

EPILOGUE

After having completed my internship at Harlem Hospital in New York, I established a general practice in Fairfield, Alabama in July, 1947. That was a time of adjustment, with both satisfaction and, at times, frustration, about a future in Birmingham. But the decision was taken out of my hands when I received a call from the army in July, 1949, to report to Ft. Bliss, Texas, in 48 hours as I was in the reserves following my army-sponsored medical training at Meharry. At Ft. Bliss, with the rank of First Lieutenant, I was assigned as a medical officer of an all-black unit just after President Truman ordered integration of the armed forces. After ten months at Ft. Bliss, I asked for and received an overseas assignment and was stationed in Wurzburg, West Germany for the remaining 14 months of my assignment with the rank of Captain.

Returning home in 1951, I lived with my father and brother, who was a senior at Fisk University. I paid all of his tuition. Daddy was still bootlegging and drinking. He exhibited no more animosity towards me as I had become a doctor.

I established an office for general practice in downtown Birmingham and found racism and segregation just as I left it—iron clad, no hospital privileges in white hospitals, and there were only two small colored ones.

As an army veteran of World War II, I applied for a staff position at the Veterans Hospital. The answer: I had to be a member of the Jefferson County Medical Society, which had in its constitution "Whites only." I had no recourse.

My practice had many pediatric patients and many more referred to me by an obstetrician, a good friend. He suggested I enter a two year pediatric training program to become a specialist. This I did. I applied and was accepted for residency training for one year in pediatrics at Meharry Medical College.

Thomas, Jr. graduated from Fisk as president of his class in June 1956. I attended and was very proud of him. Father and sister, who was living in New York, didn't attend. He became a third grade teacher with the Los Angeles Unified School District. Unfortunately, he died in 1970 from diabetes mellitus.

Father died in 1966 at a hospital in Birmingham from cancer of the stomach, possibly caused by excessive drinking of 135 proof "hooch." I didn't attend the funeral. I applied to Kern General Hospital in Bakersfield, California for a second year of training in pediatrics. Upon completion of that year, I joined a colleague in establishing a private practice in Los Angeles/Watts area. It was there I met Cordelia, my wife to be.

While serving as president of the Charles R. Drew Medical Society and continuing my private practice, I also became affiliated with the new Martin Luther King, Jr., Hospital in Willowbrook, California. In that connection, the U.S.C. School of Medicine granted me the title of Assistant Clinical Professor of Pediatrics. Later I served 17 years, full time, as a pediatrician with the Los Angeles City School System. In 1964 I took a sabbatical leave after receiving a fellowship from the National Institute of Mental Health for one year at the L. A. County General Hospital's Psychiatric Service.

In 1976 I established a pediatric practice in Las Vegas, Nevada. My wife and I traveled by train for my 50th high school reunion in Birmingham in June, 1987, a happy event I have described in detail in Part II of these memoirs. Later we took trips to Hawaii, the Philippines and China; in the latter country I was able to observe their hospital and medical practices, which were very different to ours.

Finally came retirement in 1980 and a move to Victorville, California, 92 miles north of Los Angeles between Cajon Summit and Barstow, 30 miles farther north. How convenient for lovers of train travel to be living in a town where AMTRAKs "Desert Wind" and "Southwest Limited" stop.

This, in very scant outline, is the life story of Edwin T.Witt, American.

Victorville, California